THE
ELEMENTS OF
DRAMA

BY

J. L. STYAN

CAMBRIDGE
AT THE UNIVERSITY PRESS
1960

PUBLISHED BY
THE SYNDICS OF THE CAMBRIDGE UNIVERSITY PRESS

Bentley House, 200 Euston Road, London, N.W. 1
American Branch: 32 East 57th Street, New York 22, N.Y.

CAMBRIDGE UNIVERSITY PRESS
1960

Printed in Great Britain at the University Press, Cambridge
(Brooke Crutchley, University Printer)

PREFACE

My most sincere thanks are due to Connie my wife, Professor G. E. T. Mayfield and Mrs Pat Roberts for their encouragement, advice and practical help when this book was in manuscript. My indebtedness to other writers is recorded in the text.

But I owe an earlier debt to the amateur dramatic movement, and especially to all those adult students of the theatre, in my estimate the front rank of playgoers, with whom it has been my pleasure to test and to talk about plays. For the book arose from their lively exchange of ideas, the sharing of honest opinion and the mutual desire for understanding.

Disinterested and clear-sighted, the adult student can usually be trusted to recognize the fundamental issues, and this is certainly true of his attitude to drama. His genuine concern for the value of his visit to the theatre begins with the excitement of asking what passes between an imaginative stage and an intelligent auditorium when the play is in performance.

The growing body of such playgoers could endow us with a living theatre beloved and of some account in our society.

J.L.S.

YORK
March 1959

CONTENTS

PREFACE		*page* v
INTRODUCTION		1

PART I. THE DRAMATIC SCORE

1 DRAMATIC DIALOGUE IS MORE THAN CONVERSATION   11
  Rosmersholm, The Importance of Being Earnest

2 DRAMATIC VERSE IS MORE THAN DIALOGUE IN VERSE   27
  Othello, A Sleep of Prisoners

3 MAKING MEANINGS IN THE THEATRE   48
  The Playboy of the Western World

4 SHIFTING IMPRESSIONS   64
  The Cherry Orchard

5 THE BEHAVIOUR OF THE WORDS ON THE STAGE   86
  Voice, pause and meaning, *Pygmalion*; Voice and verse, *The Confidential Clerk*; Gesture and meaning, *Arms and the Man, The Apple Cart*; Words and movement, *King Lear*

PART II. ORCHESTRATION

6 BUILDING THE SEQUENCE OF IMPRESSIONS   121
  King Oedipus, Deirdre of the Sorrows, Murder in the Cathedral

7 TEMPO AND MEANING   141
  The Importance of Being Earnest, Saint Joan, The Wild Duck, The School for Scandal, The Father

Contents

8	MANIPULATING THE CHARACTERS *Arms and the Man, A Midsummer Night's Dream, Six Characters in Search of an Author*	page 163
9	BREAKING THE CONTINUITY *The Plough and the Stars, Ardèle*	188
10	THE MEANING OF THE PLAY AS A WHOLE *The Three Sisters, Antony and Cleopatra, Point of Departure*	205

PART III. VALUES

11	AUDIENCE PARTICIPATION *Crime Passionnel, The Hairy Ape*	231
12	PASSING JUDGMENT *Deirdre of the Sorrows, The Lady's Not For Burning, The Cocktail Party*	256
13	PLAYGOING AS AN ART	285

SHORT READING LIST	290
REFERENCES	292
INDEX OF PLAYWRIGHTS AND PLAYS	299
INDEX OF SUBJECTS	302
INDEX OF CRITICS AND COMMENTATORS	306

INTRODUCTION

This book is for those playgoers interested in drama, and for those students of drama who go to the theatre. It offers to point out what to look for and how to look for it, both in the theatre and in the text of the play. And it offers to define and account for the kind of activity that being at a play demands of the playgoer.

It sets out to fill a gap among the books about plays. It hopes to convince some that the actor has a share in the play, and others that the writer has. It tries to do this by proposing a completer criticism for drama, one which embraces both its verbal and its visual and aural elements. Thus the first article of its faith is that the act of reading a play is not likely to be enough.

These aims throw up problems of drama that lie at the root of understanding. The playgoer is uncertain what he is looking for. Does he want something 'effective' in the theatre, or else something 'good' as literature? If the play falls short of being one of these, how much credit can he allow it? His natural wish to pass a judgment is thwarted.

Bickering between rival ideas of what is theatre and what is literature perplexes our understanding of drama. For an author to say he will write for the theatre is to imply that he will have to learn to play to the gallery: 'If the audience gets its strip tease it will swallow the poetry', writes Mr Eliot.[1] How often do we hear a remark like, '*That* was put in for the *groundlings*' upon a theatrical effect in Shakespeare? For a student to say he is going to study drama *seriously* is still likely to suggest that he is going to ignore the physical considerations of actor, stage and playhouse. At one extreme we hear

[1] The superior figures in the text refer to the list of references on p. 292.

The Elements of Drama

Granville-Barker telling us that the art of the theatre is the art of acting, first, last and all the time.[2] At the other we read William Archer advising the playwright not to think of the actor's performance of his play as indispensable, but only as an added illumination.[3]

What it amounts to is that we do not know where the actor fits into the pattern of effects we call the play.

There is little help to be had from the critics. Detailed criticism of drama which comments on the play for playing is very difficult to find. Mr Raymond Williams has recently insisted that a play can be both literature and theatre, 'not the one at the expense of the other, but each *because* of the other'.[4] And of course the ordinarily honest and intelligent playgoer has always sensed that the good play was both. To reconcile literature and theatre is not to compromise and lose something from each, but rather to understand what dramatic dialogue is and does, why words on the page are not the same in function as words on the stage. The methods of literary criticism may well be inappropriate by themselves: we are not judging the text, but what the text makes the actor make the audience do.

Even if we accept the play as performed as the subject for discussion, a very real difficulty is the lack of precise terms to use in talking about the composite effects always common to the stage. The commonest shovel-word between dramatic critics, I would guess, is 'effective'. It is supplied as a critical talisman, it warms like a compliment, but it means nothing. There are dozens of others: 'atmospheric', 'spectacular', 'theatrical', 'realistic', 'dramatic' itself, and so on.

We habitually depend upon terms that bring with them powers of false association. Those who know their Aristotle (and those who do not) will finger a term like 'catharsis'; the theatre-wise fall back upon concepts like 'tempo'; others feel comfortable talking about the 'response' of the audience. To

Introduction

discuss the play in the theatre we turn to medicine, music or psychology in order to talk at all.

The terminology of literary criticism may be equally embarrassing. It has been well said that the easiest way of taking a play to pieces is in terms of its characters and story, but that these are probably inappropriate as counters for dramatic criticism: a character has no meaning outside its play; the abstracted story may have little to do with the complexity of thought and feeling an audience carries away from the theatre.

It seems to me that this failure to find a way of talking in any detail about responses in the theatre can be traced to an enduring uncertainty about the sources and nature of the play's effects. We must look first to the structure of idea and emotion in the dialogue itself, how the actor is to embody it in speech and action, and the sort of work the audience must do before the play is created in their minds. An understanding of the processes of the theatrical experience is necessary for the full appreciation of the play.

Words put on the stage assume a complexity all their own, because they are words written to be acted, seen and heard.

The history of the interesting theatrical failure is the history of the play that has not acknowledged this. The effect of the words in a play, and therefore of their value, is limited if they deny the resources of the stage or if they are not valid in terms of the theatre for which they are written. When we talk loosely of the writer who is at home in the theatre we mean one who *has* acknowledged this. Yet critics still largely ignore the visual and aural requirements of dramatic language.

The word written, the word seen, the word heard: are they so different? Is there no common ground for them? Whether the writer writes 'Jack was cold', or whether we see Jack looking cold, or whether we hear Jack say 'I am cold', the concept has the same root. Words written, seen and heard must meet first in the mind of the playwright, then in the

The Elements of Drama

theatre in the person and voice of the actor, and finally, in the minds of the audience. All this is the common ground of the word dramatized. One word of dramatic dialogue has many functions to fulfil.

Thus when we are thinking of the complexity of the art of the play, we ought not only to be thinking of the variety of contributors to the finished production, author, actor, producer, designer. This topic has been discussed at length to little purpose. We ought to recognize instead that, essentially, the words which stand for a production must make for a synthesis of the elements of drama; that the complexity of drama lies in this; that this kind of complexity and this kind of synthesis is unique and peculiar to drama. Mr Peter Brook sees it as the mark of a good dramatist when he writes of the work of M. Jean Anouilh:

> He conceives his plays as ballets, as patterns of movement, as pretexts for actors' performances. Unlike so many present-day playwrights who are descendants of a literary school, and whose plays are animated novels, Anouilh is in the tradition of the *commedia dell'arte*. His plays are recorded improvisations. Like Chopin, he preconceives the accidental and calls it an impromptu. He is a poet, but not a poet of words: he is a poet of words-acted, of scenes-set, of players-performing.[5]

An understanding of this complexity is proper to the appreciation of the play.

When words written for a stage are put upon a stage by good actors the quality of this complexity is tested. It is therefore very difficult for a reader to make this test for himself. Think how difficult it is to imagine eloquent variations of pace alone, without taxing the imagination further. Granville-Barker asks us to envisage the task before the reader:

> He must, so to speak, perform the whole play in his imagination; as he reads, each effect must come home to him; the succession and contrast of scenes, the harmony and clash of the music of the dialogue, the action implied, the mere physical opposition of characters, or the silent figure standing aloof—for that also can be eloquent.[6]

Introduction

And in addition to all this he must be the audience in the theatre, since a play is the response of an audience to its performance.

The worst difficulty in thinking about a play is simply to remember that, given words written for demonstration on a stage, there is no other *completely* valid means of judging their efficiency and value except within their own terms. Leave your armchair throne of judgment, says Granville-Barker, submit for the while to be tossed to and fro in the action of the play: drama's first aim is to subdue us.[7]

These are some of the reasons why there is plenty of room for a fresh inquiry into what makes up a play. At this point the reader should be told that the argument of this book rests on a simple and empirical theory which the playgoer can test for himself without trouble. It proposes that meaning is created in the theatre by putting two or more stage ingredients together for a spectator to observe. And it holds that, if once we can distinguish clearly between what happens on the stage and what happens in the audience, then we shall be in a better position to grasp what happens during a performance.

For a reader, the concept of 'redness' and the concept of 'apple' can combine to form the verbally more complete and precise idea of 'red apple'. On a stage an actress can listen in silence to a long speech of dreamy optimism by an actor, then suddenly and for no apparent reason, take off her hat and say she will stay to lunch after all. This is the way Masha behaves in the presence of Vershinin in the first act of Chekhov's *The Three Sisters*. But this sequence of events, made up of speech, silence and gesture, *does* make sense—to the spectator in the audience. Just as a reader assimilates 'red apple' as a single concept, so the playgoer concludes that Masha finds Vershinin sufficiently interesting to make her want to stay. Thus an effect is made, whether slowly or quickly, in the mind of the

The Elements of Drama

spectator, and it comes as a result of his activity excited by the combination of particular details.

Here then are the three parts of this book: (i) the elements which go to build 'events' on the stage (The Dramatic Score); (ii) the way these may be put together (Orchestration); and (iii) the reaction of the playgoer (Values).

According to this plan, the starting point is to discover what the actor owes to the written word, and what the word owes to the actor's voice, gesture and movement. Only when the parts of the action are put together can larger effects, like tempo and the development of character, be felt. So we shall see how the play is organized until its whole meaning is created. Finally we shall be able to understand what the audience contributes to the theatre experience, and therefore what values lie in the play.

Unhappily, this plan means that in the earlier chapters aspects of the 'score' must be artificially isolated, and the discussion of a piece of dialogue is sometimes unfairly trimmed to suit our needs. But I hope the reader will listen all the more richly when he hears the full music.

And I hope that some topics, hoary but still hot, will settle into their places. Thus 'plot' cannot take precedence over the complete, multi-coloured stage action. 'Character' is seen less as a role for an actor and more as a sequence of impressions in our minds: it is not treated as an isolated instrument in the orchestra. 'Values' do not arise as problems until we have felt the play as a whole: a pocket of farce or sensation which may add hugely to the impact of the play cannot be judged separately. In particular, unwieldy arguments about 'convention' (another shovel-word, I fear, used today to shift almost any problem of dramatic theory) are broken down: a way of speaking can be conveniently disentangled from a trick of a certain playhouse; a fashion in characterization can be distinguished from expectations and beliefs held dear by a contemporary audience.

Introduction

Final points: the book's reasoning is developed by examples, and the reader will hardly need to be told that any suggestions for production are not always likely to be the only ones. But illustration properly makes this a book to look *beyond*. It takes it for granted, that is, that the reader will put it down in the interests of seeing or reading the play it is discussing. To make this possible the examples are chosen from plays easy to see in the theatre or take from a library or one's own bookshelf. And where foreign plays are used, they are used in English translation. This is not to say that a play is not better played or read in its own language, but that the play as it is seen in any theatre, with its effect and the response in that theatre, is what really matters. Similarly where the understanding of the performance is not affected by historical considerations, the approach is not a historical one. *This* play in *this* theatre is the issue.

To send the reader back to the play with a direction for his understanding is all one could wish for.

PART I
THE DRAMATIC SCORE

NOTE

The superior figures in the text refer to
the notes starting on p. 292.

I
DRAMATIC DIALOGUE IS MORE THAN CONVERSATION

Any artificial picture of life must start from the detail of actuality. An audience must be able to recognize it; however changed, we want to check it against experience. Death, for example, is something we cannot know. In *Everyman* it is represented as a man embodying some of our feelings about it. So Death is partly humanized, enough, anyway, for us to be able to explore what the dramatist thinks about it.

Conversely, the detail of actuality in realistic drama can be chosen and presented in such a way as to suggest that it stands for more on the stage than it would in life. The *Cherry Orchard* family, in the excitement of their departure, overlook their old servant Firs. Placed with striking force at the very end of the play, this trivial accident becomes an incisive and major comment on everything the family has done.

So it is with dramatic speech. A snatch of phrase caught in everyday conversation may mean little. Used by an actor on a stage, it can assume general and typical qualities. The context into which it is put can make it pull more than its conversational weight, no matter how simple the words. Consider Othello's bare repetition: 'Put out the light, and then put out the light.'[1] In its context the repetition prefigures precisely the comparison Shakespeare is about to make between the lamp Othello is holding and Desdemona's life and being. Its heavy rhythm suggests the strained tone and obsessed mood of the man, and an almost priestlike attitude behind the twin motions. We begin to see the murder of Desdemona in the larger general terms of a ritualistic sacrifice. Poetry is

The Elements of Drama

made from words which may be in use in more prosaic ways; dramatic speech, with its basis in ordinary conversation, is speech that has had a specific pressure put on it.

Why do words begin to assume general qualities, and why do they become dramatic? Here are two problems on either side of the same coin. The words in both cases depend upon the kind of attention we give them. The artists using them, whether author or actor, force them upon us, and in a variety of ways try to fix the quality of our attention.

If dialogue carefully follows the way we speak in life, as it is likely to do in a realistic play, the first step towards understanding how it departs from actuality can be awkward. It is helpful to cease to submit to the pretence for the moment. An apparent reproduction of ordinary conversation will be, in good drama, a construction of words set up to do many jobs that are not immediately obvious. Professor Eric Bentley has written of Ibsen's 'opaque, uninviting sentences':

> An Ibsenite sentence often performs four or five functions at once. It sheds light on the character speaking, on the character spoken to, on the character spoken about; it furthers the plot; it functions ironically in conveying to the audience a meaning different from that conveyed to the characters.[2]

It is true that conversation itself can sometimes be taken to do these things. 'Whatever you think, I'm going to tell him what you said' is a remark which in its context can shed light on the speaker, the person spoken to and the person spoken about. For a fourth person listening, as a spectator witnesses a play, there may also be an element of irony, in that he recognizes attitudes and a relationship between the two who are talking that mean something only to himself as observer.

In the play the difference lies first in an insistence that the words go somewhere, move towards a predetermined end. It lies in a charge of meaning that will advance the action. This is argued in a statement in Strindberg's manifesto for the

Dramatic Dialogue

naturalistic theatre. He says of his characters that he has 'permitted the minds to work irregularly as they do in reality, where, during conversation, the cogs of one mind seem more or less haphazardly to engage those of another one, and where no topic is fully exhausted'. But he adds that, while the dialogue seems to stray a good deal in the opening scenes, 'it acquires a material that later on is worked over, picked up again, repeated, expounded, and built up like the theme in a musical composition'.[3]

It is a question of economy. The desultory and clumsy talk of real life, with its interruptions, overlappings, indecisions and repetitions, talk without direction, wastes our interest—unless, like the chatter given to Jane Austen's Miss Bates, it hides relevance in irrelevances. It follows that dialogue which merely stimulates is also unacceptable. It is sometimes easy, for example, to be pleased with the wit and vitality in Shaw's dialogue yet ignore the question of its relevance to the action.

When the actor examines the text to prepare his part, he *looks* for what makes the words different from conversation, that is, he looks for the structural elements of the building, for links of characteristic thought in the character, and so on. He persists till he has shaped in his mind a firm and workable pattern of his part. Now the clues sought by the actor hidden beneath the surface of the dialogue are the playgoer's guides too.

The actor and producer Stanislavsky has called these clues the 'subtext' of a play:

The subtext is a web of innumerable, varied inner patterns inside a play and a part, woven from 'magic ifs', given circumstances, all sorts of figments of the imagination, inner movements, objects of attention, smaller and greater truths and a belief in them, adaptations, adjustments and other similar elements. It is the subtext that makes us say the words we do in a play.[4]

And in another place he says that 'the whole text of the play will be accompanied by a subtextual stream of images, like

The Elements of Drama

a moving picture constantly thrown on the screen of our inner vision, to guide us as we speak and act on the stage'.[5]

Once we admit that the words must propose and substantiate the play's meaning, we shall find in them more and more of the author's wishes. For dramatic dialogue has other work to do before it provides a table of words to be spoken. In the absence of the author it must provide a set of unwritten working directives to the actor on how to speak its speeches. And before that, it has to teach him how to think and feel them: the particularity of a play requires this if it is not to be animated by a series of cardboard stereotypes.

Dramatic dialogue works by a number of instinctively agreed codes. Some tell the producer how to arrange the figures on the stage. Others tell him what he should hear as the pattern of sound echoing and contradicting, changing tone, rising and falling. These are directives strongly compelling him to hear the key in which a scene should be played, and the tone and tempo of the melody. Others oblige him to start particular rhythmic movements of emotion flowing between the stage and the audience. He is then left to marry the colour and shape of the stage picture with the music he finds recorded in the text.

Good dialogue works like this and throws out a 'subtextual stream of images'. Even if the limits within which these effects work are narrow, even if the effect lies in the barest or the simplest of speeches, we may expect to hear the text humming the tune as it cannot in real life. Dialogue should be read and heard as a dramatic score.

The first minute in Ibsen's *Rosmersholm* demonstrates his meticulous use of words. As dialogue to open a play, the qualities in it stand out: its power to take our interest, its neatness of exposition, its planning of visual effects:

MRS HELSETH. Hadn't I better begin and lay the table for supper, miss?
REBECCA. Yes, do. Mr Rosmer ought to be in directly.

Dramatic Dialogue

MRS HELSETH. Isn't there a draught where you are sitting, miss?

REBECCA. There is a little. Will you lock up, please? *Mrs Helseth goes to the hall door and shuts it. Then she goes to the window, to shut it, and looks out.*

MRS HELSETH. Isn't that Mr Rosmer coming there?

REBECCA. Where? *Gets up.* Yes, it is he. *Stands behind the window-curtain.* Stand on one side. Don't let him catch sight of us.

MRS HELSETH *stepping back*. Look, miss—he is beginning to use the mill path again.

REBECCA. He came by the mill path the day before yesterday too. *Peeps out between the curtain and the window-frame.* Now we shall see whether—

MRS HELSETH. Is he going over the wooden bridge?

REBECCA. That is just what I want to see. *After a moment.* No. He has turned aside. He is coming the other way round to-day too. *Comes away from the window.* It is a long way round.

MRS HELSETH. Yes, of course. One can well understand his shrinking from going over that bridge. The spot where such a thing has happened is—

REBECCA *folding up her work*. They cling to their dead a long time at Rosmersholm.[6]

The scene takes our attention before this. On the rise of the curtain and before Mrs Helseth enters, Rebecca peeps from time to time through the window. It is part of Ibsen's method, as we know, to begin his play in the centre of the main situation, and this mime begins the task without delay. The dialogue makes allowance for appropriate movement about the stage and for the visual picture of the women around the window-frame, which fixes and accentuates their attitude to the man and the mill path offstage. And from the outset the necessary facts are given *while* interest is being aroused. We learn quickly of the time of day and of Mrs Helseth's relationship with Rebecca, but we also feel promptly what is habit with them and what is not. We get hints of what knowledge is common to them, but we are also urged to guess what they share as a secret.

Any playwright tries to sustain the interest he has captured. But this Ibsen does through an exposition which continues:

The Elements of Drama

an unusual relationship between Rebecca and Rosmer is implied without satisfying and killing our curiosity. Thus a statement like 'Don't let him catch sight of us' is part of the exposition of the facts: it establishes the conspiracy against Rosmer, and that there is something to hide from him; it gives us a strong, if for the moment ragged, impression of a personal relationship. But it is also at the same time inviting our question, 'Why not?' Ibsen knows we will attend closely to have the answer, helping him in the work of exposition.

'He is beginning to use the mill path again', says Mrs Helseth, and her use of 'again' compels a special attention to 'the mill path'. We try to piece together the significances: 'the mill path' leads us to 'the wooden bridge', but Rosmer's 'turning aside' startles us with an illogical 'explanation': 'It is a long way round.' The mystery is left unsolved by an appropriately vague euphemism in Mrs Helseth's cautious mention of 'such a thing'. Only Rebecca utters the word that might provide a link: the 'dead'. So we grope on. Ibsen happily combines the need to keep off-stage the movements of Rosmer with the opportunity to give us a tantalizing, but completely naturalistic, series of clues from the two women looking at him.

This is what is expected of any detective play. But it is also Ibsen's aim to convince us that his characters are anchored in a real situation. While the surface detective work is being encouraged, he is intensely concerned to give his characters a *memory*. To do this he must suggest that his characters have already grown and have the kind of depth we will believe in and the actor can work on. Some events are presented as having happened, and the attitudes of the characters to them are made to seem inevitable, in such a way that the audience will begin to anticipate, rightly or wrongly, any reaction from any character to any remark. Everything said is relevant to a conjectural memory, to a central premise of a character's

Dramatic Dialogue

past deeds and thoughts, from which are to be reasoned his present attitudes. This puts great strain upon the dialogue and gives it its exceptionally taut quality. It must be compact of implicit and relevant references: 'Hadn't I better begin and lay the table...'; 'Mr Rosmer ought to be in directly.' These commonplace comments from the two women imply a routine that is disorganized. 'He is beginning to use the mill path again.' This arrangement of words tells us precisely that he did at one time use the mill path but has stopped, and that Mrs Helseth remembers the time. Her feeling behind her observation is therefore likely to be of pleasure at finding him behave as before, but of surprise at the change. This is the kind of deduction the actress will make instinctively.

Memory not different in kind could have been suggested by less scrupulous means, by tricks with which we are all familiar in the 'hack' play. One servant might have said to another, 'I'm sure Mr Rosmer is having an affair with that Rebecca'. Or a twentieth-century Rosmer might have had a conversation with a stranger on the telephone, 'You must meet my housekeeper...'. Trite methods could certainly relieve the strain on the dialogue, and the narrative of the play could progress as well. But the spectator would be less under control, because he would not feel the pressure of a dialogue whose function is to persuade us to a conviction of the necessity of the situation. Our interest would be stimulated at the expense of our belief.

Ibsen offers much more. The edge on his words creates the tone and emotional rhythm of the opening of the play. Those first four speeches are ordinary enough, and to most readers they will mean nothing more than they appear to say: they will hurry over them. But they are written for actors in front of a theatre audience, and their intended effect in the theatre is more complex. Their very ordinariness is suspicious after we have seen Rebecca peeping. Is this 'routine'? The actress knows from Rebecca's 'He came by the mill path the day

The Elements of Drama

before yesterday too' that there is anxiety in her. Can she then take the calm of 'Mr Rosmer ought to be in directly', the apparently commonplace remark, at its face value? Its triteness has this theatrical edge to it, and we feel it when we hear it contradict what we have seen. Wouldn't we also hear a particular note of concern in Mrs Helseth's voice too? In her first two speeches she is not of course saying, 'Do come away from that window', nor, 'I should like to look through it too', nothing as strong as that. But implications of this kind are present, because the words for both the women are in counterpoint with their feelings, and the action is piquant with interest long before the 'Stand on one side'.

An alert reader now begins to fill in his picture of the action. On the stage the actor helps the audience to do this, and on the stage the details of the performance combine to establish the scene's individual tone. Rebecca turns away from the window: she has seen what she wants to see. Suddenly she says, 'They cling to their dead a long time at Rosmersholm', a statement startling because it is incongruous with the more simple statements just heard, a poetic statement because no immediate answer from any character *can* explain it to us. So it remains in the mind unaccounted for, we listen to its echoes from time to time in the course of the play, we are never allowed to forget it, and it is only elucidated by the whole play and when the final curtain has fallen. A 'literary' analysis will tend to confine itself to comments on the theme of the play, and perhaps to a statement about Rebecca's realization of the position she has reached in her understanding of the household. On the stage Ibsen gives us a larger statement.

On the stage she makes her speech after she has turned. Ibsen is saying that this is Rebecca's provisional conclusion upon what she has learnt in the past and what she has seen now. This is her comment on Rosmer's attitude to the unknown situation and his state of mind. Her intonation will reflect

Dramatic Dialogue

this. She folds up her work and this adds a touch of finality. We are still filling in the facts, and, as has been said, this first mention of death spurs us to make a more precise guess about the events that have passed before the play began. But now in addition we are trying to understand her feelings for these events. We see her in a room decorated with flowers, a visual picture in direct contradiction to what she is saying. Why this contradiction? At this point the contradiction in the setting itself is likely to strike us. Behind the living flowers we see that 'The walls are hung round with portraits, dating from various periods, of clergymen, military officers and other officials in uniform'—the dead. From the play one almost guesses what kind of faces they have, for the portraits are to reflect Beata's image, just as the flowers shed sunlight on Rebecca. The room as we see it stands for an antithesis between the dead and the living. This visual irony confirms, elaborates and deepens the meaning of what we have just seen and heard.

Behind this there is the emotional rhythm of the scene, which emerges to enrich and refine the general tone. The dialogue begins with a smooth rhythm through which we only barely perceive the conflicting undercurrent, but those calmer intonations and unhurried cues break quickly and naturally as Mrs Helseth sees Rosmer through the window. What has been below the surface and what we have partly suspected in Rebecca becomes apparent, while the mutual excitement of Rebecca and Mrs Helseth suggests the emotional state of the household. The little crisis is turned with the decisive 'No. He has turned aside' and the strong lines from Rebecca and Mrs Helseth follow only after attention has been captured. The stage is alive because this sequence is alive rhythmically, and this rhythmical unit is the first of a series which grows to great dramatic power.

In the first minute of the play a great deal has 'happened'.

The Elements of Drama

What is inadequately called the exposition not only arouses interest, but transmits a complex tonal effect. And while we are subtly being told what the author wishes us to know and *feel*, he persuades us to accept the substantiality of the make-believe. So we become involved in the tragedy: we are all the more anxious to know the meaning of what we are suffering. Ibsen works his will upon us without destroying his realism.

In *Rosmersholm* conviction is important. Does this mean 'subtext' is dependent upon depth of characterization? No. The dramatist's ordering of the network of suggestions depends upon his insight into his theme and his power to handle it. The expression of his theme may be at a distance from real life, where no depth of this kind is wanted. The first moments of the meeting between Cecily Cardew and the Hon. Gwendolen Fairfax in *The Importance of Being Earnest* submit a dramatic subtext of the same stamp, though not of the same subtlety, as Ibsen's:

MERRIMAN. Miss Fairfax. *Enter Gwendolen. Exit Merriman.*
CECILY, *advancing to meet her.* Pray let me introduce myself to you. My name is Cecily Cardew.
GWENDOLEN. Cecily Cardew, *moving to her and shaking hands.* What a very sweet name! Something tells me we are going to be great friends. I like you already more than I can say. My first impressions of people are never wrong.
CECILY. How nice of you to like me so much after we have known each other such a comparatively short time. Pray sit down.
GWENDOLEN, *still standing up.* I may call you Cecily, may I not?
CECILY. With pleasure!
GWENDOLEN. And you will always call me Gwendolen, won't you?
CECILY. If you wish.
GWENDOLEN. Then that is all quite settled, is it not?
CECILY. I hope so. *A pause. They both sit down together.*[7]

Cecily and Gwendolen have earlier been extravagantly presented as charming if perverse creatures, having flagrantly self-assured attitudes towards life, preposterously feminine.

Dramatic Dialogue

It is impossible to believe that such women exist; but we are not invited to do more than posit their existence in a world the author has invented for his own use. Nor is it possible to believe that such a conversation as this would ever be heard outside the theatre, but as long as the characters remain convinced of their own existence, and serious about themselves and about their own virtues, it is in the nature of the theatre for us to accept them and what they say without protest. They are not in essentials any different from each other. Both are cats: Gwendolen, a younger Lady Bracknell, masking her cattiness behind an affected urbanity, Cecily behind an affected rural innocence. Otherwise as characters they could be transposed without upsetting the play: this could never be done with Ibsen. It is part of the effect of this scene that they should be identical in general behaviour and in their attitudes to each other. This impression is enforced by puppet-like movement in sitting down, standing up, exchange of diaries, turning to the audience to speak their asides, and by copying each other's tones, all to shape the pattern of the scene as a whole. The style extends from the manner of speech to the manner of gesture and movement.

Because of this artificiality, we refer less spontaneously to our experience, we supply less of the data of thought and feeling about the situation. Consequently to assist the actor it is necessary for the dialogue to fill in the tone of the scene more deliberately and with more force. Why is so much time spent in introduction, in preparing the ground before the quarrel, without furthering the plot? Is it padding? It is because the author is making allowances for the *strangeness* of his conception, setting out for us the conditions upon which a disagreement between the two girls can be reached. Yet the words as they are written are flat and nearly meaningless. For this reason they show what a playgoer gains that a reader loses.

Wilde is sometimes guilty of lapses into undramatic

The Elements of Drama

diffuseness and digression.[8] The ordinary playgoer is not so ready to excuse diffuseness as the ordinary reader. The reader may be grateful for stretches of dialogue at lower tension, and for a substitute for action he cannot envisage. On the other hand, what he takes to be diffuseness may make a properly dramatic contribution.

This meeting between the two girls is dramatic and important. But why? It seems they meet, they shake hands, they speak politely and compliment each other, they sit down. But to play these words in this unimaginative way is to present dull nonsense, and to crack a very delicate relationship between the world of the actors and the world of the audience. Would two girls be ready to be friends *in these terms* at first meeting? Especially when Gwendolen must certainly be surprised to find a girl as attractive as Cecily living in her fiancé's house, and when Cecily is expecting 'one of the many good elderly women who are associated with Uncle Jack'.

Doubts should be roused by the excessive politeness in the phrasing of the words they speak:

Pray let me introduce myself to you.
What a *very sweet* name! Something tells me that we are going to be *great* friends. I like you already *more than I can say*.
How nice of you to like me....

Aren't they covering up their true feelings? This presentation is of two girls suspicious of each other. It is a keen irony, and one which strikes the note for all the ironies of the succeeding scene. How then shall we see it?

Merriman announces, 'Miss Fairfax'. If Cecily is curious to meet Gwendolen, she will hurriedly have to recompose herself before 'advancing to meet her'. Cecily will be alarmed at seeing this example of 'one of the good elderly women', but she will face up to the enemy. She 'registers' an excessive smile of welcome—'registers' because Cecily is now acting a part and the smile is false. She speaks with a defiance in her

Dramatic Dialogue

voice, 'Pray let me introduce myself to you...'. As hostess in a world of fixed social manners such conduct is expected of her, but she attacks by overplaying her part as hostess while she retreats behind that rampart of conventional behaviour.

Wilde sustains his finely balanced satire through each speech in the excerpt. The flow of ironical innuendo is to swell to a torrent as their mutual suspicion grows and as the fabric of genteel proprieties is strained. And the satire reaches the audience as dramatic action.

Gwendolen is not to be outdone. The battle, she senses, is on, and she must assert herself. This girl shall know that she, Gwendolen, is the one to stipulate the conditions of the fight. From now on the excessive politeness will seem more frigid as her voice becomes more cutting: 'What a very sweet name!...' And she makes it clear that it is her place to patronize Cecily: 'we are going to be great friends' means that Gwendolen will allow her to be a friend provided she presides at this meeting. Cecily is astute enough to recognize this. The crescendo of courtesies and compliments mounts: 'How nice of you to like me so much after we have known each other such a comparatively short time.' This is already an obvious sarcasm; both parties know what is to be expected. Gwendolen remains standing when Cecily invites her to sit: she shall decide when she will sit, not Cecily. Now that she finds Cecily after this sarcasm to be rather more formidable than she thought, she will physically assert her superiority. She dictates the terms of the bond of friendship that both know from the outset is false. But Cecily strengthens her position by allowing her this liberty, and the artificial compact is made: 'Then that is all quite settled, is it not?' They both sit down together, equal in strength, forces consolidated, ready for the first blow to be struck after the feinting. Their sitting down precisely together is more than a social courtesy: it is a mutual gesture of 'the formalities are over; now to business'. They

The Elements of Drama

will act as unscrupulously as the rules of behaviour for hostesses and guests will allow.

We have to recognize these preliminary gambits if we are not to miss the musical pattern of the whole interview, to which this is but the prelude. The rhythm of what follows is carefully composed. Whereas Cecily and Gwendolen begin on equal ground, as we have seen, quickly the balance shifts and Gwendolen is the first to be caught at a disadvantage while Cecily becomes increasingly the mistress of the situation. When the announcement of her engagement to 'Ernest' is made and is countered by Gwendolen's own claim, they are both on their feet with their weapons and their diaries drawn. After the preliminary parrying, battle is waged and rises to a crisis. At this point Merriman enters with the tea and both are compelled to resume their earlier composure: they must act their parts of hostess and guest again, while their anger boils. It is against this formal pattern of modulations in the scene as a whole that we have to measure the author's success in fixing the scale of the action.

'The scale of the action.' An aspect of dramatic speech is brought sharply into focus as soon as any comparison is made between the language of *The Importance of Being Earnest* and that of *Rosmersholm*. The use of opposed speech 'conventions', which affect the tone of the dialogue as well as its whole embodiment in voice and gesture, is unmistakable: the actress, looking for her code-signs in the text, does not need to be told that Cecily and Gwendolen do not talk in the same way as Rebecca and Mrs Helseth. For purposes of satire, Wilde gives us two-dimensional people who speak, not as people do speak, but as some would speak if their habits of thought were distorted by simplification. Two-dimensional speech precludes interest in complexity of motive, in order both to stress some kinds of basic and typical behaviour and to keep an audience detachedly critical of it. *Rosmersholm* stresses *individual*

Dramatic Dialogue

behaviour. Our interest, and often sympathy, is captured by the more personal motives and values which add that extra dimension of realism.

Although speech may rightly lead us to conclusions about what kind of play we are seeing, this is not to plead for Ibsen and pass judgment on Wilde. The proper grounds for debate are the precise nature of the convention the play is written in and its suitability to its task, not whether one convention is better than another—an academic red-herring which distracts from the business of appreciating the play as it stands.

'Conventions' of speech are simply understood when we reflect that, of course, people speak in a variety of private languages. By their words they betray many details about themselves, including their environment and their habits of thought. The playwright can fabricate 'environment' and 'habits of thought' for his agents the characters. To this the actor will add in the appropriate spirit this or that degree of stylization in his gesture and movement.

So often he does this, but forgets that convention must advertise its presence to the audience primarily by the way the dramatist composes his words to be spoken. We make a compact with the author and his actors which is a compact to accept what is heard in the way it is said.

Had William Archer wished to recognize this, he would never have written this surprising statement:

After the parting of Romeo and Juliet, what would be more natural, one may almost say inevitable, than that Juliet should throw herself down on her bed in tears? But it does not occur to Shakespeare. Probably there was no bed visible, the action passing behind the balustrade of the Upper Stage. There was nothing for Juliet to weep upon; and the gesture is an essential part of the effect. Shakespeare *had to fall back upon words*, and make her say:

>   Oh, Fortune, Fortune, all men call thee fickle.
>   If thou art fickle, what dost thou with him
>   That is renown'd for faith?[9]

The Elements of Drama

But Juliet's gesture is in those words. And Shakespeare has a more explicit thing to do than let his heroine dissolve in tears. *Because* of the speech convention in which he is working, he can demonstrate *precisely* the state of her mind. At the same time, through what she says, Shakespeare is free to strengthen our understanding of the dialectic of contrasting scenes which are characteristic of this play. We learn from the next few lines,

> Be fickle Fortune:
> For then I hope thou wilt not keep him long,
> But send him back,[10]

that the 'Fortune' Juliet is apostrophizing is not a tear-jerking capricious Chance, but the sobering relentless Fate that dogs the lovers through the play.

But dramatic poetry is the form of words furthest removed from conversation. It brings its special problems of artifice and intensity.

2

DRAMATIC VERSE IS MORE THAN DIALOGUE IN VERSE

The first demand put upon prose dialogue is that it should be an effective frame for all that is to pass on the stage. But even where the dialogue neither looks nor sounds like conversation, it is bound by rules dictated by the stage *no different in kind* from those that bind prose dialogue.

There is no question of seeing poetry on the stage merely as a relevant decoration. We can concur with Mr Eliot's proposition that verse in drama must justify itself dramatically and is more than an exercise in putting prose dialogue into verse. It is worth restating some of his findings at various stages in his researches:

Let us avoid the assumption that rhetoric is a vice of manner, and endeavour to find a rhetoric of substance also, which is right because it issues from what it has to express.[1]

We should expect a dramatic poet like Shakespeare to write his finest poetry in his most dramatic scenes. And this is just what we do find: what makes it most dramatic is what makes it most poetic. No one ever points to certain plays as being the most poetic, and to *other* plays as being the most dramatic. The same plays are the most poetic and the most dramatic, and this is not by a concurrence of the two activities, but by the full expansion of one and the same activity.[2]

I laid down for myself the ascetic rule to avoid poetry which could not stand the test of strict dramatic utility.[3]

These comments point to the same thing, that at bottom the manner of the language is a means of expressing the idea dramatically. Even as poetic imagery it must carry and particularize what passes on the stage, and its validity can be

The Elements of Drama

properly judged only through the theatre. Granville-Barker, talking about poetry in drama, defines the function of words in the theatre with an exactitude that comes of being an actor and producer:

> Language in the theatre...is not simply verbal language. The artist... thinks in terms of his material. The dramatist, then, must think in terms both of speech and action; and in terms of his structural or pictorial background besides. The artist thinks also of the proportionate importance of each item of his material to the particular piece of work he has in hand, its use for the effect he wants to make.
>
> But there is a fourth and most important item in the dramatist's means of expression; the personality of the actor...If his part is not sufficiently and appropriately filled in for him, he has no choice in its performance but to fill it in for himself.[4]

What is the justification for a line of verse in drama? When will it better embrace the details of the play than a line of prose? How can it help the expression of the author's ideas? It is fair to state a doubt that may be in the minds of those familiar with the realistic manner in the theatre: that the particularity of realistic detail may be lost in a heightened form of words. But even absolute realism would not necessarily provide a means for absolute perception.

It is quickly demonstrated how verse can better encourage, in both the actor's speech and his movements, a more accurate interpretation of the author's intentions than prose. When an author raises emotions to the surface by giving them verbal expression, as can happen in a non-realistic play, the actor may have a more particular guide to the feelings demanded of him. A Hamlet will know he must speak the lines

> How weary, stale, flat, and unprofitable
> Seem to me all the uses of this world![5]

with a feeling and a tone of voice that is 'weary, stale, flat, and unprofitable': the meaning of the words, but particularly their dragging rhythm and the despondent slither through the

Dramatic Verse

short, unaccented syllables of 'and unprofitable', emphatically point the speaking. The voice of course finds a greater resource in metrical and other poetic devices than it can in prose.

By contrast, the moment of Lavinia's personal crisis in *Mourning Becomes Electra* staggers somewhat lamely under its load of colloquialisms:

No! Don't think of that—not yet! I want a little while of happiness—in spite of all the dead! I've earned it! I've done enough—! *Growing more desperate—pleading wildly*. Listen, Peter! Why must we wait for marriage? I want a moment of joy—of love—to make up for what's coming! I want it now!...⁶

It is difficult to disentangle these easy, novelettish sentiments from the naïve shapes in which they appear; but it is clear that emphatic pointing in this instance is attempted only by an expressionless series of exclamation marks. Even hysteria has to be given a tune if we are to listen to its meaning.

As for the imagery of poetry, it can in conjunction with the sound of the syllables give a clear directive to the projection and intonation of the lines. In

> So excellent a king, that was to this
> Hyperion to a satyr⁷

Shakespeare has chosen two contrasting images to identify King Hamlet and Claudius, and the descent from the most bright and beautiful of the gods to the half man, half beast that signifies lust is a descent of voice as of meaning. The images are echoed by their sounds, the two high, firm accented syllables in 'Hyperion', stressed at the beginning of the line, are contrasted by the voice running down in four unaccented syllables to the disgusted sibilant and the flat vowel qualities of 'satyr'. Sound and image thus sharply define the vocal outline for the actor.

Mr Eliot in *Murder in the Cathedral* has been careful to practise similar effects of vocal colouring, and they are especially noticeable in the Chorus speeches, which are more direct in evoking feeling. Melody is added to meaning in these lines:

Since golden October declined into sombre November
And the apples were gathered and stored, and the land become brown
   sharp points of death in a waste of water and mud,
The New Year waits, breathes, waits, whispers in darkness.[8]

The modulation down a delicate scale of vowels from 'golden October' to 'sombre November', the bristling and incisive consonants of 'brown sharp points of death', and the sudden change of rhythm in the last breathed line, falling, shy and hushed, yet expectant with a suspense in the short alert words and the succession of pauses, provide an insistent pattern of sound to echo the imagery. An analysis of the progressive vocal effects of each chorus would illuminate the growth and direction through the play of the emotion of the audience.

   The forms in the verse that enforce a certain manner of speaking are those that enforce a certain manner of moving too: the stream of intonation of voice is intimately linked with the gesture and movement of the body. Both Shakespeare and Mr Eliot write lines that direct the actor to particular movements, because they are felt in the muscles when they are heard in the head. The freedom of a Hamlet to interpret the suggestion of movement in 'How now! a rat? dead, for a ducat, dead'[9] is limited by physically felt contradictions when it is spoken inappropriately. There is in this speech a moment to turn and to pause, a moment to thrust through the arras, a moment, already, for Hamlet's impetuosity to hesitate and reflect. And parallel with the physical action, the words themselves provide the intonation of the voice: startled, sharp, rising, vigorous, brutal, quavering. It is unwise in dramatic poetry to try to distinguish between the gesture of the actor's body and the 'gesture' of his voice.

Dramatic Verse

Mr Eliot's Women of Canterbury approach the Cathedral with lines of which these are a sample:

Are we drawn by danger? Is it the knowledge of safety, that draws our feet
Towards the Cathedral?[10]

These too are lines calculated for movement. The doubt and anticipation of the women and the sense of an unaccountable impulsion in their minds is reflected in the reluctance of the rhythm, which marks the manner and pace of their passage through the church, not as a phalanx but in twos and threes, intermittently.

But providing implicit stage-directions for speaking and moving is not peculiar to verse dialogue: conditions prevail in prose dialogue where words can to a degree of efficiency direct intonation and gesture, even if good prose cannot be as precise as good verse. No: that the verse has to carry both speech and movement is simply a condition of, not a reason for, its use. Neither Shakespeare nor Mr Eliot were concerned in the first place with writing words for a kind of dramatic opera, nor for a kind of dramatic ballet. Even a special manner of speaking and moving is but the mere mechanism of a craft.

The question remains: does dramatic verse help the play? Poetry can make the drama uniquely precise not only for the actor to work with, but also for the audience to react to. It can do this especially where the author's subject cannot be represented by the details of real life. Through dramatic poetry he can secure the depth and intensity characteristic of poetic method. The answer is, surely, that the effect of poetry in the theatre will be of the same order as the effect of words in a poem. It will extend the range and power of the author's meaning. It will compel drama on the stage of such a kind that the image of it in the audience's mind will be something wider and yet finer, something enlarged and yet more pure than it could be if it were written in prose. The poetry is there

The Elements of Drama

to express and define patterns of thought and feeling otherwise inexpressible and indefinable. This is the legitimate reason for its use.

Two examples are given, one from *Othello* and the other from a modern verse drama. The scene from *Othello* is the conclusion of the tortured 'closet lock and key' interview between Othello and Desdemona, their last exchange before he comes to smother her.

> OTHELLO. Are you not a strumpet?
> DESDEMONA.   No, as I am a Christian:
>   If to preserve this vessel for my lord
>   From any other foul unlawful touch
>   Be not to be a strumpet, I am none.
> OTHELLO. What, not a whore?
> DESDEMONA.   No, as I shall be saved.
> OTHELLO. Is't possible?
> DESDEMONA. O, heaven forgive us!
> OTHELLO.   I cry you mercy then:
>   I took you for that cunning whore of Venice
>   That married with Othello. You, mistress,
>   That have the office opposite to Saint Peter,
>   And keep the gate of hell!
>
> *Re-enter Emilia*
>   You, you, ay, you!
> We have done our course; there's money for your pains:
> I pray you, turn the key, and keep our counsel.
>
> *Exit*
> EMILIA. Alas, what does this gentleman conceive?
>   How do you, madam? how do you, my good lady?
> DESDEMONA. Faith, half asleep.[11]

The verse carries the sort of vocal and physical movements and the musical shading of emotion that have been illustrated. These communicate sensations we are sure of assimilating. While Othello is on the stage, it is apparently to him that attention is chiefly given, for it is through him that the line of narrative has been drawn. At this point we are closely

Dramatic Verse

interested to see to what length his passion will take him: Shakespeare supplies an interim crisis in Othello's progress towards the extremity of killing. Therefore, for all the quiet strength of Desdemona's defence, the dialogue will seem to keep Othello dominant, and his aggressiveness will be felt physically in the sequence of increasingly belligerent questions: 'Are you not a strumpet?' 'What, not a whore?' 'Is't possible?' While his anger is rising in these lines, and his body is thrusting them at her, his voice will move up the scale from the insolence of 'strumpet' to the menacing roar of 'whore', the more brazen and violent word, and then to the shorter, conclusive hiss and evil sarcasm of 'Is't possible?' His withdrawal, already partly present in this last rhetorical question, into the bitterness of a mock anticlimax,

> I cry you mercy then:
> I took you for that cunning whore of Venice
> That married with Othello,

is not a slackening. Though his body will turn and his voice will drop, the edge in the voice has introduced at last that sinister note to Desdemona that had been anticipated. His attitude of withdrawal at this point is the more powerful in that our anxiety for Desdemona is unrelieved. He flings off with the derisory abuse of Emilia, a touch of hysteria in the shout, 'You, you, ay, you!' which is followed caustically by the mock courtesy and sour half-laugh with which he leaves them: 'I pray you, turn the key, and keep our counsel.' Shakespeare has vividly seen and heard his Othello, and delicately moulded him by each subtlety of the language.

The astute actress supplies the outline for Emilia by her reaction to the way she is addressed, even though she says nothing while Othello is on stage. To some extent she embodies our reaction to Othello's attack, for she is an observer as we are. When he addresses her, we know from his reiteration, 'ay,

The Elements of Drama

you!' that she is startled and incredulous, and that she has not obeyed him promptly. Shakespeare's arrangement for her entrance here is a little easy and mechanical: she has to be brought on stage for the scene that follows; but it is hardly noticed in the heat of the drama and she serves a purpose in playing a part in Othello's ugly make-believe, in fixing unmistakably in our minds Othello's reference to his wife's room as if it were a brothel, and in enhancing the effect of the horror.

Desdemona, too, will feed her acting from the suggestions in the text. She will feel the dignity of her part in the firm and rational flow of the words she speaks:

> If to preserve this vessel for my lord
> From any other foul unlawful touch
> Be not to be a strumpet, I am none.

This is in strong contrast to the fitfulness of Othello's lines. Her steady logic here, following upon the protest of 'No, as I am a Christian,' suggests the effort she is making to keep from breaking down, and although her voice will waver, she will stand her ground before his attack. Her voice will rise to meet his with 'No, as I shall be saved', her final protest, but her strength goes after the last thrust:

> Is't possible?
> O, heaven forgive us!

Her silence after this is eloquent of her misery and her fear and her lack of understanding. The bare and simple 'Faith, half asleep', dazed, deflated, a whisper of momentary resignation, is utterly poignant.

Readers will, perhaps unconsciously, be reading emotions into a text in this way. But it is more difficult for anyone outside the theatre to perceive and reconstruct the tempo of the speeches in sequence, though our sensation of the verse is equally our guide to the manner in which the speeches follow one another and to the rhythmic shape of the whole sequence.

Dramatic Verse

In the scene preceding the excerpt, Othello spoke quickly on his cues to suggest the finality of his state of mind; Desdemona spoke slowly upon hers to contrast her hesitancy and her failure of understanding. The resulting rhythm enabled the audience more precisely to identify speech with character and to assimilate their attitudes. This time has now passed, and Desdemona in her despair is defending herself with a sharpness almost equal to his, a sharpness that comes of defiance. So the tempo quickens, and the pitch of Othello's voice, which through the scene regulates the general intensity of feeling, rises to a wild cry:

> You, mistress,
> That have the office opposite to Saint Peter,
> And keep the gate of hell! You, you, ay, you!

Emilia and Desdemona are left to move us by the contrast of their painful relief and the hushed, oblique conversation that follows his exit. The live arrangement of the speeches implicitly leads us by the emotions where we are to go.

But comments of this kind, even were they to take into consideration the verbal imagery, which they have not done, are inadequate to account for the total effect of the scene. What can be satisfactorily recounted in detail as vocal music, physical action, movements of the mind and shifts of feeling to be felt in the movement of the verse, cannot explain the quality of the feeling passing to the audience. Here difficulty begins in the analysis of drama, and particularly of poetic drama. We have already called up confusion by trying to verbalize a mixture of feelings. We have said of Desdemona alone that she is on the defensive, that she has dignity, that she tries to be reasonable, that some part of her wavers while another stands its ground, that she protests, that her strength goes, that she is miserable, fearful, lacking understanding, dazed, deflated and momentarily resigned. These remarks are descriptive and external. They have no power to suggest the

The Elements of Drama

impregnation of the scene with the feelings suffered, nor the continuity of the emotion as it is triply embodied by the three characters, nor how we are carried on its flood. They are inadequate to account for the depth of the audience's impressions felt in the theatre, for although it has been stated that our attention is chiefly given to Othello, and although on his exit it is possible to say that the focus changes to Desdemona, in effect there is at no point a wholly focal character. Though our eyes and ears may be upon a particular actor, we are at all times measuring what we see and hear against the situation as we envisage it: while we listen to Desdemona, we supply the Othello reaction to her, and vice versa. Any special weight put upon the emotions in, or inspired by, one character alone, tends to falsify the whole image in our minds. In a play the characters are not separable, even when they speak in soliloquy. Each speech acts as a catalyst on the elements of the situation to which each character is contributing. Were it possible to isolate the effect of the situation on the audience at any moment in the course of the performance, the task would be easier. But it is not possible. A completer analysis would involve, not simply an account of all the characters even in relation to each other, but the nature of the pressure upon those characters of what has gone before in time. The action of a play is something in transition, something that only has meaning in time passing. So what follows will be merely a gesture towards the effect of the scene, an attempt to recreate the image it forms in an audience's mind knowing that this serves only as a hint of a more complete experience.

In the analysis of speech and movement two elements have been omitted, the interaction of the characters and the imagery by which this interaction is expressed. These elements are not separable, since both have common roots in the author's poetic perception. Our not taking them into account has so far made of our description of the scene in *Othello* nothing more than

Dramatic Verse

a report of a clever piece of dramaturgy, the jealous husband rejecting the innocent wife, a situation trite, potentially melodramatic, offering opportunities of histrionics different in kind from the performance the play actually encourages.

The language through which Othello and Desdemona speak is written to raise the scene from the level of domestic melodrama. The argument between man and wife at the point we have chosen now no longer revolves round Othello's concept of 'honesty': we heard the meaning shift earlier in the scene:

OTHELLO. Why, what art thou?
DESDEMONA. Your wife, my lord; your true and loyal wife.
OTHELLO. Come, swear it, damn thyself;
Lest, being like one of heaven, the devils themselves
Should fear to seize thee: therefore be double-damn'd;
Swear thou art honest.
DESDEMONA.   Heaven doth truly know it.
OTHELLO. Heaven truly knows that thou art false as hell.[12]

The ground of the discussion has shifted to heaven and hell, and the issue in Othello's mind becomes one less of his own jealousy and more of the horror of a foul and mortal sin clothed in innocence. Desdemona's 'Alas, what ignorant sin have I committed?' touches off the explosion of all Othello's faith in the surety and order of his moral universe. Dropping the familiar 'thou', he asks her, 'Are you not a strumpet?' and Desdemona swears by her religion and in her hope of heaven that she is not. By using these words Shakespeare raises her from the level of the misunderstood wife to be a representative of Christian martyrdom, while Othello, speaking for heaven with the promptings of hell and Iago behind him (Iago is later recognized by Othello as 'that demi-devil' who 'hath thus ensnared my soul and body'[13]), is deceived in both worlds. In his eyes Emilia keeps 'the gate of hell', the brothel which is his wife's room, which stands for his home and his marriage. We remember that heaven sanctified this marriage in the beginning:

The Elements of Drama

DESDEMONA.   The heavens forbid
But that our loves and comforts should increase,
Even as our days do grow!
OTHELLO.   Amen to that, sweet powers![14]

For him to talk now of his house as if it were a brothel is fine rhetoric, and the sense aches at the idea of Desdemona, 'tender, fair', challenged with 'whore!', but for his wife to turn devil, and for the heaven of his marriage to turn to hell, is incredible to Othello. He looks upon his position with the sardonic self-contempt of a man crazed, of a man looking upon himself as a stranger:

> I took you for that cunning whore of Venice
> That married with Othello.

The verbal imagery anticipates the soul's argument to be heard in the sequel: 'No; heaven forfend! I would not kill thy soul.'[15]

The extract throws out a picture of the blasting of Othello's happiness, and of his self-torture. For him the sanctity of his marriage has become an issue as great as the salvation or damnation of a soul. It is there too to superimpose a picture of innocence martyred, of the soul within the 'vessel' tortured for the sake of human conceit, of a human sacrifice seen in its preparatory ritual. And yet it is neither the self-torture of Othello nor the torture of Desdemona that is behind our scene, but the composite picture of man in his pride doubting his own element of divinity, and in his doubt reversing all he holds valuable until the reason and coherence of his life is confused, slackened, degraded, 'Perplex'd in the extreme'.[16] Within the compass of the stage, a domestic quarrel has grown to the proportions of the mystery of man's relation to the laws of divine justice.

Some hold that the scene does not advance the play, since Othello has already decided what action he will take. In the previous scene he had said, 'Ay, let her rot, and perish, and be

Dramatic Verse

damned to-night; for she shall not live'. Thus we find our scene awkwardly argued away with excuses that Othello is still hoping to find disproof of Desdemona's guilt. A distinction must be drawn between the narrative line of the play, which hardly matters in this scene, and the concept of speech and action we are urging, one which serves to promote emotionally what might be called the 'thematic' line of the play. The scene presents the situation to the audience in such a light as to charge the drama with values, felt through the stage, that enlarge the meaning of the last act.

When modern verse dialogue is satisfying, it seems to be aiming at the same kind of proficiency and fullness as we find in the mature plays of Shakespeare. Mr Christopher Fry's *A Sleep of Prisoners* is an essay in poetic drama which is partly hindered by an uncertain idiom for the poetry. This is from Meadow's dream of the murder of Abel:

> ADAMS. Cain, drop those hands!
> *He is wheeled by an unknown force back against his bunk.*
>   O Sir,
> Let me come to them. They're both
> Out of my reach. I have to separate them.
> DAVID, *strangling Peter*. You can leave us now, leave us,
>   you half-and-half:
> I want to be free of you!
> PETER.   Cain! Cain!
> ADAMS. Cain, Cain!
> DAVID.   If life's not good enough for you
> Go and justify yourself!
> ADAMS. Pinioned here, when out of my body
> I made them both, the fury and the suffering,
> The fury, the suffering, the two ways
> Which here spreadeagle me.
> *David has fought Peter back to the bed and kills him.*
> O, O, O,
> Eve, what love there was between us. Eve,
> What gentle thing, a son, so harmless,
> Can hang the world with blood.

The Elements of Drama

DAVID, *to Peter*.   Oh,
    You trouble me. You are dead.
ADAMS. How ceaseless the earth is. How it goes on.
    Nothing has happened except silence where sound was,
    Stillness where movement was. Nothing has happened,
    But the future is like a great pit.
    My heart breaks, quiet as petals falling
    One by one, but this is the drift
    Of agony for ever.[17]

Mr Fry's episodes in this play are conceived strongly as physical movement. They are shot through with visual symbolism, with the properties of ballet. Of his experience in first producing it, Mr Michael MacOwan has said that

> the play almost seemed to stage itself. So vivid had been the picture in Christopher Fry's mind while he wrote it that, although the script had practically no stage directions, every move and piece of business seemed almost inevitable. It was lying there waiting. All that we had to do was to discover it.[18]

The actor in the part of Adams is encouraged to feel the voiced and bodily expression the verse expects. His arms are 'pinioned' and 'spreadeagled', like the statuesque wings of some great bird. 'O Sir' is his cry addressed to God, and his head and eyes are thrown up. The anguish of the appeal is caught up by the pain in the sounds of the words he is given to speak: 'They're both / Out of my reach.' The break in the sentence at the first line-ending accentuates the physical strain of the explosive 'both'; it simulates the forced intake of breath; the groan becomes shriller as he makes a renewed effort to free himself; his face and voice contort through the thin, high vowel sound of 'reach'. When he sees that his son is not affected by his cries of, 'Cain, Cain!' he tries with fresh vigour to free himself from what is holding him, and the verse repeats the muscular struggle with consonants more prominent by their alliteration: 'Pinioned here, when out of my body / I made them both.' The repetitions, 'the fury and the suffering, /

Dramatic Verse

The fury, the suffering', express the twisting of the head and shoulders, the writhing in agony of a father who witnesses the last stages of the murder of a son and recognizes a son as a murderer. His voice again rises shrilly on, 'the two ways / Which here spreadeagle me', as Abel at length dies and drops over the bed.

As with Shakespeare, the physical and visual interpretation of the lines lies within themselves. Mr Fry's range of effects is wide, and they are used to offer vigorous and colourful contrasts following quickly upon one another. We hear and see David pass from one kind of intensity, the wild and angry cry, 'You leave us now, leave us', to the low, uneasy rumble of his mind as he becomes quieter: 'Oh, / You trouble me.' Adams's change is more remarkable. As his physical pain changes to mental distress, so his arms are freed and his voice grows calm and measured in its tones. The author's control over his behaviour is in the whispered sibilants of the lines that begin 'How ceaseless the earth is'. The lines drop away with shorter phrases; the voice is hushed, the stage stilled:

> quiet as petals falling
> One by one, but this is the drift
> Of agony for ever.

This is contrasted again when Cain tries to recover his self-confidence with a rasping colloquialism, an attempt at a feeble and vain bravado that makes us wince: 'Now let's hope / There will be no more argument.'

Seen as a whole, this sequence of contrasts submits and controls its own tempo. It has been worked up through the mimed dice game and reaches a pitch of intensity when the two active figures on the stage, Adams and David, at a distance from each other and each talking to his own purpose, have their speeches counterpointed. Each cry of brutality from David is stressed by Adams's redoubled protests. Peter's last ineffectual appeal of 'Cain! Cain!' is repeated and echoed by

The Elements of Drama

Adams speaking in sympathy: this too serves to whip the tempo along. The change is strikingly abrupt when the pitch and pace is relaxed upon the release of Adams, an exhausted and helpless figure on his knees. He now ceases his struggle with God and retreats in humility to the human comfort of his wife. The silence and stillness of the stage at this moment, the shock and terror of this anticlimax, is heard in the lines

> Nothing has happened except silence where sound was,
> Stillness where movement was.

The sense of death on the stage, its horror, and the knowledge of retribution to come, make the suspense of the long pauses after the killing both fitting and effective. The simplicity of the verbal image, 'But the future is like a great pit' is appropriate, and its clipped syllables hit off the atmosphere created by the event and by the change in the tempo.

One has reservations, however, about the rhythmic idiom Mr Fry has chosen to work in. What are the advantages of Shakespeare's firmer metrical line? Mr Fry's rhythms are comparatively limp because he cannot fall back upon a standard of regularity from which any departure provides a rhythmic meaning to the ear. And although we can identify voice and gesture from the swing of a phrase, the lines in *A Sleep of Prisoners* lack momentum. They lack a cumulative pressure which comes also from this constant reference to a norm of verse speech, such as Mr Eliot has attempted since *The Cocktail Party* and Mr Fry is more aware of in *The Dark is Light Enough*. In our passage a long sequence of phrases based on a loose colloquial idiom relaxes the weight wanted behind Adams's speech of suffering, no matter how firmly Mr Fry tightens these particular lines. Some of the force of the words is dissipated before they are spoken.

The temporary effectiveness of this crisis is a result of a colourful blending of some of the properties of stage words,

Dramatic Verse

their music and their movement. This effectiveness is not exceptional to Mr Fry when he brings to his dialogue his sense of the stage. But the play's interest lies in the meaning with which he has attempted to load such effects of sensation. Already through the design of the play and its dreams, the common soldiers of modern times are urged to become figures representative of violence and resistance to violence, and are charged with what significance our awareness of the Bible can lend. Yet does the author realize these transformations on the stage? By what dramatic chemistry do the changes take place? Is this an Adam we are prepared to admit to our experience? Is what we witnessed merely an adroit stage technique or is it substantiated by admissible feeling?

Some of the visual pictures and the verbal meanings have their source in the same concept, and they are finely involved with each other. Thus, 'the fury and the suffering' suggests gesture and movement, as has been said, but these words also express the feeling of a father helpless to prevent the crime of fratricide. In addition they express the feeling of Adam, father of all men, watching the two parts of his progeny at war. He is aware of the character of David's passion, 'the fury', the passion that Peter had in the pulpit described with mock solemnity as 'the bestial passions that beset mankind'.[19] And he sees Abel's quality as an opposite, as passivity, 'the suffering' that David, the realistic soldier of the opening of the play, had indicated in suitable slang to be an attitude of 'There's nothing on earth worth getting warmed up about!'[20] They are offered as the two grounds of behaviour, the two basal attitudes of mankind. They are 'the two ways' that split the individual mind which was in the beginning a comfortable unity: 'out of my body / I made them both'. They are the Cain and Abel in man, instincts that propose clashing courses of action for his progress. Adams is summing up the significance of the event for us, and we may not object to the simplification in the symbolism since it is the business of the rest of the play to expand this elementary view of the roots of good and evil towards the sophisticated complexities of modern compassion and violence. *A Sleep of Prisoners* is a modern morality play. We are intended to follow the symbolic debate by having the visual impressions obliquely identified by such uttered explanations.

If one's complaint against the play is a complaint of its coldness, of its failure to move us, this arises perhaps because there is at times a partial separation of what we see from the meaning affixed. The text is not as close-grained as it might be because the ideas are not wholly clarified in verbal imagery that has its impulse from the whole meaning. No image can therefore be recalled to mind as can a motif in music. The theme behind 'the drift of agony', for example, is central to the emotional residue this episode is to leave. Sharp and bright at the time of speaking, it is dulled by the presence of too many other images before it recurs in the last episode of the play.

Nor does Mr Fry give himself time to develop the episodic situations in human terms: there is a limited realization of an unlimited idea. This may be the source also of complaints about the play's obscurity: the intelligence at work behind the play is not equalled at all points by the control over the action. The dangers of a play too weighted with symbolism showed themselves when the reviewers of the first production in 1951 were led either to make the charge of obscurity or to suggest meanings in the play more complex than could legitimately be found. When too many avenues are opened but unexplored, a full text complicates the simple line desirable in a morality of this kind. Even the modern mind finds it difficult to argue in allegorical dialectic.

To conclude: the reasons for verse in a play, apart from any tradition current at the time, stem from the need of the

Dramatic Verse

dramatist to write in a language specific and explicit. If we agree that a play rests on the acceptance of a convention of speech, the verse dramatist feels that dialogue in the form of conversation is as artificial a limitation in one way as dialogue in the form of verse is in another.

It is nevertheless true that prose may also provide a subtle and concentrated action, as Ibsen and Chekhov at least have proved. As we said, the rules of the stage for verse are no different in kind from those for prose: it is the way of assembling the score that creates dramatic meaning, not the raw materials used. Naturalism is not necessarily taking a lazy line of least resistance. This needs to be said in the heat of discussions about the function of verse on the stage and about the condition of English playwriting, discussions that have been going on for half a century. Yet because plays particularize and intensify, and because poems have comparable aims, some have concluded that poetry is the 'natural' medium for the stage. Extreme statements of the case are not unfamiliar:

I shall only enquire whether the assumption that prose is the natural and straightforward medium for a play be not profoundly mistaken; whether, on the contrary, it be not poetry that is the natural and straightforward medium.[21]

The dramatist who is not a poet is so much the less a dramatist.[22]

In English only the use of verse on the stage can elevate the drama to a position where its achievements may be taken as seriously as those of the novel.[23]

That a good play is a verse play, and a prose play is a novel gone wrong, is a familiar assertion. Unhelpful criticism arises because the critic ceases to think about the 'subtext' for which the words stand. The 'poetry' lies in the depth and strength of the whole meaning of the stage action, and only indirectly in the words spoken, otherwise it would be hard to justify on its own merits the verse in *Tamburlaine the Great*, in *The Lady's Not For Burning*, in *The Cocktail Party*. And only if it

The Elements of Drama

is argued that the poetry is in the whole meaning is it possible to refer to a play by Chekhov as 'poetic', as is often done, when its language remains an approximation to conversation. Misguided views on the function of verse in drama are the result of accepting the fallacy that drama is a purely literary form.

There is no conclusive evidence to support the contention that the driving force of modern English verse drama is the narrowing desire merely for full dramatic speech to replace probable conversation.[24] If a playwright uses verse today it is because he wishes by traditional methods to make his play a more universal statement, one of extended range. So he rejects representational for 'presentational' dramatic form. Doing this may affect the whole treatment of his subject: the stage may become a platform for the angular and staccato presentation of an abstract idea, and the actor may become a marionette acting in a style suited to the degree of abstraction, as in an Expressionist play like Toller's *Masses and Man*. Toller stands back from his subject and rejects the naturalistic detail which would dwarf his abstraction. The writer of presentational drama may use all the agencies of the stage to render his ideas transparent for our better understanding of them. But this is the point at issue: it is likely that *the language will lose its realistic appearance as well* and, though not necessarily, take on verse form. When language in drama moves away from conversation, then, it is because the conception behind the play has demanded it. Although it is true that the words are usually a good guide to the nature of other conventions in which the play should be played, such as the acting itself, one would be reluctant to say that a play is in such and such a convention *because of* the language: the language is only one manifestation of the original image of the play conceived in the dramatist's mind. Of plays written in realistic dialogue, Mr J. B. Priestley's *An Inspector Calls* and

Dramatic Verse

O'Neill's *The Emperor Jones* are but two examples which invite production in a non-realistic manner.

However, the poetic dramatist has this distinction, that he is using language as his strongest contributory instrument in the communication of his idea. It is fitting therefore to close this chapter with the reminder that the playgoer visiting a verse play will expect to give the same kind of discriminating attention to the detail and structure of sight and sound in the play as he would give to the detail and structure of words in a poem.

3

MAKING MEANINGS IN THE THEATRE

In a good play all the agencies of the dramatist from the literary meaning of the word to the non-literary effects of motion and stillness are brought into use as an integral expression of meaning which is indivisible in performance. Dialogue is the scaffolding inside which stage meanings are erected.

In the theatre one does not separate verbal from physical expression. The statement 'I am going to kill you' and the act of killing are extensions of the same idea. Faustus's business of cutting his arm is inseparable from his declaration:

> Lo, Mephistophilis, for love of thee,
> I cut mine arm, and with my proper blood
> Assure my soul to be great Lucifer's,
> Chief lord and regent of perpetual night![1]

The explanatory comment and the deed illuminate each other: the audience accepts what it sees and hears as a unity. Deed, statement, and silence, spring simultaneously from the author's concept. A signal for meaning may even come from something external to the actors, as when lights dim, or when music makes its comment. A stage property can be a vivid token of expression and understanding: a tattered hat in the first act of *Waiting for Godot* symbolizes the dignity of mankind. Worn by the moronic Lucky, it enables him to 'think'; used for a music-hall antic by the tramps Estragon and Vladimir, it is emphatically derided. Any device to stimulate in the audience the required degree and kind of attention is properly the concern of the playwright.

Making Meanings in the Theatre

To understand how such meaning is made in the theatre we must distinguish between what happens on the stage and what happens in the imagination of the spectator. He takes from the detail of the scene impressions that are sown and ripened in the mind. These impressions may be independent of what the character on the stage is doing: the significance of what he is doing is what only the *audience* may know. This is especially true of words spoken. When Mephistophilis promises Faustus he will be as great as Lucifer, we are not asked to believe him, but when Faustus does believe him, we with our superior knowledge recognize his folly. Marlowe has calculated that we would: one joy in the play is to see our wisdom confirmed by events. This is the true irony of drama, through which the dramatist does most of his work; it is the steady and insistent communication to the privileged spectator of a meaning hidden from the characters.

Further, the spectator's impressions taken from a scene are fluid, since they are incomplete in themselves until the play is done. An act of killing is not completed with the killing. The killer is probably asking himself what he will do next; but the audience is certainly asking the same question. The next impression has already begun to shape itself. So Faustus, having shed blood as a sign of good faith, and having called upon it to be 'propitious' to his wish, finds to his horror that it congeals when he tries to write with it. But he does not interpret this portent as we do; he defies the life within himself:

> Why streams it not, that I may write afresh?
> *Faustus gives to thee his soul*: ah, there it stay'd!
> Why shouldst thou not? is not thy soul thine own?
> Then write again, *Faustus gives to thee his soul.*

His declaration, his momentary doubt, his renewed dedication are in continuous and developing sequence by which we confirm and deepen our impression of his lust.

The Elements of Drama

But it is natural for the stage to use as agents of communication those that come easily to it and those it has traditionally relied upon: one or more actors and what they can exhibit in make-believe before spectators. Primary meaning arises from the tactical handling of actors in their elementary role as human counters in a strategic game, the arrangement of 'characters' in a 'situation'. The dramatist has always conceived embodied human relationships rather than a design of words like a poem. When the *commedia dell'arte* was performing, the simple narrative of an event was mimed. When the actors improvised dialogue, it was only as an adjunct to, and a refinement of, what they could express by physical actions. For the most part, simple representative business by characters identified by mask and costume enabled the spectators to recognize a story. Beyond encouraging that delightful anticipation of a simple self-evident plot, how could these actors add to the excitement? The typical *commedia dell'arte* plot is concerned with winning the lady or the money or both at someone else's expense. The characters are either dupes or dupers, either a Pantalone or an Arlecchino, either a Dottore or a Brighella. The pleasure for the spectator lies in his knowledge that one is outwitting another, in his feeling in league with the deceiver in the deception. The recurring element, by a simple manipulation of puppets telling their story in mime, is an irony that is not merely verbal, but intrinsic to the stage.

The vigour of the dialogue in Molière is attributed to its origins in the actors' tradition. In *The Miser* the go-between Frosine is flattering Harpagon to promote his marriage with Marianne:

FROSINE.... You are something like a man, something worth looking at. You have the sort of figure women fall in love with, and you dress the part too.
HARPAGON. You think I'm attractive?

Making Meanings in the Theatre

FROSINE. Why, you are quite irresistible. Your face is a picture. Turn round a little, if you please. What could be more handsome? Let me see you walk. There's a fine figure of a man—as limber and graceful as one could wish to see! Not a thing ails you.

HARPAGON. No, nothing very serious, Heaven be praised, except a bit of catarrh that catches me now and again.

FROSINE. Oh, that's nothing. Your catarrh is not unbecoming. Your cough is quite charming.[2]

We know what Frosine is about, and if we don't, her tone of voice and crescendo of praises would tell us. This irony is conceived, however, quite visually, and our enjoyment of Harpagon's gullibility is increased as he prances awkwardly across the stage and we witness the incongruity between her praises and the object of them. Frosine's comments on his catarrh and his cough add the last touch of the ridiculous. We balance what we see and hear, what Frosine says of him and what he says of himself, and form a view for ourselves about the flattery and the flatterer and especially about the flattered, a view which survives independently of our knowledge of the particular self-deception of Harpagon or of the particular wiles of Frosine. The meaning exists in the relationship between them, and Molière is doing more than drawing us into Frosine's deception: he is fulfilling his first purpose of making us sharply aware of how far the miser's obsession with money will take him.

The texture of a play will become finer in proportion as its author can say more to the spectators through an ironic management of the actors. The actors perform two functions: they act and talk to themselves, and they act and talk to the audience. Irony works easily in the larger narrative of a complete story, as in *King Oedipus* or *Macbeth*, and the traditional term 'dramatic irony' applies especially to Greek tragedy and to any drama in which the audience is expected to know the outcome of events—since the characters do not share our secret, our knowledge adds an edge to our pleasure in the play.

The Elements of Drama

But irony as a means of stage communication is at work constantly in a play in performance: it is a process which permeates its speech and action. Its sensitive touch is felt whenever a fusion of impressions takes place, in degrees large and small, even in the smallest detail of the intonation or gesture that quickens the word, as artlessly as a wink from Mosca in *Volpone* or as deftly as when Masha in *The Three Sisters* took off her hat. Its effect is urgent and irresistible.

Regard its function not merely as a contrivance of plot or a stylistic twist of language, but *as a way of seeing*, by bringing together chosen contradictions and disagreements. Regard it as the metaphor of the theatre which enlightens understanding and refreshes imagination with stab after stab of hint and suggestion. When Keats writes, 'Where youth grows pale, and spectre-thin, and dies'[3] in preference to his earlier version of this line, 'When youth grows pale and thin and old and dies', he has first increased attention to his subject by revitalizing the rhythm and introducing a verbal image startlingly remote, and its initial incongruity strikes the reader. He has also intensified meaning and quality by forcing together what we associate with 'youth' and what we associate with 'spectre', compelling us to see his subject in a distinct light: we now see youth as a spectre and the spectre in youth. In seeing this image as a unity we have at the poet's injunction created new meaning: and as readers we have participated in the work.

In drama is there not a function analogous with that of metaphor in poetry? We listen to character A and we listen to character B, but what we assimilate as the effect of the passage between them is a *tertium aliquid*, something the author is saying that we apprehend only as the result of the fusion of the two character-statements like the notes of a musical harmony. Or we listen to a single character speaking, and we know that what he says will work upon the situation in which

Making Meanings in the Theatre

he says it in a way more than he knows: what we receive is something beyond the mere representation of the actor. The author speaks obliquely throughout the play, and by forcing upon our attention this or that speech or deed, he is working to guarantee our co-operation in the joint enterprise of communication. The audience follows a play by discovering it; it is constantly interpreting signs, looking beyond the actors, listening between the lines. The play only has meaning through what the audience in this way is allowed to perceive. So in the extracts we have used there is a central ironic moment in each, if we care to recognize it.

Recall our fusion of impressions when Rebecca is at the window:

MRS HELSETH. Isn't that Mr Rosmer coming there?
REBECCA. Where? Yes, it is he. Stand on one side. Don't let him catch sight of us.

Mrs Helseth gives us impression A, that there's a man outside of whom we know nothing other than his name. Rebecca gives us impression B, that these women wish to see but not be seen. From the conjunction of the two impressions we gain an insight into a situation, and already we know something more than the character Rosmer does. This provides a frank visual irony that gives *Rosmersholm* an impetus from its first moments. It would have been as strong had Rebecca been in the room alone and conveying these words in mime, but of course with Mrs Helseth there as *confidante* visual meaning is made more precise. The irony is at the expense of a character who will enter later: we therefore anticipate his entrance more keenly. And it has told us about Rebecca's certain state of concern for Rosmer: we therefore regard her more shrewdly after this, to find Ibsen's hint taken up in her subsequent behaviour.

The entrance of Gwendolen presents a more complicated irony, because it operates on the assumption that we will supply

The Elements of Drama

our interpretation of Gwendolen and Cecily from previous scenes to point it:

CECILY. Pray let me introduce myself to you. My name is Cecily Cardew.
GWENDOLEN. Cecily Cardew. What a very sweet name! Something tells me we are going to be great friends.

What has gone before in the play leaves us well aware of trouble to come between Gwendolen and Cecily. Impression A is therefore of the context of the scene, of two young ladies likely to be unhappy in each other's company. Impression B is of the courtesy with which they greet each other and is emphasized by Gwendolen's implication of a predestined friendship, contrary to what we expect. Wilde's irony of their dissembling is technically a finer piece of drama than Ibsen's: as detached and critical observers on the comic scene, we relish our superiority as the characters wriggle in their embarrassment behind their curtain of coventional manners.

The ironies underlying the passage from *Othello* run deeper. The force of the whole 'brothel' scene rests upon the innocence and ignorance of Desdemona and upon the guilt and error of Othello, but taken in such crude terms the irony is in quality not unlike that of the Molière extract. The scene is made more meaningful by forcibly translating the house into a brothel, the wife and husband into whore and client, and Emilia into bawd. Thus in

OTHELLO. Are you not a strumpet?
DESDEMONA.   No, as I am a Christian,

impression A is of Othello incensed and carried to a bitter extremity in thinking of his wife as 'a strumpet'. Impression B however, is one of Desdemona's nobility of demeanour, of her purity as it has been built up for us, and of the quality of her love, strengthened by her introduction of Christian values into her declaration of it. Shakespeare stresses the clash by marking it with discordant images of vice and virtue. As a result, we do

Making Meanings in the Theatre

not simply feel sorry for a misunderstood wife; instead, we are jarred by an ambivalent effect of a Christian lady in a black brothel, an angel pulled into hell.

As in the *Othello* extract, the poetry in *A Sleep of Prisoners* helps it to be implicit with ironies. In the latter play, irony is in general more absolute, because the narrative outlines are taken from familiar Bible stories. Because we know the biblical sequence of events, we experience the overall effect of classical dramatic irony, but within this framework we accept the detailed ironies as they are induced by the author's particular interpretations of the events. Our previous knowledge of the outcome serves naturally to put an edge on the interpretations, and on the peculiarities of the author's own conception when they diverge from the original tradition. We remember Cain's first prickings of conscience:

> DAVID. You trouble me. You are dead.
> ADAMS. How ceaseless the earth is. How it goes on.

Mr Fry might have followed that with emphatic admonition from Adams, but this would have been dramatically hollow. He chose instead to throw up as impression B a wholly contrasting sensation, one of Adams's premonition of larger and impalpable consequences: 'How ceaseless the earth is.' We deduce that death is an event in time, but that life is measured in eternity. Immediately the subject is raised from that of mere murder to a universal and a more urgent level. This would have been the whole effect had we no biblical background to see it against. But because we are conscious of the traditional religious significance of the Cain and Abel story, the irony is redoubled, the meaning is transposed into another key. A murderer becomes the first murderer, and the killing is the blood-spilling that will taint man's life on earth.

Already the reader will have felt differences between the ironies in these examples, differences in quality, differences in

The Elements of Drama

kind. To recognize how they work is important, not only because irony is drama's essential tool, but because it is our chief means of examining the quality of the texture of a play and of evaluating the whole, and as such it cannot be disregarded.

The actor may ask, Am I to be bothered with irony if it is only something to be taken by an audience at my expense? If it is the unspoken matter of a play, perhaps it does not concern me? A moment's reflection will suggest that this cannot be the case: if the actor is the agent, he must be aware of his act of agency. In *The Play Produced* Mr John Fernald discusses variety and dramatic contrast: this is what in fact the actor contributes to the play upon his recognition of an irony. Mr Fernald writes

> it is as a matter of course expected of a producer that he should give proper expression to what the playwright has presented to him. But his work 'of bringing something' to the play begins with the supplementing of the author's contrasts with a perpetual variety in the performance.[4]

Variations of tempo, volume and pitch in speech, variations of tone of voice, of type of movement, and so on, must be calculated to stress contrast where the author intends irony, not in another place, otherwise meaning becomes nonsense. This is because dramatic meaning derives from the play's ironies. Mr Fernald's contrasts are the metaphors from which are projected our dramatic impressions.

Thus in the example from *A Sleep of Prisoners*, both David and Adams are caught in wonder after the killing of Peter, but the differences between them are striking, and must be sufficiently felt by the actors to be felt in the auditorium. David is looking inward, is self-centred; but Adams is looking outward, aware in a new way of his environment. David's fear is directed towards the dead; but Adams has turned away from it and senses its repercussions upon a wider world. David is struggling for an understanding he will never attain; but Adams

Making Meanings in the Theatre

has already learned to seek his answers from beyond his own reason. The tempo of their speeches is the same, the pattern of their sentences is almost parallel, but the actors will try to provide the essential contrast in Adams's lower pitch and quieter speech, in the contrary movement of their bodies, and particularly by intonations which express Adams's greater understanding, a quality of calm, even of resignation. Where David's voice rises towards a suggestion of frenzy, Adams's will drop towards a suggestion of wisdom gained and growing from the event.

Dialogue between characters proceeds by assents and dissents, by one speaker echoing another or differing from him, with all the degrees of harmony or discord between these extremes. Since we receive our dramatic impression when we apprehend a discord in a certain context, it follows that judgment upon the quality of a performance rests upon our ability to see how it clarifies the variety of the text. Not that the playgoer needs to read the text to prepare the ironies before he sees the play. The intensity required of his attention will indicate the delicacy of texture in the play and its performance. Conversely, the spectator's degree of attention, as well as whatever the scene has to say to him, will be dependent upon the gradation and shading of the speech and action. Each actor will indicate in the appositeness of his reactions both his dependence upon another actor and his independence from him, that is, the integrity of his character. For such is the way the good dramatist sees the play as he constructs it.

The Playboy of the Western World is good drama for this reason, that the plot is simplicity itself, but nevertheless the response of the audience is subtle and delicate and of considerable complexity. In urging this it has the economy of great playwriting. It is an amalgam of ironies, and the complexity of the audience's response is due to the way in which the author manages with the visual and aural detail of his dialogue to flex and vary and refine our impressions. The meaning of the scene is intenser, its outline sharper, its importance greater, although by comparison the narrative action on the stage is bald. Thus the triple twist to the tail of the play is not a perversity, but a natural outcome of a play which is a mosaic of twists.

The first act carefully sets the tone and drift of the ironies. From Christy Mahon's first entrance, the stage presents a pattern of fluctuations in the tempo and movement of the characters as they veer between doubt of and respect for Christy. At first those in the shebeen patronize him:

PEGEEN. There's a queer lad. Were you never slapped in school, young fellow, that you don't know the name of your deed?

Their interest in the crime increases rapidly upon Christy's 'I'm not calling to mind any person, gentle, simple, judge or jury, did the like of me', to the crisis, 'Don't strike me. I killed my poor father, Tuesday was a week, for doing the like of that.' On this admission they retreat from him in some respect. But it remains a doubtful respect until they hear the manner of the crime: 'I just riz the loy and let fall the edge of it on the ridge of his skull.' From here Christy's confidence begins to grow with their esteem.

This is a severe summary of the line of the action, but it shows how the audience's regard for Christy will contrast with Pegeen's and Michael's, Philly's and Jimmy's. The life of the whole play is in that contrast. Our attitude to him was in part determined by his bathetic entrance:

For a perceptible moment they watch the door with curiosity. Some one coughs outside. Then Christy Mahon, a slight young man, comes in very tired and frightened and dirty.
CHRISTY *in a small voice.* God save all here!

The first impression of his slightness is the foundation of the spectator's estimation of him. Interest in Christy will grow

Making Meanings in the Theatre

as the characters' interest grows, but the nature of our response will differ in inverse proportion. When they glorify Christy

> PHILLY. There's a daring fellow.
> JIMMY. Oh, glory be to God!

our instinct is to vilify him. We do not do this because, of course, we do not readily jump to conclusions when a scene is still in progress. We are more bothered by the difference between our reaction to Christy and that of the characters. Christy is the focus of attention for the characters on the stage, but the spectator's attention embraces the whole stage picture.

Having thus prepared his audience, Synge goes on to sharpen the impression with this:

PEGEEN. That'd be a lad with the sense of Solomon to have for a pot-boy, Michael James, if it's the truth you're seeking one at all.
PHILLY. The peelers is fearing him, and if you'd that lad in the house there isn't one of them would come smelling around if the dogs itself were lapping poteen from the dung-pit of the yard.
JIMMY. Bravery's a treasure in a lonesome place, and a lad would kill his father, I'm thinking, would face a foxy divil with a pitchpike on the flags of hell.
PEGEEN. It's the truth they're saying, and if I'd that lad in the house, I wouldn't be fearing the loosed khaki cut-throats, or the walking dead.
CHRISTY, *swelling with surprise and triumph*. Well, glory be to God!
MICHAEL, *with deference*. Would you think well to stop here and be pot-boy, mister honey, if we gave you good wages, and didn't destroy you with the weight of work?
SHAWN, *coming forward uneasily*. That'd be a queer kind to bring into a decent, quiet household with the like of Pegeen Mike.
PEGEEN, *very sharply*. Will you whisht? Who's speaking to you?
SHAWN, *retreating*. A bloody-handed murderer the like of....
PEGEEN, *snapping at him*. Whisht, I am saying; we'll take no fooling from your like at all. *To Christy with a honeyed voice*. And you, young fellow, you'd have a right to stop, I'm thinking, for we'd do our all and utmost to content your needs.[5]

The question arising in the discussion is, Will a murderer make a good pot-boy?—one grotesquerie among the many that compose the fabric of the play. All the characters except Shawn are trying to persuade Michael to employ the stranger; superficially, therefore, we get an accumulation of arguments for it. Christy is reluctant to say where he killed his father, so Pegeen attributes to him 'the sense of Solomon'. The peelers have not followed him, so Philly twice suggests they 'is fearing him, and if you'd that lad in the house there isn't one of them would come smelling around'. And finally, to complete this trio of advisers, Jimmy points out that killing one's father takes bravery, so it is argued that Christy is brave, and 'Bravery's a treasure in a lonesome place'. We are not intended to feel incongruity between the three speeches, since they are in accord. Irony does not arise therefore by any comparison between what they say. But each echoes the illogicality of the other, the folly of the reasoning in each case making the total argument more and more ridiculous, especially as each contributor raises his voice a tone higher and speaks with increasingly assertive Irishisms. We are being asked to believe by implication that a killer would be just the one to have in a lonesome place with you, that black is white, that two and two make five. There is irony in the wit here of course, and we laugh at the incongruity of it, but such irony and such laughter are of the surface only.

The real incongruity, the real irony and the real control over the spectator springs from their *agreement*. We would have expected Philly to contradict Pegeen, Jimmy to contradict Philly, and finally we would have expected Pegeen to stop the progress of an argument moving so quickly towards the ludicrous. Instead she pursues it with a note of flirtatiousness in her voice and manner. Pegeen the single girl, Pegeen who will have to work with him, live in the house with him, caps them both with, 'if I'd that lad in the house, I wouldn't be fearing the loosed khaki cut-throats, or the walking dead'. She would prefer Christy to a Tommy and to a spectre; if she

Making Meanings in the Theatre

had with her a killer with a loy, she would not fear a killer with a knife; if she had with her a man whose conscience was burdened by the ghost of a dead father, she would not fear a ghost itself. Impression A does not confound impression B: it underlines it, and underlines impressions C and D as well. Our imagination is daringly distorted. The spectator asks himself what statement Synge is making, what to believe. Because there is a strict antithesis between our logic and theirs, and because they are thinking in unison, we can only deduce by our standard of behaviour that they are mad, the more so for appearing so serious in what passes for their reasoning. We bridge the theatrical gap between our minds and theirs with a mental gesture of half-dismissal: we laugh. But now Synge can weave his bizarre magic on us.

Christy is surprised too: 'Well, glory be to God!' So they are not all in a conspiracy of madness, and their response was not wholly to be expected after all. Perhaps our first impression of Christy as rather a contemptible young man was a right one: Christy's remark evidently confirms us in this. But the attention of Pegeen, Philly and Jimmy has been directed on Michael, and now our attention is led there too. Michael will surely resolve the contradiction. We wait in the slight pause, savouring the situation and trying the weight of Michael's decision. We anticipate something like 'The saints forbid that ever I should do the like of that!' but instead we hear a gentle, deferential voice: 'Would you think well to stop here and be pot-boy, mister honey....?' And Michael goes on to offer good wages and light work. The gap is strained again. We are not certain what to think. Is impression A in relation to impression B unmeaning? Is our recognition of a criminal, supported as it is by a code of right and wrong, to have no support from the characters on the stage and to bear no relation to any code of values within the play? We are left wondering again at the characters' irrational behaviour.

The Elements of Drama

Perhaps we are to dismiss it as we dismiss it in farce? But the stage action as it has been described is not complete.

Our critical response is not allowed to be so simple, because Shawn is on stage too, cowering in the corner, and, observe, reacting to Christy in a manner quite different from the others. Synge has been at pains through the first ten minutes of the act to fill out the character of Shawn. He is not there simply to contrast with Christy. He is there in chief to establish and show the conventional response to a murderer and a patricide. Is it then intended that he should be our chorus, and as *raisonneur* represent our feelings towards Christy? No, for how could this be? His is an excessive physical cowardice and a fanatical and hyper-religious attitude. We must be reluctant to let this sort of example be our guide: 'God help me, he's following me now, and if he's heard what I said, he'll be having my life, and I going home lonesome in the darkness of the night.'

Yet it is Shawn who now speaks our *own* comment: 'That'd be a queer kind to bring into a decent, quiet household.' Was it accident that we phrased the comment we anticipated from Michael as Shawn would have spoken it? So Synge judges us, and uses Pegeen, who was earlier taking her death with the fear, to reprove Shawn and us: 'we'll take no fooling from your like at all'. We observe she says 'we', and draws together the majority against Shawn. By the movement of her body and the change in her tone, she isolates him, the outsider, one not in the compact. And she reduces his eminent reasonableness to 'fooling'. But who is fooling?

We are left undecided, our attitude unsettled, with no certain finger left us to wag, our received impression askew. But we are forced to reconcile and make shapely this grotesquerie if we are to sit comfortably through the play. If we choose to accept Synge's coloured view of his Irish peasant characters, and can stomach this extraordinary method of

Making Meanings in the Theatre

revealing it to us, the play will supply a nice insight into human nature. We may even care to echo what Mr Edmund Wilson said in 1931, that this was the most authentic poetic drama the century had seen.[6] If not, we may boo with the first audiences who saw it at the Abbey Theatre in 1907. There are not many plays in which the author is so playful with his audience, or juggles with its feelings and adjusts the focus of its imagination so sportively to achieve his ends. *The Playboy* is a bold use of the theatre, and a good example of how extravagant a dramatist can be.

It was suggested at the beginning of this chapter that the spectator's impressions are fluid, and therefore one unit of meaning cannot be separated from the next. All drama will utilize in some degree the power the stage itself possesses to modify those impressions. It deliberately creates a shifting 'image', an impression changing in time, since drama moves in time. With four dimensions capable of working the machinery of his medium, the good playwright will not hesitate to throw all four switches. The score of dramatic dialogue must be examined again to see how it urges this convenient instability of impression and makes use of this precious fourth dimension.

4
SHIFTING IMPRESSIONS

The quality in a play that distinguishes it is its animation—not of actors acting and speaking, but of our imaginative impressions. If we can understand how these move in time, flex and vary, develop, lend themselves to exploitation, we shall come closer to knowing how effective drama arises. A play is not an art of words, any more than a film is an art of pictures: it is the art of exercising them. *The Playboy of the Western World* cannot be flatly summarized as 'a satire on human perversity': how fixed and solid this sounds! The play is alive like gossamer, and it teases and woos us towards its discoveries.

What is 'dramatic'? It is difficult to find two people who agree, because it is difficult to draw principles from many plays each working to its own ends. Clearly it is not in any particular subject to be dramatic. It is possible for Shakespeare or Ibsen to communicate a state of mind, for Molière or Shaw to examine a social situation, for Goethe or M. Sartre to expound a philosophy, for Aeschylus or Mr Eliot to demonstrate a religion, and all can be dramatic. The secret lies in the way a degree and kind of attention is elicited from the audience.

Does a stage killing elicit a degree of attention? It does, but it is not in itself dramatic. It can be exciting, like a report in a newspaper or a good dinner. But each of these is static. Were it possible to prolong in time the act of killing or the fascination of the news item or the appetite for the dinner, any of these would provide a fully engaging attraction. But none of these renews its interest of itself. What matters more is the *kind* of attention.

Shifting Impressions

Once our attention is taken it must develop from one state of interest to another. When our impressions are changing, we in the audience pursue them because the pursuit is urgent to us, just as the eye follows a moving object. Interest, given life and sap, burgeons like a growing plant. We are interested in a character's future when he is changing, because it is unstable. We are interested in a situation when it is changing, because it is unresolved. The schoolteacher knows that when a question asked becomes a question answered, the subject of the question immediately begins to lose some of its interest for the pupils—unless the answer stimulates a further question. So it is that a stage event is undramatic when it is static. To be dramatic a play must start, elaborate and sustain a pattern of interest.

'I am going to kill you' is a threat. At once we are anxious to know if it will be carried out: a threat is inevitably dramatic. We speculate, that is, on the relationship that will exist between killer and potential victim after the threat is made. And we anticipate the situation the more keenly because we know it is pregnant with further possibilities. Faustus accepts Lucifer's offer, but this is a dramatic acceptance because it is not an end but a beginning.

Beyond this restless demand for a plastic stage action, there can be no initial assumptions about dramatic form: each play will dictate its own. How is Dylan Thomas's portrait-like radio play *Under Milk Wood* dramatic?—there is no plot; not one of its many characters 'develops'. It is because its theme, the spirit of a living community, starts the dramatic momentum within itself, like a round in music. *Under Milk Wood* presents one village in one day in one season, but the characters think of the past and dream of the future and take on typical qualities till their life becomes life itself revolving from day to day and from year to year. Our attention is held by the widening of the play's meaning in our minds through the intimate and imaginative conditions of the radio medium.[1]

The Elements of Drama

Unpretentiously, an audience looks for 'life' in a play, a source of interest; an actor looks for a strong part, one having a vitality he can embody to create character; the producer looks for good theatre, material worth developing for its latent interest. They are all looking for qualities of *change and development* implicit in the dialogue.

This does not mean that there must be a constant bombardment of new thoughts and feelings from the stage. If we believed this, we might condemn any dialogue which did not display a fidgety activity. There is a place for dialogue at rest, as there is a place for a speech repeated: the activity resides in the audience's mind, just as a pause in speech provokes a greater vigilance. We cannot agree with the suggestion that a long speech is a person agreeing with himself out loud, talking 'yes' language.[2] Romeo's final soliloquy, with its long rhetorical catalogue of the attributes of death, proves its worth by giving pause for reflection:

> Shall I believe
> That unsubstantial death is amorous,
> And that the lean abhorred monster keeps
> Thee here in dark to be his paramour?...[3]

The emotion of Romeo in the vault is painted in thick colour. But its justification is to let us mark and digest meaning, to evaluate the unity and purity of young love fighting the disintegration and corruption of powers beyond itself, of which 'unsubstantial death' is the chief. Seemingly slack playing can be dramatic if we acknowledge the animation of the audience before that of the actors.

Again, it would be facile to condemn Maeterlinck on these grounds. Here is a little of the dialogue from *Interior*, in which two characters are observing a family through the lighted windows of their house upstage:

THE STRANGER. They have raised their eyes....
THE OLD MAN. And yet they can see nothing....

Shifting Impressions

THE STRANGER. They seem to be happy, and yet there is something—I cannot tell what....

THE OLD MAN. They think themselves beyond the reach of danger. They have closed the doors, and the windows are barred with iron. They have strengthened the walls of the old house; they have shot the bolts of the three oaken doors. They have foreseen everything that can be foreseen....[4]

This is dramatic, not because it is possible to see some of the actors moving in mime, but quite simply because the audience has foreknowledge of an accident that has happened to one of the family. Maeterlinck is dwelling with care upon the susceptibility of the spectator who waits in suspense. The action on the stage is held up while the muscles of the mind overreach themselves. It might be a real criticism of the technicalities of the piece that unrelieved strain, as of a balloon inflated resolutely to the point of bursting, will destroy the image from within itself. But Maeterlinck attempts to impress his statement about fate in his chosen theatrical terms. The drama is alive, at least, in the audience, and this author should be judged on other counts than that he is sluggish.

It is more than a truism, then, to insist that a play stands or falls with its reception by the audience. The playwright's object at all times is to set the audience to work. Although in *Interior* the Stranger and the Old Man seem to be telling and describing activities improper to drama, and in Romeo's soliloquy Shakespeare himself seems to be telling and describing, they are not really doing so. They are providing a channel, though not the most usual or necessarily the best, down which our thoughts can flow, a means for us to 'tell and describe' to ourselves at the author's pace. The playwright, like any artist, works circuitously, giving us, so to speak, sunshine's colour to suggest its warmth, water's sound to suggest its motion. To do this, he makes special use of the feature of our image-making faculty most pronounced in the theatre, its changeability.

The play animates the audience by a goad placed in the

The Elements of Drama

hands of the actors. The interest in the drama creates and recreates impressions that move in a progression exactly determined by the progression in the action. Just as in the cinema sound must be matched or counterpointed with picture to produce the complex polyphonic 'imagery' of the whole, as Eisenstein realized,[5] so each sequence on the stage implies a harmonic or discordant 'image' that moves with it, giving the scene depth, as an orchestral score is written vertically in several staves. The concept can be expressed diagrammatically:

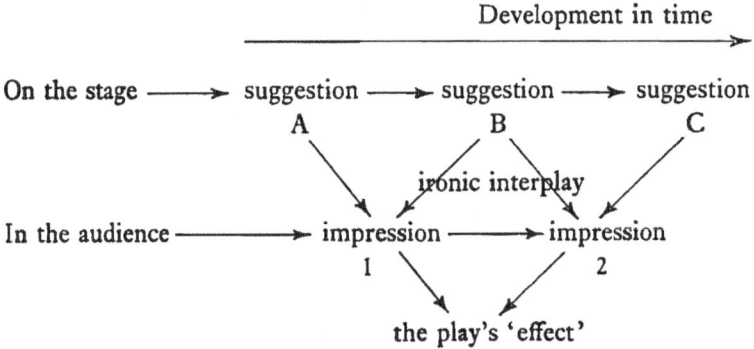

Impressions are received by the dramatic process of ironic deduction. But, again like the film, impressions alone are static and without dramatic value. V. I. Pudovkin, discussing the proper movement of a screen picture,[6] claims that every object shown on the screen is a dead object, even though it has moved before the camera. Only if the object be presented as part of a synthesis of separate objects is it endowed with filmic life. By a similar synthesis suggestions from the stage are given life, the good playwright fosters on us shifting impressions, and—behold!—his drama moves in time. The good critic measures and assesses the development between impression 1 and impression 2, a development which is the true source of effect in a play. But the primary activity in the theatre is simply that of the alert playgoer absorbing meaning-

Shifting Impressions

ful impressions by an accurate scrutiny of idea and feeling, his eyes and ears finely attuned to the actors' suggestions.

The simplest form of animation is one of regular development. The links in the chain of impressions become increasingly stronger. An example is provided by the quarrel between Brutus and Cassius, of which this is part:

> CASSIUS. When Caesar lived, he durst not thus have moved me.
> BRUTUS. Peace, peace, you durst not so have tempted him.
> CASSIUS. I durst not?
> BRUTUS. No.
> CASSIUS. What? durst not tempt him?
> BRUTUS. For your life you durst not.
> CASSIUS. Do not presume too much upon my love.
>   I may do that I shall be sorry for.
> BRUTUS. You have done that you should be sorry for.[7]

It is noticeable that most of this exchange finds a quick and ready response from an audience, because there is no ambiguity in the pattern of suggestions. Its emotions are running steadily in one direction, and quickness on the cueing is naturally demanded from the actors. Brutus challenges Cassius with a series of taunts, almost mocking him by echoing his words. Cassius responds with a display of feeling that is half incredulity, half a further challenge in the veiled threat behind his questions. They are two men spoiling for a fight: a simple sequence accumulates power to shape one intense impression. As their anger with each other increases, that fight seems more and more imminent. This meaning is, of course, overlaid by the context of the play, especially evocative because it suggests a reversal of their earlier comradeship and recalls the motives behind it: Cassius now likens Brutus to their former common enemy.

But no progression can remain as simple as this for long without monotony and consequent dispersal of interest. For how long can we listen to an 'I didn't—You did' squabble?

The Elements of Drama

The achievement of this quarrel scene lies in Shakespeare's ability to draw out their enmity, while at the same time varying it within itself. Already the impression has not merely magnified, but has shifted too. Go back to the words: how does the actor who has to speak Cassius's line 'Do not presume too much upon my love' know to change his tone of voice? True, there is a stronger threat in this, and the words are more level and measured, and therefore to some extent more weighty after the staccato 'I durst not?' 'What? durst not tempt him?' The real answer is that Cassius varies his approach and withdraws from the same kind of attack. Although this is only momentary in time, it is enough to suggest a violent change of impression, which unexpectedly cries to us that Cassius is giving a sign of reluctance, that he is the wiser of the two. On the other hand, Brutus returns to the attack, but we have had a significant relief and a hint of a subtler implication to look for in the exchanges that follow.

Already the less complicated has become more complicated, and it is in the nature of good drama that this should be. The pattern is a kaleidoscope recast from moment to moment, just as a detective story will shift the centre of its interest from chapter to chapter, the reader following a winding and deceptive trail through to the solution. Like this a dramatic moment from *Romeo and Juliet* shifts its impression:

> *Enter Romeo*
> TYBALT. Well peace be with you sir, here comes my man.
> MERCUTIO. But I'll be hang'd sir if he wear your livery:
>   Marry go before to field, he'll be your follower,
>   Your worship in that sense may call him man.
> TYBALT. Romeo, the love I bear thee, can afford
>   No better term than this thou art a villain.
> ROMEO. Tybalt, the reason that I have to love thee,
>   Doth much excuse the appertaining rage
>   To such a greeting: villain am I none.
>   Therefore farewell, I see thou know'st me not.[8]

Shifting Impressions

Tybalt has come looking for Romeo, and Mercutio has been tempting him to draw his sword, but he is keeping that for Romeo. We are keenly aware of the situation, and of their mood, burning like the heat Benvolio told us of earlier. Into this net from his marriage with Juliet comes Romeo: the ugliness of this scene is sharply contrasted with the 'dear encounter' of the previous one, and Romeo serves as the physical link between the two. Now, at the moment of his entrance, we hear and see Tybalt's fiery preliminary 'here comes my man', and we hear Mercutio speak, as he thinks, for Romeo. The challenge is virtually given, received and taken up already. We in the audience, like Tybalt and Mercutio on the stage, anticipate a particular reply from Romeo, and the fight itself. Suggestion anticipates suggestion. Tybalt raps out his challenge:

> Romeo, the love I bear thee, can afford
> No better term than this thou art a villain,

running the words together with the rhythm with which he in one motion draws and swings up his sword. Granville-Barker describes our anticipation at this moment:

What is Romeo's answer to be to an insult so complete in its sarcastic courtesy? Benvolio and Mercutio, Tybalt himself, have no doubt of it; but to us the silence that follows—its lengthening by one pulse-beat mere amazement to them—is all suspense. We know what is in the balance.[9]

Neither what is in the balance as Shakespeare has arranged it, nor the 'one pulse-beat' the producer will demand of his actor, adequately accounts for the effectiveness of Romeo's speech. Shakespeare has suddenly refused us what we wanted, and refocused the image. The shock we receive when we find that what we anticipate is contradicted, enables the author to make his effect more overwhelming. By it we *learn* what is in the balance, for we are shocked into suffering the meaning of his silence, that since Romeo has married Tybalt's kinswoman,

The Elements of Drama

and since he is now therefore his kinsman, both are in an impossible position of which only Romeo knows. The impression that has been modified by the quiet, controlled, casuistic answer grows screwed and tortuous as the climax of the scene rushes towards us.

Drama is composed of the infinite combinations and permutations of such impressions moving in time. There never were *trente-six situations dramatiques*. Indeed, no two productions, nor even two performances, can be the same. Why? The smallest change of intonation, lengthening of pause, lingering of gesture on the part of but one actor can form a substantially different impression which may modify all the rest. The barest pause before Romeo speaks, a frantic moment on a stage absolutely still and absolutely silent, can electrify the spectator. A pause, calculated or not, can be eloquent, as we know when an actor 'dries': if the lapse is at a crucial moment, the scene can be destroyed irreparably. But if the pause is imaginatively managed, its reflection can dazzle all the subsequent action. Anything an actor is capable of doing on a stage potentially illuminates or obscures, enlarges or narrows, a dramatic impression. An author whose stage suggestions are most delicately made will show how brittle the texture of a dramatic impression can be, how evanescent its shifting in our minds.

The great last plays of Chekhov have a structure in which every scrap of the dialogue is strictly relevant, but this can only be proved by scrupulous examination. Because of their close texture, deceptive in its loose appearance, his plays are difficult and demanding in production, while to read them at all adequately is wellnigh impossible. His achievement in the art of the theatre makes the effort worth while.

As has often been pointed out, Chekhov makes the largest concession to realism by discarding the concept of the hero or heroine. Each character is to a degree a centre within itself

Shifting Impressions

and has its own story, just as in life each man is his own hero, an axis round which other people are merely players. But on a Chekhovian stage we look at a whole group, and all the actors act all the time, so that one 'hero' cancels out another. An event, or even a general mood, will affect all the characters, but each in his own way, making one happy, another sad maybe. Adding up their sum we conclude within ourselves precisely what that event feels like, or what it is to experience that mood. We are made uncommonly aware in a new way of what it feels like to be alive. By refusing to put the usual theatrical emphasis on any one character, Chekhov's great achievement is to put the important stress on *relationships between* characters rather than on the characters themselves. Accordingly, events as such fade into the background of the play, and we are left only with their effect on relationships. For us to apprehend the links between characters, a method of shifting impressions must be prosecuted vigorously. The last interview between Lopakhin and Varya in *The Cherry Orchard* will demonstrate this facet of Chekhov's art.

MME RANEVSKY, *through the door*. Varya, come here a moment, leave what you're doing for a minute! Varya! *Goes out with Yasha.*
LOPAKHIN, *glancing at his watch.* Yes....*A pause. Suppressed laughter and whispering is heard from behind the door, and finally Varya comes in and starts examining the luggage. After some time she says:*
VARYA. It's strange, I just can't find....
LOPAKHIN. What are you looking for?
VARYA. I packed the things myself, yet I can't remember....

A pause

LOPAKHIN. Where are you going to now, Varvara Mikhailovna?
VARYA. I? To the Rogulins. I've agreed to look after the house for them...to be their housekeeper, or something.
LOPAKHIN. That's at Yashnevo, isn't it? About seventy miles from here. *A pause.* So this is the end of life in this house....
VARYA, *examining the luggage.* But where could it be? Or perhaps I've packed it in the trunk?...Yes, life in this house has come to an end... there won't be any more....

The Elements of Drama

LOPAKHIN. And I'm going to Kharkov presently....On the next train. I've got a lot to do there. And I'm leaving Yepikhodov here....I've engaged him.

VARYA. Well!...

LOPAKHIN. Do you remember, last year about this time it was snowing already, but now it's quite still and sunny. It's rather cold, though.... About three degrees of frost.

VARYA. I haven't looked. *A pause.* Besides, our thermometer's broken. ...*A pause.*

A voice is heard from outside the door: 'Yermolai Alexeyevitch!'

LOPAKHIN, *as if he had long been expecting it.* Coming this moment! *Goes out quickly.*

Varya, sitting on the floor, with her head on the bundle of clothes, sobs softly. The door opens, Mme Ranevsky enters quietly.

MME RANEVSKY. Well? *A pause.* We must go.[10]

In this scene we are not asked to show more sympathy for, or interest in, either Lopakhin or Varya. We know that the sale of the cherry orchard will take Varya to Yashnevo, seventy miles from her home, and that it will leave Lopakhin behind with more work to do, but we are not primarily interested in the individual futures of either of them. We are interested rather in what they feel towards each other. Their relationship as a couple expected to make a match has been hinted through three acts, and we have just heard Mme Ranevsky say

> You know very well, Yermolai Alexeyevitch, that I'd been hoping to get her married to you...and everything seemed to show that you meant to marry her, too. She loves you, and you must be fond of her, too...and I just don't know, I just don't know why you seem to keep away from each other. I don't understand it.

Now, through Mme Ranevsky's agency and the urgency of the departure, we are interested to see whether their regard for each other will bring their engagement about, and to see how they will behave towards each other in such circumstances. Lopakhin's proposal to Varya does not come off: again there is no direct emphasis placed upon an event. And so we are

Shifting Impressions

bound to ask ourselves how Chekhov is to avoid a theatrical vacuum, an absence of effect in the auditorium.

We read that Chekhov supplies a substitute for action and event, that he evokes a 'mood' or an 'atmosphere': by a series of theatrical stalemates he is supposed to put an overwhelming pressure of feeling upon the audience, which must pass for its catharsis. Or else we are told that we swallow a mixture of the comic and the pathetic in his ineffectual and frustrated characters, and then pronounce, 'Such is life'—and this must pass for a satisfying evening in the theatre. The 'laughter and tears' theory of Chekhov is dangerously easy.

Nearer the mark, perhaps, might be the view that Chekhov's trivialities and apparently inconsequential dialogue are there to show us how people appear, and against such appearances we are to balance what they momentously represent. It is a view seen through Chekhov's own statement, now a *locus classicus* of Chekhovian comment:

> It is necessary that on the stage everything should be as complex and as simple as in life. People are having dinner, and while they're having it, their future happiness may be decided or their lives may be about to be shattered.[11]

In other words, the Chekhovian triviality becomes an ironic symbol, which is irresistible in its effect because it is so like life, and yet which provides an intensely exciting evening in the theatre because its meaning is wider and fuller than in life. The more commonplace the triviality, such a theory might run, the greater the contrasting meaning, and consequently the greater the thrill of incongruity.

But some such examination as ours is indispensable if we are ever to become articulate about Chekhov's methods and effects, or ever to decide about the meaning his relationships contain or how the commonplaces of his dialogue point to it. In particular Chekhov's unique capacity for conveying a sensation of time passing can only be discussed in terms of shifting

The Elements of Drama

impressions. This capacity does not ultimately depend upon his skilful deployment of three generations, as in *The Cherry Orchard*, or upon his explicit dwelling upon the past, or upon his talent for demonstrating the growth of individual characters. The time motifs in Chekhov, which bring him closer to revealing a truth about experience than any other modern dramatist, lie deep within the action he puts upon the stage. The idea of the mutation of things springs through a succession of innumerable minute insights that are discovered to us while we assimilate his suggestions as they change.

First, how will the actor interpret the chosen passage of dialogue? The following is a description of a probable performance, the likely sequence of the action. All three characters concerned know what the interview is to be about. Lopakhin is to propose marriage to Varya: 'Let's settle it at once—and get it over!' he says, concealing his doubts and nervousness behind a show of decisiveness and a businessman's tactical approach, which even he will sense as inadequate for a delicate human problem. Mme Ranevsky goes out calling 'Varya!' and he is left alone on the stage awaiting her imminent appearance. Chekhov gives him one thing to do, to look at his watch, and one word to speak, 'Yes', which is in immediate and flat contrast with Mme Ranevsky's livelier conversation. It might mean, 'Yes, there is just time to do it'—he is the one who has arranged the details of their departure; or it might mean, 'Yes, I'll get the affair over and done with'. But it means neither of these, for they are the faint voices of a Lopakhin trying to deceive himself. The slight waver in the voice we hear tells us what the scene is going to tell us in the next few moments, that it means, 'Yes, I cannot avoid it now'. And the act of looking at the watch is the act of a man barricading himself behind a comforting defensive gesture. He starts as he hears the little burst of suppressed laughter: he feels that it is Anya, Charlotta, Mme Ranevsky, even Varya,

Shifting Impressions

indeed the whole family, enjoying the joke at his expense, as they have done before. He turns away and tries to appear unconcerned.

Varya is pushed in. Her excitement dies quickly, just as Lopakhin's gaiety had slipped away from him when Mme Ranevsky tripped out. She dare not look at him, and in hasty pretence she examines the luggage left about the room. But she must say something, the ice must be broken, and she must be the first to break it or neither of them will. What shall she say? 'It's strange, I just can't find...', she says, half excusing her presence in the room. She continues to rummage through the luggage. I ought to take advantage of this opening, thinks Lopakhin, and in the bright tone of one about to introduce a good topic for conversation, he says, 'What are you looking for?' He is looking at me now, she thinks—for neither of them to this point has dared meet the eye of the other. I must act away furiously, but what can I answer to his wretched question? I'll pretend I didn't hear it. 'I packed the things myself, yet I can't remember....' But, Varya, this is quite unlike you—you have never forgotten a thing in your life before. Lopakhin is too preoccupied to observe her lie.

Because she cannot be more definite about what it is she is looking for, Lopakhin's conversation is killed, and for an unhappy instant he struggles for another subject. He looks away again: I wish she would stop pulling that luggage about! Why not go straight to the point? Well, perhaps not quite *straight* to the point....' Where are you going to now...?' He has begun, thinks Varya with a fleeting sense of relief. This is the moment for the recognized forms of my maidenly modesty. The first rule is to express surprise: 'I?' There's no one else in the room, of course! The second rule is nonchalance: she tells him she is to be a housekeeper. She doesn't *need* marriage; she can look after herself. But she must not seem too final—that would never do. She must allow him a tiny loophole: '...to

The Elements of Drama

be their housekeeper, *or something*'. I must pursue this, thinks Lopakhin; this is making good progress. Perhaps I can bring the subject back to the cherry orchard, and then, perhaps, invite her to remain with me. He says breezily, 'That's at Yashnevo, isn't it? About seventy miles from here.'

What have I said? Did she sob? What was it Mme Ranevsky told me a minute ago?—'She cries a lot, poor thing'. What a blunder! What can I say? A little sympathy cannot be out of place: 'So this is the end of life in this house....' But Varya is hurt; the tears are spurting. He mustn't see me like this; he mustn't think it matters at all to me. So, back to the bundles on the floor: 'Where can it be?' Why can he not say what he is here to say? And in a tone of voice which says, I am very busy, I cannot be concerned about sentiment, and if you are going to propose to me you must hurry, she repeats his words: 'Yes, life in this house has come to an end....' That was a bad gambit, thinks Lopakhin, the man who so often seems to say and do the wrong thing. A more cheerful beginning is wanted. For safety's sake, it would be wiser to discuss myself first. So he begins again with an even brighter chatter, but still describing circles round his subject: 'And I'm going to Kharkov presently....' What is he saying? This is intolerable —I cannot keep up my pretence much longer. The voice which comments is distinctly bitter and dull: 'Well!...'

Lopakhin is thinking: I have made another mistake; I must have offended her; I must change my tactics; I must find a new subject; I must cheer her up. What can I see through the window? With a last strangled effort to be good humoured, he remarks on the weather: '...it's quite still and sunny'. Now, suddenly, the atmosphere of the half-deserted, dust-sheeted room and of the house that is to be abandoned permeates him; perhaps he even anticipates his own loneliness. He adds with a shudder, 'It's rather cold, though...'. His instinct as a man of method, maybe his desire to impress her,

Shifting Impressions

make him add his last clumsy offering of a quite inappropriate contribution to the conversation: 'About three degrees of frost.'

He has gone further and further away from the matter in hand, and Varya feels this more than he. It is too much for her, and in a voice now broken with tears she sobs at him, '...our thermometer's broken...'. She is really crying, 'You fool, you fool!' And there's another wretched moment when she halts, knowing that she has gone too far. Not knowing what he should do next, he flaps his arms as he always does, until—his name is called. Saved! 'Coming this moment!' Varya is now free to relax: she is alone. The episode, with the cruelty of its pain and its maddening ineffectualness, is over. She can collapse on to the bundle at her knees; the cry-baby can weep to her heart's content. But didn't she know this would be the result? She did, and her sobs grow softer and more resigned. Mme Ranevsky comes in quietly, and asks with a gay expectancy: 'Well?' In a flash she sees her foster-daughter in tears on the floor, and she reads all the details of the episode that has passed—she has no need to ask. Perhaps she, too, knew this would be the result. She moves more boldly into the room and her tone changes to the flat, bare understatement, 'We must go'.

So much for the actors and the sequence of suggestions. This outline can be largely substantiated, not merely by the elimination of alternatives, but by the carefully wrought hints throughout the play, hints which make a firm pattern for the interpretation of the essential action. The details of the episode are selected and arranged to be so close to life, so precise in characterization that even Stanislavsky's painstaking rehearsals might not plumb the depths of the dialogue. Yet to leave consideration of this passage at this is to dismiss it merely as a brilliant piece of virtuosity in the naturalistic manner. That is surely not enough. The quality of the drama is not in

The Elements of Drama

how actable the dialogue is: what does our imagination contribute?

In the theatre the episode passes in a few seconds, but even if the audience were not giving it full attention it achieves a strong effect at a simple level. It is made abundantly clear that this scene is to represent two people trying to agree upon marriage. What actually happens is measured against our expectations. Nothing is agreed: it is an anticlimax. But the general plan of this anticlimax is anticipated before it has occurred: Mme Ranevsky's enthusiasm before Lopakhin is quickly juxtaposed with his lack of enthusiasm when he is left alone. In addition, the excitement of the girls behind the door is well on the way to being reversed when Varya hunts through the luggage in embarrassed silence. These counteractions, together with the hints previously dropped by Mme Ranevsky and Lopakhin that there was not much hope that anything would come of the interview, lead the more alert spectator to pay a different kind of attention to the scene. It is not an empty anticlimax, not just one more failure devised to depress the atmosphere of the play: those who have seen it well played will know that this scene is oddly stimulating. Because we are prepared for the anticlimax, we pay a special attention to its nature. We look beyond the explicit details of the scene and ask, What is blunting the purpose of these characters?

By deduction we diagnose their relationship. Thus, although the actor is bound by his art to place as definite an interpretation as he can upon Lopakhin's 'Yes...', we in the audience cannot. If the actor chooses to read it as 'Yes, I cannot avoid proposing now', as is likely, we see it more subtly as, 'Here is a man who is going to propose marriage, but who is not really fitted for the task (we have already had under observation his particular symptoms of embarrassment and shyness), who seems to have his mind on other things (we make a note of the impatient gesture with the watch), and who probably does not

Shifting Impressions

want the match anyway (we sound the intonation of his voice)'. This goes on in our thoughts during the brief time Chekhov, by one of his neatly placed pauses, has allowed. We then hear the lie from Varya, perhaps the most efficient character in the play: 'I packed the things myself, yet I can't remember....' What does the lie tell us? Not that she wants him to think her inefficient, nor, certainly, that she doesn't want the marriage. But it tells us all at once that she is embarrassed, that she is pretending, that she is inviting him to make the first approach to the subject that is in both their minds. Therefore there is another pause. In that same pause we are asking deeper questions, since the impression has begun to shift. We are asking, Is this method of Varya's going to produce results? With a man in Lopakhin's state of mind? We know on the instant it will not: he needs a more forthright invitation. As the exchange proceeds Chekhov supplies a dramatic definition for us of what lies behind the situation, and what has been suggested about it throughout the play.

The forms of male and female social behaviour, the discretions of Lopakhin, the decorums of Varya are not sufficient to cope with the modern condition. Lopakhin had again told us a few minutes before when he was in conversation with Trofimov, that he was a peasant without manners, but it is not because he lacks manners that he cannot bring himself to propose. It is precisely because his peasant background and his lack of manners tell him he must think, if he can, as a gentleman would think, and assume what he takes to be the behaviour of the gentry, that he speaks his circumlocutions, beats about the bush and achieves nothing. When he gives up the fight with 'Do you remember, last year about this time it was snowing already...?', it is as if, in turning back on a favourite topic, he is confessing that he could never adjust himself to the ways of these people. Varya's weeping confirms him in the feeling that he can never say anything that is not

The Elements of Drama

out of place, just as his gesture over the purchase of the cherry orchard and his celebration with champagne of the family's departure had been misplaced. In the same way, Varya's maidenly proprieties reveal a failure to understand that the time for such observances is past.

None of these people, except Trofimov, who is representative of the younger generation, and who can say to Lopakhin, 'Your father was a peasant, mine had a chemist's shop. But there's nothing in that', has sensed the need for reorienting by the times their social attitudes towards each other. The loss of the cherry orchard is a full and filled-out symbol of their failure. Chekhov presses his point home in case it is missed. Varya says she is going to the Rogulins: 'I've agreed to look after the house for them...to be their housekeeper, or something.' The mistress becomes servant, albeit a very respectable kind of servant, but nevertheless a servant. Do we not also detect a distaste in her afterthought?—'...or something'.

What of Lopakhin? 'And I'm going to Kharkov presently. ...On the next train. I've got a lot to do there....' Yes, to Kharkov, the big city! Had Varya ever been there? Life in this house has come to an end, but go to Kharkov, where one is busy, where the life is. Servant becomes master. Isn't it clear to the characters now that their positions are reversed and that Lopakhin and Varya can put aside conventional behaviour? Chekhov's dramatized statement insinuates itself unmistakably. This is not a farcical scene between two rather unsuitable and doubtfully comic aspirants to love and marriage. It is a statement in little of what the whole play is about. We in the audience view it not coldly as farce, but warmly as comedy because we are not quite detached, but in part involved by our discoveries. There, but for the grace of God, go I. How utterly understandable is their short-sightedness. This scene represents dramatically a particular instance of the

Shifting Impressions

meaning of time passing. It is one variation on the theme of mutability to which the twang of the string snapping at the end of the act is the refrain: perhaps nothing else but this sound could adequately sum up the whole meaning of the play.

These ironies must operate in a sphere beyond the actors, but they do not bring their effect independently of them. We put together our impression of what this exchange of dialogue means, and its details give it strength. It is echoed by Varya's weeping, it is underscored by Lopakhin's apparently irrelevant reminder of time passing, and it is given colour by his apparently irrelevant comment on the cold weather. As all our conclusions are confirmed in our feelings, and as the particular emotion is established, we are aware that the characters know nothing of this. The climactic thrust of Varya's unhappy '...our thermometer's broken...', and the call, 'Yermolai Alexeyevitch!' are followed by Lopakhin's quick reply and hurried exit. His reaction contrasts with the painful hesitancies, breaks the strain of the suspense, and reminds us what the characters are about. But our image is yet incomplete. We have recognized that Lopakhin and Varya stand for two magnetic fields that repel each other, but Lopakhin on the stage is thinking, 'I'll have to give it up as a bad job; thank goodness I have the chance to get away; I am not the marrying kind; she would never be happy with a boor like me'. And Varya, left on the floor crying, is thinking, 'He doesn't understand; he has no love for me; I will have to be a housekeeper after all; I am condemned to spinsterhood'. Lopakhin and Varya, that is, are both thinking entirely in personal terms, as all they have said and done has indicated. They are thinking about proposals and marriage. They are thinking naturally as egoists, and their purpose does not extend beyond their own immediate happiness. Yet through all this, Chekhov has been thinking of what the *I* represents when set against *you*. He has

The Elements of Drama

been seeking the solution to the problem of a larger happiness, of how the destruction of one society need not in its wake destroy the happiness of the next. He has not been concerned only with a marriage between individuals, but of a marriage between classes and generations. The final impression from this episode, the author's final statement here, must spring ironically from a comparison between what the spectator knows and what the character does not know. Of course marriage for Lopakhin and Varya is not *trivial* for them. Nor could one insist that their trifling, abortive remarks are trivial, because they are the expression of their deepest feelings. Triviality is relative. It is what we feel as momentous that makes the breaking of Varya's individual heart a matter of small significance. Our attention has been directed and focused elsewhere, and we therefore do not wholly sympathize with her over the cruelty she has sustained, nor with Lopakhin who might deserve our sympathy as well as she. There is only partial identification: we look beyond the puppets, yet we feel their shadows cast up large and ominous behind them. The shallowness of the 'laughter and tears' view of Chekhov, this labelling him as a sentimental comedian, does him great injustice. It is too starved an account of his achievement.

The picture of humanity in the mind of the spectator grows in proportion as its preposterous pettiness and weakness diminishes it. We are occupied with measuring time and place against the eternal and the infinite in this last act of *The Cherry Orchard* because our restless impressions continue to move after the action on the stage has ceased. The Lopakhin and Varya episode slips smoothly into place with the others, a symbol for one aspect of the theme, a small but important unit in the arithmetic of the play. The analysis which will explain how Chekhov's parts create his whole may never be written. The traditional classification of function of comedy and tragedy cannot help. As the performance on the stage is light and

Shifting Impressions

enchanted, so the dramatic imagery is mercurial and the response of an audience elusive. But chasing his impressions as they flit by must be the chief concern of the critic investigating Chekhov's text, if he is to demonstrate at once its effect upon an audience and its qualities as dramatic literature, at once its stageworthiness and its value for the twentieth-century theatre.

5
THE BEHAVIOUR OF THE WORDS ON THE STAGE

We are in a position to get our bearings and to re-examine what the words have to do. We touched on the author's directive in dialogue for speech and movement: the actor cannot obey it without full reference to those critically shifting impressions the play must create. To suppose he can is to reduce him to an automaton. As for the spectator, he will cease the sooner to regard dialogue as dramatized conversation or as literary rhetoric if he judges it for its properties of making active and plastic images in the mind.

To the dialogue the actor contributes his voice, his gesture and his movement. It is convenient to consider separately how these interact on the words, and the words on them, to illuminate the impressions.

VOICE, PAUSE AND MEANING

Words that possess any degree of feeling lose some of their force if spoken without intonation. The movement of the voice is as restless and as meaningful as the movement of the emotions, and is inseparable from them. The dramatist knows he is throwing away an asset if he does not fully invite the vocal contribution.

The text is a tune to be sung. The most inexperienced actor knows how infinite in number are the tunes applicable to the smallest phrase, and all of us have amused ourselves at one time or another by playing variations on the pitch, power and pace of our own voices. In preferring one actor to another, we

The Behaviour of the Words on the Stage

depend for our choice more than we know upon his vocal range and flexibility: the actor who has the resource of a wider and more distinctive intonation serves us better. The listener is unconsciously thankful for a voice that clarifies a meaning for him, while the actor is thankful for a line telling him how to chant it significantly.

It follows that if the actor does not listen for the exact intonations supplied by the particular arrangement of the text, he will easily be disloyal to his author, and any private efforts at embellishing his speeches will be clumsy and false. Stanislavsky insisted that the actor must make 'a tonal plan with the necessary perspective to lend movement and life to a phrase'.[1] Conversely, if the author has not chosen and assembled his words for precision of dramatic meaning, they cannot offer a precise intonation. Neither author nor actor will have a chance of achieving that true collaboration necessary for transmitting a well-defined suggestion to the audience.

As the actor works upon his part, so its more exact meaning is interpreted as a more and more closely heard tune in the head. Shaw is one who composed as it were musically, and the unmistakable strength of his dialogue, even where a speech is far beyond the limits of conversation, lies in its tune. A Shavian speech has a vocal music which corresponds strictly with its logical structure, and it does not tire the listener. From Professor Higgins of *Pygmalion* we hear this Shavian tune:

Give her her orders: thats enough for her. Eliza: you are to live here for the next six months, learning how to speak beautifully, like a lady in a florist's shop. If youre good and do whatever youre told, you shall sleep in a proper bedroom, and have lots to eat, and money to buy chocolates and take rides in taxis. If youre naughty and idle you will sleep in the back kitchen among the black beetles, and be walloped by Mrs Pearce with a broomstick.[2]

Higgins has just told Colonel Pickering that Eliza cannot understand explanations and arguments. She is less than a reasoning creature. 'Give her her orders', he declares, and

The Elements of Drama

this he proceeds to do. All he says is coloured by what he thinks of her—a mixture of private soldier, child, a primitive, an animal, a thing of crude and undeveloped feelings. The actor's patronizing tone must dance to the fluctuating meaning: first peremptory, then condescending, then grandiloquent, then winning, now threatening. The speech proceeds from condition to condition, the voice changing for each 'if' through a range of assumed emotions—it is Higgins acting a part for the benefit of Colonel Pickering and Mrs Pearce, and he performs with what skill he can muster. This then is recognized first, that the tune is pointed and balanced to offer the actor a tonal plan that so fascinates the ear it cannot be misread.

Yet the intonations of Higgins's speech serve a further purpose, of subtilizing an impression in the auditorium which follows rapidly upon the initial surprise of his manner. His tone of course tells the audience immediately how he regards his new protégée: he is talking so that it can be stated plainly that he is amusing himself. He thinks she will not see beyond the surface of his words: hence his acting a part. His tone is also to give us a strong hint that, although Eliza may not be articulate enough to express her indignation and her recognition of his vanity beyond a limited 'Youre a great bully, you are', which perfectly places him, she cannot in fact avoid instinctively knowing how she is being treated, and sensing something of the motives of her tormentor. Hear the tune of 'you will sleep in the back kitchen among the black beetles' as slowing, grave, ominous, like a voice telling a nursery tale, with an unmistakable mockery of exaggeration, and it must ironically give the lie to any unsound impression of her complete simplicity. For the audience is already being prepared for the crisis of Act IV.

While intonation is as subtle an instrument as the human voice itself, and is an invaluable way of underlining a covert

The Behaviour of the Words on the Stage

innuendo of meaning, 'pause', the momentary cessation of the song, can assist in its own distinctive way.

The pause is planned by the author and prepared by the actor for the sake solely of the audience. It is unhelpful to think of it as an imitation of a mental reaction as in life, although it is true that in realistic drama the actor will find a realistic excuse for it. The dramatic pause is essentially a means of implanting a dramatic impression and schooling the audience to hear and see what the author wants. I cannot do better than quote an extract from Mr Fernald's summary of its function:

> For an audience to react fully to any one effect it must be given a period of time during which it can consider that one effect, to the exclusion of all else.
>
> In practice this means that any line which is intended to convey a particular effect and which it may be of dramatic importance to emphasize, should be followed by a Dramatic Pause, in order that the particular effect may have time to sink into the consciousness of the audience....
>
> The length of the dramatic pause is to some extent governed by the degree of dramatic value of the line or action or piece of business or scene which precedes it, since the more substance there is to an effect, the longer does it take to sink into the audience.[3]

It remains to ask what effects to emphasize and what degree of dramatic value to place on each. The pause being essentially of the theatre and not of life, there are no rules to govern its use except the order and nature of the dramatic impression which dictates it. Take another brief example from the same play to show how a pause is prompted and planned. The following is the immediate context of the major pause in *Pygmalion*:

> HIGGINS. I wonder where the devil my slippers are! *Eliza looks at him darkly; then rises suddenly and leaves the room. Higgins yawns again, and resumes his song.*[4]

The pause falls when 'Eliza looks at him darkly', when for a brief space of time there is no other speech or movement to

The Elements of Drama

prevent the spectator from assimilating its meaning. It is indicative of the kind of quality a pause assumes that it is necessary to hunt back through three acts to weigh its full value, and it is quickly evident that a special interest, gathered and stored through the whole performance, explodes upon this pause and makes it momentous.

In Act IV of *Pygmalion*, Shaw, in his fashion, provides an anticlimax that is, paradoxically, a climax. In watching for three acts the creation of Eliza the duchess, watching the fairy-story come true, we had not noticed that Shaw had subtly changed the style of his play from the realism of the first scene in Covent Garden to the artificial high comedy of the tea party in Act III. As much at Eliza's expense as at the Eynsford Hills's, we had laughed at the incongruity of the flower girl in the parlour. We had all but forgotten the happy Eliza of Act I, when she was at home in her proper environment. And perhaps we had forgotten the warnings issued to Higgins by the other women in the piece, by Mrs Pearce in Act II:

Mr Higgins: youre tempting the girl. It's not right. She should think of the future,

and by Mrs Higgins in Act III:

Dont you realise that when Eliza walked into Wimpole Street, something walked in with her?...you two infinitely stupid male creatures: the problem of what is to be done with her afterwards.

Suddenly Shaw reverts to the convention of Act I, Eliza matures and emerges from the pasteboard duchess a woman. The statue comes to life, social comedy becomes human comedy, and Shaw wakes his self-assured audience with a shock. This he does entirely in terms of theatre, not by the theatrical verbosity of which he often is accused. If Act IV is an anticlimax, it is instinct with excitement—as soon as we are awake. Here is one dramatic pause that must do all this, that must, indeed, mark the turning point of the play. It must

The Behaviour of the Words on the Stage

violently readjust for us the idea we have of an Eliza who has apparently achieved her desire in a relationship with a Higgins who has satisfied his vanity. It is important enough to shift the whole ground of the play's meaning.

This shift does not occur upon Eliza's hurling the slippers at Higgins some four minutes later in the action: this is merely the consummation we had been expecting as a result of the pause after 'I wonder where the devil my slippers are?' The action that passes during those ensuing four minutes is contrived, as examination would prove, to earmark and define the change that has occurred. They would be meaningless if the shift in the impression had not already been started by this pause.

Higgins, Pickering and Eliza are back from the ball. The men's tired voices are heard on the stairs, but it is Eliza we see. She has a long moment on the stage by herself sufficient for the actress to establish her exhaustion. She cannot further indicate her state of mind until she is given the chance to react to specific words, and it is important that the audience shall be told of her resentment as soon as possible, so that it can divine and relish the full meaning of her new mood and see the new direction of the play. But it is dramatically impossible to use the pause directly upon their entrance since it would have no substance of itself without a detail or two in the immediately preceding action to give the audience a bearing for its feeling and understanding. So the men come in and ignore her silent figure; Pickering refers to hat, overcoat, letters; Higgins yawns and sings. It is only then that he wonders where the devil his slippers are in a tone that clearly gives the order, 'Fetch me them!' These are the hints that set the imagination in motion. Eliza has to turn her head to look at him, the physical movement she makes after so long sitting motionless cannot fail to take the eye, and thus our whole attention is upon that dark look. Upon the pause, we accept

The Elements of Drama

in a flash the change in relationship between Higgins and Eliza, and that Eliza has felt the first stirrings of rebellion. We begin to recognize the serious import of the development of the action over the three acts. We see Higgins as a Shavian villain and begin to understand the nature of his act of inhumanity. Through the pause we almost hear Shaw crying out gleefully that we have been misleading ourselves. Eliza's sudden rising from the chair, in contrast with the sleepy movements and gestures we saw before, stresses her anger, and we are now alert to watch its consequences. The play is suddenly illuminated.

It would be false, however, to give more importance to the silence of a voice than to its sound. Intonation and pause take effect together. When in this scene Eliza at length speaks, Shaw gives her words that in their phrasing carry a violent intonation that requires no explanation:

> There are your slippers. And there. Take your slippers; and may you never have a day's luck with them!

With the added emphasis of the throwing of the slippers, the inverted Galatea has surely come alive at last. But to bolster up the action by this intonation would be ridiculous, if not meaningless, had the pause and the dark look not been supplied previously.

VOICE AND VERSE

In verse rhythms a voice has a stricter monitor. We saw how the form of the language dictates the manner of speaking: the mere noise of the lines is often the most persuasive guide. We can hear the fury of the 'f's and the staccato guttural sounds in the quiet venom of the Lear who must say

> infect her beauty,
> You fen-suck'd fogs,

The Behaviour of the Words on the Stage

or the decisiveness of the consonants and the triumphant ring-ringing of the rhyme in Hamlet's

> the play's the thing,
> Wherein I'll catch the conscience of the King,

or the breaking against the metre of the words that carry Hamlet's disgust in

> I should have fatted all the region kites
> With this sláve's óffal.[5]

Mr Eliot talks of Elizabethan blank verse as being 'capable of expressing complicated, subtle, and surprising emotions'.[6] The vivacity of the mind, the veering of feeling, are properly to be felt in the flow of the verse.

It is now possible to see that the form of the language will be dictated by the form of the impressions and the direction in which they are to move. The position has been reached where it is wrong to talk about the meaning and its value as something separate from the shape of the language, since the author's creative intention is the source of both.

The metre or stress of the verse alone, however well aided by the actor's sense of rhythm and by his ear for vowel and consonantal qualities, will not tell him all he needs to know. Such a procedure was responsible for much of the declamatory speaking of Shakespeare in the past. The speech work of William Poel did a great deal to break the actor's slavery to the iambic: it refined the speaking of Shakespeare by aiming at a more freely inflected speech based upon the rhythm of the meaning in conjunction with the rhythm of the line.[7] He tried by 'tuned tones' to hit the delicate medium between the metronomic regularity which kills feeling and the naturalism of prose. It is clear, and it is worth saying again, that the speaking of Shakespeare with a twentieth-century idiom of intonation is equally dangerous.

Common sense reminds the actor to look to the verse form

to clarify the way he is to present an unclouded impression. How he wants to affect the spectator must be clear within his mind, especially in non-representational drama where the rules of ordinary speech and behaviour may not apply, and he turns to the verse form for confirmation and guidance.

For example, the proud and sarcastic Coriolanus pretends privately to Menenius to plead for his 'voices', inviting an imaginary crowd to inspect his wounds. These are his words:

> I got them in my country's service when
> Some certain of your brethren roar'd and ran
> From the noise of our own drums.[8]

Apart from the change from the iambic to the trochaic foot in the third line, this metre is marked by its regularity. The actor in the first place knows from the sense of what he is to say that, after a deferential beginning, his tone must change to one of contempt for those he pretends to be addressing. The switch in the impression the spectator is to receive will accentuate the contumely in the soul of the hero. It is then that the actor will discover how aptly the rhythm will serve him, the very smoothness of the metre providing for the mincing tones of the first line, the end-stopped 'when' at the end of that line momentarily breaking the rhythm and slightly reorienting our attitude to the speaker, and then the regularity of the metre of the rest of the speech running quickly away as his venom rises and he throats the last few words. The unexpected double stress on 'ran / From' marks this as the most intense point of his anger in these lines. As might be expected, rhythm and meaning are a unity, making it possible for the speech of the actor and the action of the scene to reach the audience also as a unity.

It is generally agreed that any heightened rhythm of speech makes for intensity of meaning, and that a good dramatic poetry must be able to carry an extra charge of emotion. But what is meant by 'intensity' and by 'carrying emotion'? Not simply that the words are emotional, but rather that, at bottom, the

The Behaviour of the Words on the Stage

words charge our minds emotionally, infecting our image. In doing this the words themselves and the rhythm they assume may be quite lacking in 'emotion'. This is a secret Shakespeare held. How else can we account for the extraordinary simplicity of voice in certain lines spoken at moments of highest tension? So in *King Lear*, to choose one play, we remember:

> Are you our daughter?
>
> ...as I am a man, I think this lady
> To be my child Cordelia.
>
> Pray you, undo this button: thank you, sir.[9]

Shakespeare knows the thrust of the play creates its own effect, and he knows it needs no further enhancement, that such enhancement might damage it.

Indeed, there are as many places in Shakespeare where the movement of the verse is planned specifically for the audience as there are signposts for the actor. Hamlet approaches the praying Claudius with

> Now might I do it pat, now he is praying,
> And now I'll do it, and so he goes to Heaven,
> And so I am revenged.[10]

These are not the idioms nor the intonations of conversation, and conversation provides no guide. The repetitions of 'now ...now...now...', and of 'and so...and so...', prefacing each brief sentence, could be argued readily as the speech of a man slowly turning a problem over in his mind, groping for his decision. They could be argued equally as the abrupt utterance of a man taking hasty action, with a step forward on 'now', and a sword drawn on 'now I'll do it', and so on, as we customarily see it played. But how is it we are sure the second interpretation is right? Because the suggestion to be passed to the audience must demonstrate the riot in Hamlet's brain after the revelations of the play scene; it must balance and render effective the shift to the calmer withdrawal of 'O this is hire

The Elements of Drama

and salary, not revenge', as 'Heaven' echoes round his mind and he remembers his father is

> Doom'd for a certain term to walk the night,
> And for the day confin'd to fast in fires.[11]

How else is the audience to be told decisively that Hamlet's delay in taking revenge is not entirely of his own volition, that there is a pressure of circumstance upon him? That all his extremes of mood are but enacting the oscillation of his mind as it reflects like a fine needle the complexity of the values he must gauge the world by? How else can Shakespeare demonstrate to the audience that a remote prince is not merely individualistic, but that his tragedy matters to it? The actor looks to the whole impression deriving from the play to confirm his idea of how perhaps one line shall be spoken. Likewise, one line heard spoken correctly may confirm and solidify for the audience the whole statement of the play.

Is the problem a different one for predominantly 'conceptual' poetry? In Mr Eliot's post-war comedies the language rarely takes on the vocally and physically coloured Elizabethan style in which it is so comforting to act. His verse barely moves out of the idiom of conversation; for the most part it is visually at rest; the beats of the line urge themselves only on strictly reserved occasions. What guide has the actor here?

A typical example of Mr Eliot's new dialogue is taken from *The Confidential Clerk*, a play criticized by some for its flat and spare poetry:

> LUCASTA.   I think I'm changing.
>   I've changed quite a lot in the last two hours.
> COLBY. And I think I'm changing too. But perhaps
>   what we call change...
> LUCASTA. Is understanding better what one really is.
>   And the reason why that comes about, perhaps...
> COLBY. Is, beginning to understand another person.
> LUCASTA. Oh, Colby....[12]

The Behaviour of the Words on the Stage

It is too easy to condemn these repetitions of phrase and word for giving a forced and undramatic strength to the concepts of 'change' and 'understanding' by dint of mere insistence. Mr Eliot has set out to sum up what we have remarked between Colby and his half-sister Lucasta since the act began. We have had the suggestion of Lucasta's development from her own direct declaration of her insignificance, 'Not that *my* opinion counts for anything', to the point where Colby can reply to her comment that she would like to understand him, with a carefully judged: 'I believe you do already.' Perhaps we were startled to see Colby open himself to her, but he did it soberly, with no romanticizing. The scene emphasized that these two have come together in understanding. Lonely people, they begin to suppress their loneliness by a mutual consideration of the apparent desirability of a private retreat, a 'secret garden' of the mind. Now, with words that drop below the pictorial quality of a moment before, with a flat conceptual diction, Mr Eliot feels he can consolidate his gains and legitimately have his characters state what their drama has amounted to.

Their speeches are made softly incantatory by the gently compelling beat of the lines. By reason of the pressure of meaning on this sequence, the words quicken with associations that seem almost to be held in the tone of the voices that utter them, as their mutual feeling gathers strength. We hear 'I think I'm *changing*. / I've changed quite a *lot*.' 'And I think *I'm* changing *too*'—here the author, with the emphases of ordinary conversation, has charged the idea of 'change' with what we know of Lucasta's and Colby's mutual development. 'But perhaps what we call *change*'—here the author returns to the first motif and restates it with its accumulated meaning, the third repetition of the word helping the illumination that has accrued. 'Is *understanding* better'—here the author transfers one impression of what these two have become to

The Elements of Drama

the control of another, one which allows us to see the 'change' of two individuals as a relationship between them: individual change becomes mutual understanding.

Thus the key words extend their meaning through the play, accumulating strength and widening their scope. The intonations of the actors' voices confirm the impression the action had begun already to suggest. The technical achievement of this verse is that it here offers a medium for a three-cornered tossing of ideas between them and us, it makes quite acceptable a colloquial manner of finishing each other's sentences, it permits their drawing together physically and the rising excitement that they share with each other, until complexity of feeling is at last sounded in Lucasta's cry of 'Oh, Colby...'. The verse permits a variety of functioning within its one framework. The spectator must derive a strong impression of two people in tune, and the effect comes off with sincerity and depth, although it has not apparently departed from a natural level of speech.

GESTURE AND MEANING

'When you are in verbal intercourse on the stage, speak not so much to the ear as to the eye.'[13] Stanislavsky's paradox is easily resolved, since intonation and 'gesture', the term by which is specified any motion by one actor for himself, are twin and inseparable. They stem from the same roots of feeling in the speaker. They grow together and they die together. They reflect and exemplify each other. It is as easy to describe a gesture with an intonation as it is to describe an intonation with a gesture. If you regard words as signs for sounds, by their nature you must also regard them as signs for gestures. This quality in speech has been neatly summarized by Dr Samuel Selden:

The Behaviour of the Words on the Stage

The tonal design of dramatic speech is founded solidly on a concept of action.... The real significance of 'woman' or 'house' does not begin to emerge until the utterance gives some intimation of the speaker's personal feeling regarding that particular object, his inclination to do something about it—to approach or to avoid it, to extend its activity or to destroy it, to sense it more fully or to cast it forth from the realm of his experience. The kind of movement implicit in the speaker's mind at the moment of utterance is reflected in a vocal colouring which affects the sound of the word. Therefore we say, in general, that human voice-tones are connected with the sense of muscular tensions. They are kinaesthetic.[14]

Much of the success of radio drama, even though it is using a blind medium, is due to the fact that the sound of a voice has the power to stimulate the listener's motor imagination, to excite him to reproduce imaginatively some muscular activity, as when spectators at the ringside go through the motions of boxing. The visual and motor elements in the play on the wireless can readily be embodied in his mind as he listens.

It follows that words written for radio might be specially chosen for their clarity of expression in this respect. We find any dialogue lends itself to more intense expression if it is felt physically, since this is a supplementary way of clarifying its sense. It is not unexpected, therefore, that we find drama frequently depicting its meaning strongly in physical terms, as if the actor were a ballet-dancer embodying the music of the text. As the action modifies the impression transmitted, the degree of weakness or violence in the change is likely to be reflected in a greater or lesser physical tension in the words.

A common criticism of Shaw's drama is that he depends too much upon his stage directions, and that the words are a verbose and undramatic vehicle. A typical comment on his dialogue, for example, is that it is 'strikingly easy, too dazzlingly witty, too close to the brilliant discursive style of the prefaces'.[15] Shaw would seem to be a poor source for examples of gesture. In fact, every speech is alive with it in its

The Elements of Drama

proper sense, and upon examination it can be seen that Shaw is fully an actor's writer. An early and a later play will prove he did not lose his propensity for sensing the body behind the voice.

Arms and the Man (1894) is an early play. It is brisk and quick with the kind of gesture that is serving a first purpose in drama in compelling new and cumulative ironies. The play advances from shock to shock, each visualized and integrally animated. The curtain rises on a wholly visual picture of Raina, the youthful idealist at second-hand, draped on a balcony, studiously romanticizing herself. When she speaks, her voice confirms what her body shows:

RAINA, *dreamily*...I wanted to be alone. The stars are so beautiful! What is the matter?
CATHERINE. Such news! There has been a battle.
RAINA, *her eyes dilating.* Ah! *She comes eagerly to Catherine.*[16]

Her 'Ah!' is of course not seen in 'dilating eyes', but in her whole change of physical posture as she turns to her mother. We register our first ironic impression: that she was posing. When she continues 'ecstatically', 'Tell me, tell me. How was it? Oh, mother! mother! mother!' it is her impatience and excitement that we see as she bounces with a childlike glee on the ottoman. This forms for us the second major impression modifying the first, and we are certain now of her immaturity. Before our eyes a young hussy becomes a silly kitten. By this immediate irony, one deriving strongly from gesture, is defined the nature of her imposture.

Arms and the Man is a clear-cut play about *poseurs* and the quality of posing. The key revelations are marked throughout its course by emphatic and unmistakable gesture. The biggest disclosure and the inevitable irony falls in Act III:

RAINA, *standing over him, as if she could not believe her senses.* Do you mean what you said just now? Do you know what you said just now?
BLUNTSCHLI. I do.

The Behaviour of the Words on the Stage

RAINA, *gasping.* I! I!! *She points to herself incredulously, meaning 'I, Raina Petkoff, tell lies!' He meets her gaze unflinchingly. She suddenly sits down beside him, and adds, with a complete change of manner from the heroic to a babyish familiarity,* How did you find me out?

These gestures of pointing and sitting, set in contrast, clinch our pervading impression of Raina the cheat. The actress cannot avoid 'overacting' the 'heroic' and the 'babyish familiarity', thus stylizing her part to make the message striking and effective.

Shaw was writing this play as high comedy, nearer to the Restoration style than to the pseudo-realism that passes for a style of comedy in England today. It is a mark of artificial comedy, as we find it in Shakespeare, in Jonson, Congreve and Sheridan, that the special mode of gesture is married to a special manner of speaking. This has not only to do with a deliberate consistence of style within the type of play, but also with the predisposition of exaggerated words to dance sensually. Shaw declared he was not writing in the 'cup-and-saucer drawing-room style'.[17] As he progressed, his unique manner did not desert him, but evolved until he could write lengthy dialectical speeches which kept all the athleticism of his more active plays.

In these later plays, the dialogue seems at a first glance to be little more than awkward rhetoric. Yet this rhetoric arises legitimately from the character, the situation and the subject, and the words dance to a fittingly artificial tune. True Shavian music continues to reinforce the meaning, and his old flair for the sinewy line is still present. In *The Apple Cart* (1929) King Magnus is haranguing his mistress Orinthia, and attempting to explain her place in his household:

MAGNUS....Do not let us fall into the common mistake of expecting to become one flesh and one spirit. Every star has its own orbit; and between it and its nearest neighbor there is not only a powerful attraction but an infinite distance. When the attraction becomes stronger

The Elements of Drama

than the distance the two do not embrace: they crash together in ruin. We two also have our orbits, and must keep an infinite distance between us to avoid a disastrous collision. Keeping our distance is the whole secret of good manners; and without good manners human society is intolerable and impossible.

ORINTHIA. Would any other woman stand your sermons, and even like them?

MAGNUS. Orinthia: we are only two children at play; and you must be content to be my queen in fairyland. And *rising* I must go back to my work.[18]

Comparatively, Magnus is a low-toned character, and any emphatic, virile gesture is not in keeping either with him or with what he says. But the actor cannot avoid beating a time to the imperative melody of his speech, though he remains sitting on the settee, with the inclination of head and eyes. For he is playing the parson to her, and with gentle modulations of tone, admonishing, reasoning, warning, Magnus reaches the end of his lesson with a decorous flourish, addressed as much to himself as to her. Orinthia's reply, completely irrelevant to the substance of the sermon, puts it in its place and breaks the magniloquent tension he has built. He turns back to her, sees he may be becoming pompous, changes his tone, brings the abstract analogy down to a more homely metaphor, takes a final, half-mocking fling at her with 'you must be content to be my queen in fairyland', and then, and only then, allows himself his strongest visual gesture to blast the accumulated rationality of his disquisition with a superb anticlimax: he rises and says, 'And I must go back to my work'. This dialogue is as delicately and resiliently modulated for tonal gesture as a Pinero farce is robustly wooden.

It is important to a full understanding of this scene to notice that Magnus's abstract way of talking offers through gesture a central irony that is irrepressible. Is he not after all talking of his physical intimacy with Orinthia? With words and figures, he is trying to keep her at a distance in more senses than one.

The Behaviour of the Words on the Stage

Is she not, on the other hand, the sort of woman who is instinctively going to use all her feminine intuition and sexual prowess to combat and destroy his argument? She refuses to answer him in his own terms, and jerks the conversation down from the realm of abstract reasoning, down from the 'stars', back to their particular and personal relationship, back to the settee on which they are sitting: 'Would any other woman stand your sermons, and even like them?' She reproves him and refutes the logic of keeping their distance by, in fact, coyly inclining herself towards him, ignoring his rationalistic 'good manners' in favour of the 'powerful attraction'. She denies his logic with an unanswerable gesture until he is forced to rise to release himself. It is remarkable that Shaw has never for a moment forgotten the living presence of the actors, and to argue that the scene is conceived verbally and not visually is quite wrong. The truth is that Shaw has found a way to point our impression of a Shavian man, an intelligence, in conflict with a Shavian woman, an intuition and a creature of the flesh. Mind and body are the stars in collision. So, by words against gesture, the author persuades us.

Is it fair to complain that because there can be no exact relation in modern realistic drama between the arrangement of words and the method of enacting them, 'the performance will inevitably be an "interpretation" of the text and hence subject to wide variation'?[19] Mr Raymond Williams makes an original attack upon the acting tradition of the realistic theatre which is well worth reading. He suggests that, whereas in the formal drama of the Greeks and the Elizabethans the dialogue necessarily controls the actor's gesture, modern prose dialogue, lacking the strictures of verse rhythms, leaves the actor free to do what he likes. He instances *The Seagull* and Stanislavsky's treatment of it. He complains, for example, that while Konstantin delivers his long speech in Act I, Sorin is directed to comb his hair and do other things apparently irrelevant to

The Elements of Drama

the speech he is listening to, and that these gestures help to determine the effect of what Konstantin is saying without the authority of the author. But it needs to be said that it is not the combing of the hair that matters, but *how* it is combed, the gesture properly offering unspoken comment. It is a reaction inside a realistic play which is as surely legitimate as any reaction of one actor to another in formal drama. In both it is the particular impression in the context of the whole scene that directs the non-speaking actor what to do when he is not speaking. In both the actor is free to use or abuse the text. It is entirely fitting for Stanislavsky to make the precise evidence of the dramatic image the excuse for appropriate gesture. The relation between speech and gesture in Chekhov is no different in kind from their relation in Shakespeare.

Mr Williams tends to rate Stanislavsky for describing how Sorin in his production shall rock on the bench: 'A pause of ten seconds. Sorin rocks on the bench, and hums, *or* whistles, *or* strikes a match and lights a cigarette.' Mr Williams italicizes the words to emphasize how these gestures are merely 'something for the character to do', and therefore that they do not 'embody a state of feeling'.[20] But of course each of these gestures does embody Sorin's state of feeling, although the actor is not free to feel *what he likes*. Sorin's unspoken comment arises from the facts of the dialogue: what Konstantin says and what Sorin does not say. The rocking, humming, whistling or lighting a cigarette all have one thing in common, and so are not arbitrary: they point to Sorin's indifference and thence to Konstantin's isolation. The audience is not interested in the gesture, but only in what the gesture *means*, its irony. This irony arises from the gesture as a direct extension of the text. Throughout the history of the stage the author has of necessity left the acting to the actor. It is Chekhov's strength to have so arranged Sorin's silence that it must convey an incontrovertible meaning: silence is written into the text as

The Behaviour of the Words on the Stage

part of the text itself. Chekhov does it knowing that the actors are free only to fulfil his purpose and that the audience is free only to take from it what he intends.

WORDS AND MOVEMENT

Intonation implies a voice persisting in time. Gesture is the plastic embodiment of the voice, and thus gesture too is effective by its duration in time. Both are the expressions of thought and feeling that reside in the words of a character speaking. But the ironic images of drama are for the most part derived from the exchange between two or more characters, and therefore the plastic embodiment of such an exchange will emerge from the gestures of these characters *between* each other. Since 'mutual gestures' of this sort call up a large new field of stage activity, it is helpful to use a distinctive term in referring to them, 'movement', although it will be appreciated that there is no firm dividing line between a gesture by one character to another and a movement by that character to or from another, nor between that movement and what is loosely called the 'grouping' the movement must affect. Stage movement also has its effect in time, and since it is not different in origin from intonation or gesture, it will also be an expression of the thought or feeling in the scene, and its form will be determined by the impression the author wishes to beget.

What is loosely called 'the stage picture' does not, therefore, exist in practice. Although obviously there are moments when the stage will be quite still, and although there are moments when it is desirable that the grouping of characters on the stage shall present a pleasing and harmonious composition to the eye, as at a final curtain, it is nevertheless true to say that an arrangement on the stage must not be determined by any vague aesthetic of pictorial composition, but by the shifting impressions to be created. Good grouping of actors will always

The Elements of Drama

prepare the audience to receive the next impression. Even where the subsequent action is to involve surprise, the preceding movement and grouping will prepare the audience so that the shock shall be greater: the impression must lie in the relation between the expected and the unexpected. When therefore it is said that the stage picture is 'good', we mean that it is an exact embodiment of our feelings as ushered forward to that point. When it is said that it is 'exciting', it ought to mean it offers a bright prospect of what is to come. But if the movement in a play is as dependent on the dramatic image as we say it is, it would follow that even general rules for movement are inadequate and out of place: each text must be examined for itself.

Scenes conceived wholly in terms of movement are unmistakable. They design their own choreography, as when in Congreve's *The Way of the World* Lady Wishfort prepares for the arrival of Sir Rowland, her counterfeit lover:

FOIBLE. All is ready, Madam.
LADY WISHFORT. And—well—and how do I look, Foible?
FOIBLE. Most killing well, Madam.
LADY WISHFORT. Well, and how shall I receive him? In what figure shall I give his heart the first impression? There is a great deal in the first impression. Shall I sit?—No, I won't sit—I'll walk—ay, I'll walk from the door upon his entrance; and then turn full upon him—No, that will be too sudden. I'll lie—ay, I'll lie down—I'll receive him in my little dressing-room, there's a couch—Yes, yes, I'll give the first impression on a couch—I won't lie neither, but loll and lean upon one elbow; with one foot a little dangling off, jogging in a thoughtful way—Yes—and then as soon as he appears, start, ay, start and be surprised, and rise to meet him in a pretty disorder—Yes—Oh, nothing is more alluring than a levee from a couch in some confusion—It shows the foot to advantage, and furnishes with blushes, and recomposing airs beyond comparison. Hark! There's a coach.[21]

And as she scuttles away from the sound, she is thrown into a confusion she had *not* prepared.

The affectations of the decaying lady are modelled on the

The Behaviour of the Words on the Stage

airs and graces of the coquette. They are used as much to burlesque the behaviour of the younger members of the sex as to ridicule Lady Wishfort's own self-deception. She mimes across the stage, striking a pose with each 'Yes' and breaking it with each 'No'. Her agitations are contrasted with Foible's still, silent merriment, for Foible is a party to the deception Sir Rowland is to practise on her mistress. The whole scene has been painted visually the better to make a clown of her. The words are hardly more than stage directions, and might even have been dispensed with altogether. Gesture merges into movement, since Lady Wishfort's delicious rehearsal is performed before an imaginary Sir Rowland, in whose stead we and Foible stand. As a result we speculate on any man's reactions to this prodigy of misdirected enthusiasm.

Visual and verbal integration is regularly to be found as a working method of defining the impression felt to be either difficult to grasp, or particularly abstract, or of special importance. Thus it often marks a central crisis: a producer studying the text may quickly put his finger on the core of a play, since at such a point the writer may be expected to bring to bear all the dramatic agencies he can muster. Can we miss the point of a Shavian crisis even when the play's meaning is perverse? Shaw supplies vivid visual summaries of his arguments, as when his Caesar leaves Cleopatra, when his Eliza leaves Higgins, when his Candida takes Morell, when Ann Whitefield takes Jack Tanner.

It would be difficult to find closer visual and verbal unity than in *King Lear*. That the stage movement Shakespeare plots is inherent in our total impression, is consummately demonstrated in the scene before the hovel—this in a play Lamb, the first of many, declared to be 'essentially impossible to be represented on a stage'.[22]

To limit examination to the passage in which Gloucester discovers Lear and offers him shelter is not possible without

The Elements of Drama

reference to what Lear says just before Gloucester enters, since, like the distribution of the balls about a billiard-table in preparation for the next cue, movement must grow out of movement.

LEAR. Thou wert better in a grave, than to answer with thy uncover'd body, this extremity of the skies. Is man no more than this? Consider him well. Thou ow'st the worm no silk; the beast, no hide; the sheep, no wool; the cat, no perfume. Ha? here's three on's are sophisticated. Thou art the thing itself; unaccommodated man, is no more but such a poor, bare, forked animal as thou art. Off, off you lendings: come, unbutton here.
  Enter Gloucester with a torch
  . . . .
GLOUCESTER. Our flesh and blood, my Lord, is grown so vile,
  That it doth hate what gets it.
EDGAR. Poor Tom's a-cold.
GLOUCESTER. Go in with me; my duty cannot suffer
  T' obey in all your daughters' hard commands:
  Though their injunction be to bar my doors,
  And let this tyrannous night take hold upon you,
  Yet have I ventured to come and seek you out,
  And bring you where both fire, and food is ready.
LEAR. First let me talk with this philosopher,
  What is the cause of thunder?
KENT. Good my Lord take his offer, go into th' house.
LEAR. I'll talk a word with this same learned Theban:
  What is your study?
EDGAR. How to prevent the Fiend, and to kill vermin.
LEAR. Let me ask you one word in private.
KENT. Importune him to go once more my Lord,
  His wits begin t' unsettle.
GLOUCESTER. Canst thou blame him?
  Storm still[23]

First, what was the probable way Shakespeare intended his actors to be disposed about the large area of the platform? If one character expresses sympathy for another, he is naturally drawn towards him; if he feels antipathy, he is naturally repulsed. If we work on this assumption, there is one un-

The Behaviour of the Words on the Stage

doubted and centrally important regrouping of the characters to be deduced from these passages: Lear marks his sympathy with Edgar and antipathy for Kent and Gloucester by leaving them for him.

Lear's
> Is man no more than this? Consider him well...
> Ha? here's three on's are sophisticated...

makes it plain he is at this point regarding Edgar as the same sensational object of curiosity he is presenting to Kent, the Fool and the audience. On the stage this is marked by the physical separation of Lear, Kent and the Fool from Edgar. These three must be downstage, where in the Elizabethan theatre they would be standing in nearly the centre of the auditorium, and looking at the phenomenon before them with the spectator's eyes. Their being grouped together signifies their sanity, and their regard for a bedlam beggar is at one with the audience's own view: we are thus invited to join in the general judgment upon him. Edgar upstage, framed against the background of the tiring-house, is acting his part: 'Still through the hawthorn blows the cold wind: says suum, mun, nonny, Dolphin my boy, Boy Sesey: let him trot by', in his gibberish conjuring up the storm with his voice, and in his antics imitating the simpleness of both a farm-boy and a farm-boy's horse.

But Lear, contemplating what he sees, is already changing his attitude towards Edgar. As his sympathy for the creature becomes stronger, and as his understanding of his affinity with the 'poor, bare, forked animal' grows clearer in his mind, so the passive prayer from Lear we heard two or three minutes before, 'Poor naked wretches, whereso'er you are...', is translated by sudden illumination into the active desire to look and to be like him. With the abrupt cry, 'Off, off you lendings...', Lear strides clear of Kent and the Fool, faces the audience as Edgar is doing, tears off his clothes, and

The Elements of Drama

immediately in a fiercely direct manner aligns himself with the madman. Shakespeare provides a visual climax to the scene and stresses as vigorously as he can Lear's change of mind and his repentance.

The entry of Gloucester serves to re-emphasize what has happened. He peers through the 'storm': 'What are you there? Your names?' It is Edgar, acting his part with greater energy to escape detection by his father, who replies. Gloucester now looks towards the madman and recognizes—Lear! And naked. Horrified, he cries, 'What, hath your Grace no better company?' He sees Lear beside Edgar, a monarch intimate with a madman.

Gloucester attempts what he has come to do, and begins to plead with his king to take shelter. But Lear has linked arms with Edgar, and King of England urges bedlam beggar round the periphery of the platform marked out by the pillars, like two peripatetic Greek philosophers at their teaching: 'First let me talk with this philosopher....' Gloucester is left in the centre of the platform as Lear and Edgar circle away from him. Kent joins him there and adds his own plea: 'Good my Lord take his offer, go into th' house', but Lear's comment on this is as before: 'I'll talk a word with this same learned Theban....' As those in the centre follow with the turn of their bodies these two whom they cannot understand, Lear leads his new companion downstage with words that dismiss all but Edgar, words that echo what the grouping itself states visually. Lear says, 'Let me ask you one word *in private*'. The 'privacy' perhaps suggests also a confidential proximity to the audience which Kent and Gloucester cannot hold at the same time. Our recognition of the absolute separation between the two groups is confirmed the next moment when Gloucester makes a last appeal which Lear rejects in irritation:

GLOUCESTER. I do beseech your Grace.
LEAR. O cry you mercy, sir: noble philosopher, your company.

The Behaviour of the Words on the Stage

Lear flings off upstage, drawing a startled Edgar with him. They go into the hovel in the pairs which mark their alliance and their alienation. The Fool, neglected, follows as best he can.

That is a likely pattern of the stage movement and grouping, as would seem to be clearly visualized by Shakespeare from moment to moment as the scene proceeds. The physical link between Lear and Edgar is more than symbolic of the tragic humiliation of Lear, however: it details and clarifies the author's statement of the impalpable concepts behind the play. We can now begin to appreciate more fully how his words integrate the physical and mental action, and what together they stand for.

The scene is conceived visually to make transparent the paradoxes that lie within it, demonstrating the enigma of Lear's mind. Edgar's raving must seem sense; the despised must seem worthy, poor Tom a philosopher; the impure and the false is to be pure and natural; the genuine are to be 'sophisticated'; man must seem animal and animal must seem man. Lear's new humility and compassion must fit with his old arrogance; the wisdom of a king outside a hovel must seem greater than of a king secure in his own court; Lear the superman defying the storm and its gods must fit with Lear the animal embracing his Edgar; his rejection of sane advice must fit with our intuitive knowledge of his wisdom; madness must seem an illumination of the mind. The injustice of heaven must seem just, its justice unjust; the storm must seem divine and yet petty; the open heath must seem a prison, as later a prison must seem free for Lear and Cordelia to 'sing like birds i' th' cage'.[24] As these complexities of feeling accumulate, the action on the stage must enact and clinch them, else the significant pattern of the play will disintegrate. The immaterial state of man and nature is to suffer a dramatic test of its substantiality, man's place in the scheme of things is to be visibly demonstrated, the subjective made objective.

The Elements of Drama

We are reminded of a notable statement in Professor J. F. Danby's essay on the play:

> Drama is an especially apt vehicle for the handling of meanings. Meanings are always meanings-for-people. And people move among other people with their ideas. Under the pressure of truth or circumstance one meaning can be adopted or another discarded. We watch the development of an idea and a man, people animating meanings and meanings animating people. Over the province of meaning which a play takes for its own we can watch the manifold inflections of the idea.[25]

The ambiguities at the centre of the play must be cut into the mind by clear, hard action. Thus before our extract begins we are prepared for the visual extension of the abstract. 'Poor naked wretches, whereso'er you are', apostrophizes Lear, half thinking of himself, and straightway we see Edgar, naked and wretched, the lowest form of human life that Elizabethan Shakespeare could envisage, leap out: 'Away, the foul fiend follows me...!' Again, more than half thinking of himself, Lear cries,

> take physic, Pomp,
> Expose thyself to feel what wretches feel,

and in a moment the passive attitude implied in the cold, figurative words has become animated and vitalized when Lear tears at his clothes.

Already the paradox is being argued in terms of the stage as the idea of the 'naked wretch' first suggests Lear himself, is then demonstrated by Edgar, in fact and flesh, and then linked again with Lear as we see him unbuttoning. How far is the abstract and the concrete already a unity before we actually see Lear embrace Edgar? Are they already identified? At all events, the identity between the two forming in our minds is established when we hear from Lear 'Didst thou give all to thy daughters? And art thou come to this?' Lear sees Edgar as himself. We are prepared now not only for the conjunction of the two, even to modern eyes something against the nature

The Behaviour of the Words on the Stage

and order of things, but also for them to seem in their identity to be two parts of the same man, which is exactly what Shakespeare wants his audience to imagine. The author secures our consent to this arrangement through the pressure of our sympathy with Edgar, and, by identifying Lear with him, he induces us to pity them equally. We are also induced to accept the ravings of Edgar as a restatement that Lear's 'gods' in the storm are of the Devil, that the order of nature is now topsy-turvy, that the 'thunder' has indeed cracked 'Nature's moulds' that any complacent view of the universe and its justice needs re-examination: 'Away, the foul fiend follows me, through the sharp hawthorn blow the winds. Hum, go to thy bed, and warm thee.' Edgar and Lear are talking the same language, and this becomes more apparent in the subsequent hovel scene. We are already prepared for the intimacy of Lear and Edgar, since it is but an extension of the dramatic reasoning we have been assimilating.

Kent protests, 'He hath no daughters, sir', but here it is *Kent's* sanity that is in question, and we are aware he has not the picture of his master in the same sharp focus as we have. The Fool, too, who up till now has been self-sufficient in his criticisms of Lear and Lear's perplexity, cannot in this crisis comprehend what is happening. He retreats with a feeble witticism, 'This cold night will turn us all to fools, and madmen'. The cynicism of this is inadequate to reflect the image we have formed, and, like Lear, we tend to dismiss him with Kent. For all his own suffering, he begins to lose his protector when Edgar takes his place, and as they go into the hovel he is left a misplaced figure, being neither sane nor mad. The limitations of Kent and the Fool in the light of the situation make it impossible that Lear should not partly reject them. The balance of alliances is stressed when Lear ceases to speak verse, but speaks instead with the looser prose rhythms and the illogical inconsistencies that echo Edgar's. The seeming

The Elements of Drama

assurance of the verse spoken by Kent and Gloucester must be incongruous.

The paradox prepared, it can be explored. Lear's 'animal' speech is a summary of the scene till now, and the elements that have been impressed upon us are pulled together. He declares, 'Thou wert better in a grave, than to answer with thy uncover'd body, this extremity of the skies', and forthwith unbuttons: he is beyond the solution of the grave, for he is dealing in the elementals of life. These he goes on to stress: 'Thou ow'st the worm no silk; the beast, no hide; the sheep, no wool; the cat, no perfume', and so he will strip himself: and acquire the purity he sees in Edgar. 'Unaccommodated man, is no more but such a poor, bare, forked animal as thou art', and Lear will be 'unaccommodated' like Edgar: and render himself animal. The one physical gesture of stripping himself of his clothes will equate him with Edgar, the socially despicable, raise the bedlam beggar to royalty, reduce nobility to animality. The two parts of man, the Edgar and the Lear, animal and divine, passion and reason, the part that must endure the storm and the part that can defy it, shall now in visual irony be equal. It is irony because what we know contradicts what we see, and it shocks us into realization. But we know too it is through his own experience that Lear has arrived at this degradation, that it is therefore a personal triumph of humility for him to accept and resign himself to it. We know he is of his own volition prepared to prove himself animal, not angel; whereas we know Edgar has been forced by circumstance to assume madness, and that he is a fake. The madness of Lear therefore signifies ironically for us that he has found what lay already within himself rather than found identity with Edgar. We know, seeing him to a degree objectively from the auditorium, that Lear has arrived at a position to feel the unity of man-animal within himself, and that fundamentally he is on his own. Whatever Shakespeare

The Behaviour of the Words on the Stage

will have Lear think he finds in Edgar is only a way of having us see that Lear has discovered it within himself: Edgar is not to become a second hero in the tragedy. When Lear cries, 'Off, off you lendings: come, unbutton here', this is Shakespeare's theatrical method of saying the two parts of man are now one in Lear, and that whatever Lear shall do after this will be the interaction of the two extremes working their purpose.

Shakespeare is yet to intensify this impression, when Lear spurns the apparently sane advice of Kent and Gloucester. When he does this, the argument changes from a discussion of what constitutes animality to a discussion of what constitutes sanity. The impression of Lear, animal-man, shifts to the impression of Lear, mad-sane, and the mad trial scene in the hovel is to justify its place in the play. In saying, 'First let me talk with this philosopher', Lear tells us that the affinity he feels with Edgar is an affinity of wisdom, but of a kind of wisdom which the 'sane' Kent and Gloucester cannot understand. It is not a wisdom, of course, that we are likely to comprehend by whatever semi-gibberish Edgar speaks, nor by whatever conversation there is between the two of them. It is only to be comprehended through the image the scene has created. When Lear turns to Edgar as his 'philosopher', it is to reveal to us that, in finding his affinity with him as an animal, he finds him 'noble'. This is his new wisdom. By becoming mad, Lear has understood what sanity is, just as by becoming animal he took the incredible step towards discovering what man was. These two concepts are at the conclusion of this scene modifying each other. They are interwoven by the physical movement that accepts Edgar and at the same time rejects Kent and Gloucester. Thus Lear can say, 'Noble philosopher, your company', whereby at once he grants the mad beggar the height of wisdom, but by standards other than those of accepted reasoning, and implies that he

The Elements of Drama

has a supremacy of rank, but by standards other than those of conventional social distinctions. We can better understand why Shakespeare has given so much of the dialogue over to Edgar *before* Lear recognizes him as the embodiment of wisdom: it is to persuade us that the company on the stage can receive only one impression of him, that he is mad. It is to make unmistakable the rhythm of the scene's mood: Edgar's gibberish shall respond to, harmonize with, and finally replace the effects of the storm now that Lear has ceased to resist it. We begin to be able to characterize the total effect of the scene. The fury of

> the great gods,
> That keep this dreadful pudder o'er our heads,

and reduce man to animal, has, in the upsetting of the natural order, become merely their madness. That madness has now been transmitted to Lear, for whom Edgar with his capering and his gibberish is the spokesman. 'What is the cause of thunder?' is the cool question Lear asks of Edgar. Cool, because on this question, spoken in a light, almost cynically jaded, tone, rests ironically the whole central contest of the scene and the paradoxes of the play. The question puts point blank man's query about the universe and his relation to it,[26] it poses the radical problem of suffering. Yet the effect of their playing with an empty metaphysical speculation, as of cold theological controversy, sharpens by contrast the importance of the question. The scholastics could make this sort of inquiry because they knew their faith was safe; so Lear too, in his self-discovery, has almost gone beyond the point where the answer really matters to him. He is now beyond suffering and beyond reasoning. His mind and spirit are dissociated from the cruelty of his daughters and of the gods. The physical movement of that seemingly casual promenade of the two grotesque and incongruous figures, casual after the racket and rage of the previous action, prepares us

The Behaviour of the Words on the Stage

to understand and accept the wisdom Lear is acquiring. This wisdom will enable him to be reconciled with Cordelia and to rediscover his place in nature.

Intimations of something about ourselves are the most valuable offerings drama can make. Its deepest intimations require all the means at the disposal of the stage if they are to reach us. Shakespeare makes his most profound statements, not in spite of any physical handicap a stage presents, but by using its properties to the full as indispensable instruments for his ends. Far from being its slave, he makes the stage and its actors, with their voices, their gestures and their movements, servants of his purpose.

A producer needs a special set of equipment to read a well-written dramatic score such as this. For the full appreciation of the play, the serious playgoer can begin to understand the absorbing and exhilarating complexities of the medium only by setting out himself to acquire some of this equipment.

PART II
ORCHESTRATION

6

BUILDING THE SEQUENCE OF IMPRESSIONS

The bad play is one which fumbles its action, sacrifices clarity in its impressions and loses control of its theme. The better play is one which efficiently manipulates its action to steer its ideas resolutely home. It takes them along a planned course, a 'line of intention'. This is not a question of 'plot'. Extracting a plot from a play rarely helps us to know it, any more than telling the story of *Emma* offers a morsel of Jane Austen's real content. Dig out the story from *King Lear* or *The Cherry Orchard*—what do we have? A cold, stiff, shapeless, unlovely skeleton. So we abandon a misleading path and look instead for the sequence of impressions. Thereby we come closer to the line of intention, to the theme of the play, as communicated by the whole theatrical experience. Real coherence is possible because good dramatic impressions possess some quality of synthesis, something that binds one to another, that provides a temporary centre for interest while showing us a direction along which to look.

Lopakhin and Varya seem superficially to demonstrate that they are sensitive about themselves, but really insensitive towards each other; that a proposal of marriage is unlikely; that in any case they would never have suited each other. The line of the action would seem to open a dramatic discussion of, say, the fitness of the parties for marriage. But it does not. The subject of marriage is closed. Nor are we allowed to follow their separate careers with an irrelevant biographical curiosity. Chekhov, least of all dramatists, is not merely telling a story. He wants us to see his characters as he sees them; he does not want them to perform stock tricks we supply; he wants us to see them as representative of *his* comic view. Otherwise what happens to them cannot fall into place beside what happens to Dunyasha, Yepikhodov, Gaev, indeed to all of them. For together they make up a pattern of well-selected impressions succeeding each other by design.

In *King Lear* interest is caught by one central, towering character, and less by a relationship between two or more characters. Lear towers through his relationship with Goneril and Regan, with Cordelia, and in our instance by discovering himself through Edgar. But again the sequence we receive is planned to lead us to a definite goal. Prepared as we are by hints of Lear's humility, the appearance of Edgar tests and demonstrates the quality of his feeling. When Lear takes Edgar's part, he is in effect saying first, 'I will be animal, if *that* is godliness', and second, 'I will be mad, if *that* is sanity'. We have already perceived, through the 'unnatural' scenes of Lear's rejection of Cordelia and of his rejection by Goneril and Regan, not only that this animality and this madness is an immediately fitting sequel, but that they intimate another Lear to come, one nobler for his animality, wiser for his madness. An effective image reflects the past and the future within the play.

The synthesis of its parts which a play attempts comes of its adroit handling of a certain sequence of impressions in a preconceived relationship. The detective pieces together his clues and finds a solution: the clues have no value unless pertinent to the problem. The dramatist manufactures his impressions so that under his influence his meaning shall be our meaning: they have no value unless they possess an imaginative relevance. Just as each speech must seem to provoke the next, just as in the 'well-made play' the fall of a curtain is designed to raise it again, so the impulse of the play's intention will dynamically determine what form the next impression will take.

Building the Sequence of Impressions

Thus the producer sees the links by scrutinizing the whole chain. Thus the actor traces the development of his part by keeping the whole play in perspective and his own part in proportion. Thus the audience apprehends the creation of a character, the development of a situation, the unfolding of the play's theme.

It should be possible, therefore, to abstract any effect from a scene and measure its relevance to the whole. The impressions behind this dialogue from Sophocles's *King Oedipus* are marshalled and disposed with deceptive simplicity. The effects in the vast Greek theatre were of necessity strong ones, but for all this the images were delicate, or we should be more ready to find much of the melodramatic plot structure in Greek tragedy merely sensational.

> TEIRESIAS. I know, as you do not, that you are living
>   In sinful union with the one you love,
>   Living in ignorance of your own undoing.
> OEDIPUS. Do you think you can say such things with impunity?
> TEIRESIAS. I do—if truth has any power to save.
> OEDIPUS. It has—but not for you; no, not for you,
>   Shameless and brainless, sightless, senseless sot!
> TEIRESIAS. You are to be pitied, uttering such taunts
>   As all men's mouths must some day cast at *you*.[1]

Teiresias is introduced as a blatant antagonist to Oedipus to make the battle of words between King and conscience immediate and prominent. Oedipus, in all the strength of his position as king, is actually accused of sinning by Teiresias, old and blind. The mere opposition of hot temper and reverend calm heightens and intensifies Teiresias's assertions and Oedipus's denials.

Within this generally emphatic framework, our short passage provides a succession of strong impressions. First there is Teiresias's imputation of the King's sin and ignorance, to which Oedipus's doubtfully positive answer in a threat, 'Do

The Elements of Drama

you think you can say such things with impunity?' is not padding, nor is it a further expression of the King's anger to give an opportunity to an actor to grace himself. We deduce a power in Teiresias which belies the figure he cuts. The power is greater than the power of personal courage. It is one of the authority of 'truth', and we are granted a premonition of what Oedipus in all his might will be fighting. Teiresias qualifies and complicates this premonition when his next speech makes the further suggestion, with tragic implications for the future, that 'truth' may work and destine Oedipus as much for destruction as for salvation: '...if truth has any power to save'. A new and more perplexed impression carries the ambivalence the play is to explore.

Oedipus, incensed further, abuses Teiresias, flinging out words seemingly as they come to his lips, but each of which resounds ironically for an audience familiar with the legend: 'Shameless and brainless, sightless, senseless sot!' They are particularly pointed and barbed when Teiresias describes them as,

> such taunts
> As all men's mouths must some day cast at *you*.

Oedipus's thematic words echo down the play, and even at this point the audience is questioning their application and preparing itself for the sifting of their ambiguities. 'Sightless', we say to ourselves, is Teiresias, will be Oedipus. But if Teiresias knows the truth, he has insight, which Oedipus has not; when Oedipus has insight, he will be sightless. Then and then only, when the torments of the body have paid for and relieved the torments of the mind, shall Oedipus possess the truth. 'Shameless', we say, is Teiresias the subject thus to address his sovereign, and Oedipus is right to punish. But Oedipus is bearing a greater shame: his is the shame of patricide and incest, and punishment will be answered by juster punishment. Yet Teiresias's accusation of shameless-

Building the Sequence of Impressions

ness has truth on its side; truth is shameless, and he admits and bears his shame. When Oedipus admits and bears *his* shame, then he too will acknowledge the truth and truth will be victor.

The impressions now pursue each other. Truth can save or destroy, we continue; Oedipus will find insight when he loses his sight, but his new knowledge will destroy him, and in destroying him may save him. In bearing his shame he will live again with truth, and both his destruction and his salvation will depend upon his accepting his shame and his penance for his sin. Oedipus will lose his life to find it. A modern Christian or an ancient Greek audience would see in this the terrible greatness of man stung by self-knowledge and bitter in resignation, noble in his readiness to accept and atone for his sin.

Even in a compressed sequence impressions can be clear and sharp. No audience, of course, would rationalize its deductions in this way, nor is it desirable that it should. Such deductions in the theatre are arrived at as it were intuitively, and as a felt experience as the theme of the play asserts and reasserts itself in variety. On the surface of this scene, what immediately moves the audience is the power of an old man to make a king angry, and the impulse to life on the stage is Teiresias's increasing command and Oedipus's increasing wrath. But even while this is affecting us strongly, we are moved to perceive the complexity of the hints which itch in our minds. We are taught dramatically that the old man's confidence comes of the truth of what he is saying, that the King's anger comes of his error, and that Teiresias and Oedipus symbolize a right and a wrong. While the prominence of these symbols firmly establishes them as a frame of meaning to circumscribe the action, already Sophocles can begin to hint at refinements of reason and feeling which are to synthesize the play as a whole. Awaiting elaboration, they will organize

The Elements of Drama

a subtle imaginative experience which has nothing in common with the grosser indulgences of melodrama.

The experience in the auditorium is inevitably cumulative. An emotional sequence, especially, is not easily restrained once begun: it makes its own momentum. The author must take this into account when he requires his audience suddenly to become more detached and critical, or when he wishes to alter the direction of the emotional impulse he has set up. This is why the Epilogue to *Saint Joan* upsets us: it irrationally surrenders the valuable charge of feeling from the previous scene; nor can even Shaw's wit reassert itself before the final curtain. The last part of *Murder in the Cathedral*, after the Knights have dropped into another convention and lent a new satirical tone to the action, so unsettles the audience that it finds it difficult to take up again the drive of the play, recapture the experience and get back on the line of its intention. A similar reason can be given for the doubtful success of the last act of *The Cocktail Party*. The emotional experience behind Celia's self-sacrifice is uncomfortably and immodestly blunted by the lapse into the more trivial world of the Chamberlaynes, which Mr Eliot cannot raise to a corresponding level of importance. On the other hand, the transference of interest from Antony to Cleopatra after his suicide is accomplished successfully, because there is no rootedly antipathetic feeling between them in the first four acts. The twin heroes have been standing passionately together against the same kind of opposition, the forces of politic reason, so that in Act v the load of our emotion is lifted readily on to Cleopatra without disturbing the balance of our regard.

Another successful disturbance in a sequence is to be found in Synge's *Deirdre of the Sorrows*, like *King Oedipus* a far more complex play than its surface simplicity suggests. In Act II Fergus attempts to draw Naisi back to Ireland by suggesting that domesticity does not offer an appropriate life for a hero.

Building the Sequence of Impressions

Naisi confesses his own doubts about living with Deirdre in retirement, taking the argument further while she overhears him. This is the episode:

> FERGUS.... You'll do well to come back to men and women are your match and comrades, and not be lingering until the day that you'll grow weary, and hurt Deirdre showing her the hardness will grow up within your eyes... You're here years and plenty to know it's truth I'm saying. *Deirdre comes out of the tent with a horn of wine, she catches the beginning of Naisi's speech and stops with stony wonder.*
>
> NAISI, *very thoughtfully.* I'll not tell you a lie. There have been days a while past when I've been throwing a line for salmon or watching for the run of hares, that I've a dread upon me a day'd come I'd weary of her voice, *very slowly* and Deirdre'd see I'd wearied.[2]

Deirdre of the Sorrows is a play about love, its strength and beauty. To begin, it is told sparely and simply, with nothing detracting from the steadily increasing urgency of emotion. Forebodings of the outcome, the irony of the wild girl in royal robes that befit her but must not belong to her, the sense of nature playing its part, the pressure of time the lovers are fighting, the desire for safety they know can never be theirs except in death, the jealousy of Conchubor—all contribute to the weight of the emotion. Now the perfection of Deirdre and Naisi's passion is challenged when the first test is applied.

There had been some preparation for the shock of Naisi's fear of disaffection, for we had already heard something of Deirdre's doubts: 'It's lonesome this place, having happiness like ours, till I'm asking each day will this day match yesterday....' The series of interviews between Deirdre and Lavarcham, Owen and Fergus pass to the tolling tune of 'Queens get old...', which betokens her state of mind. It is as if she is trying her lover when she leaves Fergus and says she will give Naisi the choice of returning to Ireland or staying with her. This is true enough. Its larger effect has been to encourage our wonder at the honesty of Deirdre's love, and to make us feel with her how strongly she was committed by her action in leaving

The Elements of Drama

Conchubor. The mutual security of the lovers then remained intact: Naisi, we assumed, was as strong as Deirdre herself.

Fergus on our behalf throws out a feeler. He suggests to Naisi he might grow tired of her: '...not be lingering until the day that you'll grow weary, and hurt Deirdre showing her the hardness will grow up in your eyes'. He does not say more, and we take this to be one more phrase of the strain sounding through the play, of the consequences of growing older. But there is a new tone in Naisi's voice that stops Deirdre as she enters, and the sudden alertness of her movement promptly draws our attention to the way he speaks. Naisi follows Fergus's suggestion with an unwitting cruelty: 'I've a dread upon me a day'd come I'd weary of her voice, and Deirdre'd see I'd wearied.' Their mutual sense of security can now never be regained, except in death. Naisi goes on with confidence, 'She's not seen it.... Deirdre's no thought of getting old or wearied'. She *has* seen it now; we know this as we watch her.

How are our impressions affected? They are almost revolutionized. The smooth course of our sympathy with the lovers is rudely halted. For a precarious moment the audience has no direction for its emotion. Then, the weight of tragic foreboding the two have been carrying is shifted on to the shoulders of one, on to Deirdre. Because we have been schooled into believing she would survive her doubts about the onset of age and its effect upon her love, we easily concede her the extra burden and dismiss Naisi. Our feelings for Deirdre assert themselves with new vigour, the emotion released again after a momentary restriction surges out with more intensity than before. This is Synge 'aggravating' his image. He directs its progress towards a destination whose significance we are led to appraise by implication: 'There's no safe place, Naisi, on the ridge of the world.' This play demonstrates a deft manipulation of impressions leaving in their wake a trail of resounding overtones.

Building the Sequence of Impressions

The structure of the play unrestricted by the particular curbs of realism can allow an exciting freedom in the sequence of impressions. Bold experiment with their juxtaposition, to persuade the spectator to undergo unfamiliar and disconcerting experiences, makes of course for remarkable successes and remarkable failures in the theatre. It is a delight to see the Elizabethan dramatists discovering what use they can make of their free stage and in what variety of ways they can call up a response from their audience. One feels there must have been a similar delight in the theatres of Strindberg and Pirandello earlier in this century.

Shakespeare is a mine of discoveries. Even in an early play like *Romeo and Juliet* Shakespeare is exploring the characteristics and scope of his theatre, and there already we may spot his peculiar dramatic rhythm. The realistic opening of the play, vividly, visually and systematically built to prepare and foreshadow the entry of the Prince, is followed by 'unreal', quasi-Petrarchan lines spoken as prelude to Romeo's entry. By this expedient Shakespeare is perhaps only partially successful in dramatizing at the outset of the play that ideal love has no place where the coarse society of man is at odds with itself. Later, Mercutio's ribald, mocking, earthy lines are used to preface Romeo's colourful abstractions of the balcony scene. He cries with healthy unfeeling,

> Romeo! humours, madman, passion, lover!
> Appear thou in the likeness of a sigh,
> Speak but one rhyme and I am satisfied:
> Cry but ay me, pronounce but love and dove...![3]

The poignancy and ethereal quality this throws up in the immediately subsequent love-scene dominated as that is by an abundance of contrasting celestial verbal imagery, is strikingly successful in stressing the uniqueness and the loneliness of Romeo and Juliet's love; Mercutio might even be said to enrich

The Elements of Drama

the tragic overtones of its cosmic significance. In Act III the violent stage on which Romeo banishes himself, and the crowded scene in which his sentence is passed, is juxtaposed melodramatically with the solitary figure of Juliet, who appears immediately afterwards above the departing crowd. Its brutal impression upon us does not quickly fade, and Shakespeare skilfully torments the image by having her, in her ignorance of what has happened, call upon the night to bring Romeo to her. Again, the lovers appear just as father and future son-in-law have jovially fixed the wedding-day. The juxtapositions in the action are big and bold, often near to sensationalism, and it is not until his maturer plays that Shakespeare more subtly regulates the audience's feelings.

The second scene of *Hamlet* in structure follows and develops the method of the first scene in *Romeo and Juliet*. Attention is forcefully and visually drawn to the lonely figure of Hamlet replacing the pomp of Claudius and his council. But in this play the second element of the sequence has been weighted with meaning already, so that the ferment of Hamlet's misery contrasts desperately with Claudius's smooth control of his court. We think of the structural ordering in Hamlet's play scene, the stiffly stylized play-within-the-play with its simple message and the restrained sarcasms from Hamlet himself, broken suddenly by the hysterical reality of the call for lights and the frantic bustle that ensues, leaving an exultant Hamlet alone with Horatio. An examination of the sequence of impressions is the way of knowing the full function of the Grave-diggers, as in *Macbeth* of the Porter.

Macbeth is a play compact of transitions to provoke the audience into imaginative alertness. The typically confident sequence of ironies is the leap from Macbeth's humble genuflection to Duncan,

> I'll be myself the harbinger, and make joyful
> The hearing of my wife, with your approach...,

Building the Sequence of Impressions

to Lady Macbeth's remorseless

> Come you spirits,
> That tend on mortal thoughts, unsex me here...,

and back again to Duncan's

> This castle hath a pleasant seat....[4]

This is familiar, but constantly effective because these are not logical ironies but emotional ones. They are not dependent upon our following a process of reasoning we may have followed before but dependent upon our submitting freshly each time to an emotional pressure which begins to grow from the moment we see the witches. The telescoping of time which the Elizabethan stage permitted at once makes these ironies more forceful, and makes the approach to the crisis of Duncan's murder almost unbearably urgent. Shakespeare exploited the susceptibilities of his audience while exploiting his free stage. His control of the stage during the sequence of the murder itself is, at the least, brilliant craftsmanship, a lesson to any writer of melodrama in how to thrill.

But Act III offers an interplay of visual and aural impressions to elaborate the theme of pride which shows a control over his material as fine as any in the canon. From the moment when Banquo alone on the stage intimately acknowledges his fears to himself and then to the audience at large, and from the moment when Macbeth and Lady Macbeth enter with the full ceremony of a king and queen, our interest is prompted by increasingly sinister ironies. Macbeth with seeming self-control makes his plans for the deception of Banquo, while we are granted flashes of insight into the real instability of his soul: so we learn a dramatic lesson on the divided mind. This is developed and emphasized in the succeeding scene by the oscillations of fear and confidence in the diseased minds of the husband and wife. Strong suggestions of supernatural evil are worked into the verbal imagery, until we are made to see 'night's black agents' themselves in the persons of the cloaked figures of the murderers. As they enter stealthily on to the platform, while Macbeth is still apostrophizing the night perhaps from the gallery above, the audience takes their appearance as a tangible expression of all the witches stand for, a savage actualizing of the motif of evil. The play grows until Macbeth's meditation on the death of his wife is blazingly enlightened, for us as much as for him, by the report 'The wood began to move!' So we, as always urged to complete the pattern of tragic meaning before the hero himself reaches self-knowledge, cannot miss recognizing 'th' equivocation of the fiend'.

This fluid rhythm of impressions constitutes an effect in the theatre that cannot be captured in reading the play, for each exists as part of a design that is shaped emotionally, the one calling up the other only in the conditions of the theatre. In reading, one may doubt that the putting out of Gloucester's eyes adds meaning to the complexity of Lear's madness, until scenes vi and vii of Act II of *King Lear* are seen in juxtaposition in time and place on the stage. The meaning of punishment and suffering is extended and redoubled. Nor does one question in the theatre the logic of the time scheme in *Othello* when the sweep of the play's emotion makes the jealousy scenes one tight, intervolved, emotional unit. The stage for poetic drama is an illogical one, and therefore an inexhaustibly experimental one.

A similar freedom is found on the Restoration and eighteenth-century stages. While the non-representative proscenium doors and the neutral ground of the 'apron' persisted, the dramatists continued to take effective liberties with the pattern of a scene. The fantastic elements of Restoration plays were as comfortable on the stage as those of earlier plays. This was to last as long as the doors provided entrances close to the spectator, and as long as the actors on the apron were permitted intimate extravagances with the audience. In particular, the 'aside',

Building the Sequence of Impressions

lost in recent years as a theatrical weapon and a dramatic stimulus, was at its best an acute method of sharpening the edge of a sequence.

The cumulative effect of the Screen Scene in Sheridan's *The School for Scandal* does not owe its success so much to the contriving of a situation in which in turn the deceiver Joseph Surface is embarrassed by visits from Lady Teazle, Sir Peter, Charles his brother, and then threatened with Lady Sneerwell—which, after all, the bedroom farce in today's style can do as well. The success is due to the refreshing manner in which each actor swiftly and appetizingly engages interest at the expense of, chiefly, Joseph's and Sir Peter's peace of mind. The comic zest that characterizes the scene is largely the result of the rapid and direct succession of conflicting impressions made possible by the brisk reinforcement of the asides. Sir Peter says to Charles,

Joseph is no rake, but he is no such saint either, in that respect. *Aside.* I have a great mind to tell him—we should have such a laugh at Joseph.[5]

The purpose of this aside is quite different from that of soliloquy: it is a quickening address to the audience (Sir Peter's 'we' specifically includes the audience to whom it is spoken), not a revelation of the character's mind, which is in any case apparent. The effect is wholly ironic. We cannot care whether or not Sir Peter tells Charles about 'the little French milliner' for their own pleasure of laughing at Joseph's expense. The confession of the aside interests us only because we know the French milliner is Lady Teazle, and that laughter will come not only at the expense of Joseph, but at the expense of Sir Peter also. These motions are made towards the final revelation in throwing down the screen, which is a simple gesture of our release from the cumulative effect of restriction and suspense. The acceleration of the rhythm of our impressions to this moment suggests that Sheridan had

The Elements of Drama

calculated very finely how daring he could be in stretching his fantasy.

Goldsmith's *She Stoops to Conquer* depends for its success upon a series of strong situations, but each situation is composed of as bold a sequence as a non-realistic play permits. Again and again the interplay between actor and audience promotes the excitement of an episode, while at first sight it might seem, especially in reading, that the actors remain entirely within the play's framework. Look at the scene of the stolen jewels:

> MRS HARDCASTLE. We are robbed. My bureau has been broke open, the jewels taken out, and I'm undone!
> TONY. Oh! is that all? Ha! ha! ha! By the laws, I never saw it better acted in my life. Ecod, I thought you was ruined in earnest, ha, ha, ha!
> MRS HARDCASTLE. Why, boy, I *am* ruined in earnest....[6]

Mrs Hardcastle's real distress is properly deserved, and her meanness now reflects justly upon herself. But no audience is bothered at this juncture to pass moral judgments upon her. It is laughing with Tony because it was witness to his scheme to get the jewels from his mother, and it sees his success. This is in a sense morally gratifying, but what chiefly pleases is the pleasure of seeing him successfully pretend to be in conspiracy with his mother while at the same time able to give free expression to his own elation at having deceived her. Tony's 'Ha! ha! ha!' is therefore two edged, but the point is sharper still. Tony's laughter invites laughter at a woman herself hypocritical, herself a character acting a part. There we see her, behaving more and more earnestly to try to disown the figure she is cutting for Tony. The more she tries, the more it pleases Tony, and the more we laugh. Our laughter is, through Tony's agency, a spontaneous expression of our pleasure at having understood her discomfiture. The image is unusually involved, although in performance its effect is keen and immediate. It is involved because previous impressions

Building the Sequence of Impressions

in the play, of Tony's plans to secure the jewels, of Mrs Hardcastle's plans to keep them, and of what Tony knows that Mrs Hardcastle does not, have been brought almost mathematically together to explode in this one joyful scene. Dramatic impressions have the power to affect one another without their being juxtaposed in time.

Sometimes verbal thematic insertions in the dialogue help provide a greater synthesis of its parts, elaborate or intensify impressions to come, give an absolute direction to the spectator's curiosity, and sanction his valuation of the sequence. The insertion of such elements is a legitimate procedure where the response of the audience is insecure.

One of Mr Eliot's problems in writing his religious drama is the uncertainty of an accepted set of beliefs among his modern audience, and of any symbol or ritual common to it. He is at pains to assert the values he wants placed on his subjects. This is especially true of *Murder in the Cathedral*, in which he is initially trusting to a body of acceptable symbols to mark out his ground, and thus reach out to a religious experience. In *The Cocktail Party* and *The Confidential Clerk* he makes no such assumptions, but is excessively preoccupied with starting from a secular, almost pagan standpoint, and using commonplace, almost unenlightened, experiences, dramatizing them in such a way as to recreate belief, inspire a near-Christian valuation of them, and promote a near-religious experience. But in *Murder in the Cathedral* his framework is firmly fixed: in this sequence leading to the murder of Thomas there is no compromising:

THOMAS. It is the just man who
  Like a bold lion, should be without fear.
  I am here.
  No traitor to the King. I am a priest,
  A Christian, saved by the blood of Christ,
  Ready to suffer with my blood.
  This is the sign of the Church always,

The Elements of Drama

    The sign of blood. Blood for blood.
    His blood given to buy my life,
    My blood given to pay for His death,
    My death for His death.
FIRST KNIGHT. Absolve all those you have excommunicated.
SECOND KNIGHT. Resign the powers you have arrogated.
THIRD KNIGHT. Restore to the King the money you appropriated.
FIRST KNIGHT. Renew the obedience you have violated.
THOMAS. For my Lord I am now ready to die,
    That His Church may have peace and liberty....[7]

It is essential that the murder of the Archbishop should not slide into physical sensation. The uncouth entry of the Knights into the church is likely to be exciting in the wrong way, and the actual murder has to be lifted from a thrill in the stomach to an elevation of the mind. The electric effect of a performance in a church building of the Knights' hammering on the door behind the audience, of the terror of the Priests with Thomas, of the Knights' iron-shod boots clanging down the stone flags of the nave and aisles to converge on the altar from three directions, of their strident voices mouthing the consonants of 'Where is Becket the Cheapside brat?' will every time 'involve' the spectator as witness to the murder. By extending the acting area to the auditorium, reinforcing the effect of merging the Women of Canterbury with the audience, and by Thomas's speaking the Christmas sermon directly to it from the pulpit, the spectator will feel he is in a living congregation. For this to be followed by any realistic sword-work by the Knights would be dangerously destructive of the conceptual meaning of the scene of Thomas's temptation to martyrdom. It would be enough to dissipate the subtle impressions already established, of which the murder must be the consummation. There is need for a pause in the progress of the action, both to give an extra twist to the suspense and to guide the spectator's sensibility into a spiritual channel. The action must be elevated by some dramatized reminder

Building the Sequence of Impressions

and summary of the theme, lest this crisis should pass without its intended significance.

Thomas offers himself to the Knights quietly and submissively. The words he speaks seem a challenge in themselves in their simplicity and in the evenness of their emphasis: 'I am here'—this line is evidently intended by the author to carry his three stresses. They give pause after the rapid tempo of the previous action, and give quiet after the raucous voices of the Knights cease to echo round the church. They suggest a gathering of strength for the next pronouncement, which, though hardly suited to the situation as it might have been in reality, is important to the proper appraisal of the event. Thomas's words are rhetorical, heavy with incantatory rhythm, gathering pace and shaped to a climax like a good evocative parliamentary speech, and dying away at the conclusion as the total meaning replaces the weight of the voice. This speech is therefore the vehicle for a statement of some substance.

In effect Thomas is saying this to the audience: 'The murder these Knights are about to commit, and the murder that you, audience, are about to watch, is a matter of some religious significance. When you see me die in a moment or two—and of course you are expecting it because in any case you know the story—you must please remember my death is in the pattern of all the deaths that have been suffered in the cause of Christianity since the Crucifixion itself. Therefore my author wants the action to take on as great a degree of stylization as possible, so that you will be sure to recognize this death as a symbol of other things than the mere decease of Thomas, a colourful archbishop of Canterbury. What are these other things? I will sum them up in one word for you, and repeat it in a number of different ways so that you cannot miss its special meaning. That word is "blood", and I hope by the time I have finished manipulating it, its accumulated meaning will

The Elements of Drama

be clear to you. Thus when you "see" my blood spilt, so to speak, you will have no doubt that what you think you see is that very same "blood" I have been speaking to you about.

'You may remember in the story of the Crucifixion that, when in Matthew xxvii Pilate washed his hands before the multitude, all the people answered and said, "His blood be on us, and on our children". The Church, therefore, has traditionally acknowledged its blood-guilt, and that is what I, as Archbishop of Canterbury, am doing now. You will remember too that Christ shed his blood that we might be saved. Thus we are inextricably involved in rather an interesting conundrum, which should be stated now. Christ's death inevitably means any Christian's life is dedicated to him, and that the supreme confirmation of this dedication lies in giving up his life to him. Indeed, as we acknowledge that his death was for us, we are in that acknowledgment also committing ourselves to an act of self-sacrifice. A matter of buying and paying, if you like, in which the act of buying is also the act of paying. Accordingly, when you see me die, look also at the Cross on the altar before which you will see me slump. If you remember what the Cross stands for, the conundrum will come clear to you in a flash. Perhaps you might even identify the two deaths, mine and his, in your mind, and then you may be sure the play will make its point. My death for His death.'

The concentration in Thomas's speech is the sign of its appropriateness. Its close-packed verbal imagery is felt immediately; it is all the more forceful for its simplicity of organization and the direct Anglo-Saxon monosyllables of its diction. Parallels to its manner of repeating and accumulating meaning more musically than dramatically can occasionally be found in Shakespeare, as in *Macbeth*,

> Methought I heard a voice cry, Sleep no more:
> Macbeth does murther Sleep, the innocent Sleep,
> Sleep that knits up the ravell'd sleeve of care,[8]

Building the Sequence of Impressions

or here in Mr Eliot's own poetry, where the meaning of the key words is stressed and explored by the rhetorical device of anaphora:

> We had the experience but missed the meaning,
> And approach to the meaning restores the experience.[9]

The words of the Knights that follow are written again in that vigorously objective manner the author had temporarily dropped, and they are written for movement, as Thomas's lines are written for stillness. The severity of the words is a Latin severity, heavy, threatening, legal, material, deliberately out of key with Thomas's own way of speaking. The Knights' words are of the narrow world that lacks spiritual values, the gross and mundane world the Knights come from and understand and fall back upon. Their words contrast in form as well as in meaning with what Thomas has said, and our impression is one of horror that they cannot speak or understand his language, now our language. We can believe these men can never see, as we can, the meaning of what they are about to do.

Other effects, too, are being created in these lines. The hammer blows of the stychomythia of the four sharp lines they speak quicken the tempo after the lull, and all but bring us abreast of the climax. The echoes of the half-rhymes, 'excommunicated...', arrogated..., appropriated..., violated...', with dragging, sneering feminine endings that contrast with Thomas's decisive end-stopped lines, begin to ring round the church as their feet and their voices did before, and as will their cries to come. In gesture, each 'Absolve...', 'Resign...', 'Restore...', 'Renew...' impels the body of the actor one pace nearer to Thomas and the altar. Reginald, the First Knight, finds himself a pace ahead of his fellows, so that the ensemble takes shape automatically, and his threat becomes the immediate one. It is to Reginald that Thomas will speak. Most unusual is the effect of earlier hints that these Knights are not individuals,

The Elements of Drama

but an expression of a prototype force. They become a symbol of no specified authority, rather of a general tyranny of the material over the spiritual, of the temporal over the eternal. This impression is enhanced if the Tempters double for the Knights. The effect is emphasized by the stylized, almost choric, nature of their speech. How they speak makes it entirely appropriate to play the murder itself in the non-realistic manner of traditional pantomime, and this in itself suggests a ritual murder. The martyrdom is suddenly illuminated as a symbol of the death of Christ, as Thomas's

> This is the sign of the Church always,
> The sign of blood...,

had foreshadowed, and completes a sequence that is wholly successful.

Verbal concepts can help the dramatist to embrace a greater universe of mind and spirit, and to expand the effect of the play's whole sequence. 'Atmosphere' is a much abused term. In every case it wants breaking down. We most frequently mean by it that a particular sequence of impressions designedly reverberates in our minds and calls upon common associations of thought or feeling. These we ourselves unwittingly bring into the theatre for use in the construction of the play.

This is by no means an exhaustive summary of all the possible types of permutations and inflexions of a sequence in a play's orchestration. Here are only hints of how its fabric can be knit and laced, how determined and controlled, woven through the play, how ravelled and cut and stretched. The playgoer will multiply and classify his own theatrical experiences.

7
TEMPO AND MEANING

When dramatic impressions follow one another in a related sequence, a new quality arises because they must follow one another at a certain speed in time. We call this new quality 'tempo'. It is a quality every dramatist is anxious to command, because it affects the rhythm of his play and enhances its effect. When he orchestrates his action, his sense of the rhythm of his scene may be the deepest of his motives for adopting a particular structural arrangement.

Who can think of what follows the discovery of Duncan's murder by Macduff in anything but the tempo Shakespeare ordained by the dialogue? It was clear in his mind as he wrote

> Ring the alarum-bell: murther, and treason,
> Banquo, and Donalbain: Malcolm awake...![1]

The frenzy on the stage, a storm of noise and light, of people and their cries, is carefully arranged to succeed the silent, dark, sinister scene of Macbeth and Lady Macbeth at their crime. It in part fixes its meaning, impressing tempestuously the idea of chaos following the destruction of an order: 'Confusion now hath made his masterpiece.' The scene of the alarum-bell would of course have no meaning without the preceding scene of the murder, and even less without the Porter's references to his function as 'devil-porter'. But how much affective meaning would have been lost had the tempo of the first repeated the tempo of the second?

Trace the scene's rhythm by its smaller climaxes: of Macduff's urgent, unwitting exit, balanced by the anxious delay of Lennox's recital of omens; of the discovery itself, followed by the rapid succession of entries to the point of Macduff's

The Elements of Drama

pertinent question to Macbeth; of Macbeth's falsely ebullient explanation, marked by his Lady's swooning; and finally of Banquo's hot declaration,

> In the great hand of God I stand, and thence
> Against the undivulg'd pretence I fight
> Of treasonous malice.
> MACDUFF.   And so do I.
> ALL.   So all.

As excitement leaps from crest to crest, it passes for us from external sensation to a true crisis of inward reflection. The scene is orchestrated rhythmically, so that when Malcolm and Donalbain are left in silence alone in their horror and perplexity, their exchange is not the anticlimax sometimes supposed, but a climax of *meaning* which in this lull the audience digests. We think and feel in accord with the distraught Malcolm and Donalbain.

Tempo is therefore not a polish on the surface of the action: it is an intrinsic element in its whole structure. It cannot be imposed afterwards in stage directions. Nor can it be superimposed by the actor upon the author's text to make this brighter and livelier than it might otherwise be. Do not see it as a garnish of variations of speed: tempo must reside in the author's conception, or nowhere. If the actors press it where no provision is made for it, what will result? If they do not contradict the author's meaning, they may at least muddle it.

For a satisfactory understanding of a play's orchestration, we have to find what special contribution tempo makes. For every play moves at a pace of some sort. If that pace remains constant, the playing strangles the play. But once a rhythm is felt, then a powerful source of feeling has been called upon. Tempo always exists to evoke meaning.

The simplest form tempo takes is a steady progression: a formula is repeated and a pattern is uniformly built up. In

Tempo and Meaning

The Importance of Being Earnest the meeting of Cecily and Gwendolen grows to a quarrel which takes this shape:

GWENDOLEN, *quite politely, rising.* My darling Cecily, I think there must be some slight error. Mr Ernest Worthing is engaged to me. The announcement will appear in the *Morning Post* on Saturday at the latest.

CECILY, *very politely, rising.* I am afraid you must be under some misconception. Ernest proposed to me exactly ten minutes ago. *Shows diary.*

GWENDOLEN, *examines diary through her lorgnette carefully.* It is very curious, for he asked me to be his wife yesterday afternoon at 5.30. If you would care to verify the incident, pray do so. *Produces diary of her own.* I never travel without my diary. One should always have something sensational to read on the train. I am so sorry, dear Cecily, if it is any disappointment to you, but I am afraid I have the prior claim.

CECILY. It would distress me more than I can tell you, dear Gwendolen, if it caused you any mental or physical anguish, but I feel bound to point out that since Ernest proposed to you he clearly has changed his mind.[2]

Here is all the evidence of a repeated formula changing in its tempo of presentation. Both Cecily and Gwendolen are attacking. They challenge each other by the way they echo remarks and gestures; they rise together and they copy each other's tone of voice; together they mention the engagement to 'Ernest', its date and time; they exchange rival diaries; and equally they insist upon priority. What then suggests that this dialogue is not to move monotonously?

The excessive politeness between them shows they are concerned to conceal feelings, but nevertheless both are furious. The angrier they are, the more restrained their words: 'I am afraid you must be under some misconception'—meaning, of course, 'You've made a ridiculous mistake'. This develops to 'I am so sorry, dear Cecily, if it is any disappointment to you...'—meaning, 'I take the greatest of pleasure in upsetting your plans'. This in turn develops to the incongruously excessive 'It would distress me more than I can tell you, dear Gwendolen...'—meaning something like, 'Oh, what sheer joy it would be to hurt you!' This progression could conceivably be taken at an even pace with an effect of whimsy, but

The Elements of Drama

how much more striking if the pace changes. Should the tempo grow fast or slow? Without our requiring psychological reasons why their icy control of language would slow down their speaking, the irony of teatime manners overlying real feelings can probably be completely savoured by an audience only if the pace is moderated.

This can be checked when the scene proceeds as follows:

GWENDOLEN, *meditatively*. If the poor fellow has been entrapped into any foolish promise I shall consider it my duty to rescue him at once, and with a firm hand.

CECILY, *thoughtfully and sadly*. Whatever unfortunate entanglement my dear boy may have got into, I will never reproach him with it after we are married.

GWENDOLEN. Do you allude to me, Miss Cardew, as an entanglement? You are presumptuous. On an occasion of this kind it becomes more than a moral duty to speak one's mind. It becomes a pleasure.

CECILY. Do you suggest, Miss Fairfax, that I entrapped Ernest into an engagement? How dare you? This is no time for wearing the shallow mask of manners. When I see a spade I call it a spade.

GWENDOLEN, *satirically*. I am glad to say that I have never seen a spade. It is obvious that our social spheres have been widely different.

The stylized asides they speak 'meditatively' and 'thoughtfully and sadly' suggest that their self-control is complete, enough for each, indeed, to have the complete conviction she is mistress of the situation and of Ernest. Each gently dramatizes her position. But the change comes quickly.

There is more to the determination of tempo. Its ultimate sanction must be the sequence of impressions. After this temporary slackening, the use of deliberately provocative terms like 'entanglement' and 'entrapped' bring them together again in a different state of mind, to prepare the miniature crisis to come. The sentences lose their laboured self-control, the genteel turns of phrase all but disappear, and their comments are shorter and sharper. Anger rises to the surface, and forms are all but submerged. The puppets face each other with surnames, height of insult, and with claws

Tempo and Meaning

bared. In the last three speeches before the entry of Merriman with the teatray, Wilde intends the pace and tension to increase quickly to the point where a sarcasm from Gwendolen shall produce a certain laugh. Why?

What clarity does this particular tempo, elementary as it is, lend to the sequence, first slowing, then quickening? The irony behind the exchange of diaries has not only to be felt, it has to be interpreted. We are to perceive how women of breeding conduct themselves in a simple case of animal rivalry. Their technique in managing a human relationship when strong emotion rules it, when passion discards reason and when feminine intuition, not rational social forms, determines behaviour, is put up for our scrutiny. We need a fraction of time to assimilate and criticize. At the change, a new tone and a new pace mark the contrast and offer a further statement. We are reminded that even women of this kind surrender their control when they must, that their manners are but a mask. We are happy to discover that these ladies, whose values a second or two before were apparently unassailable, can after all behave in a way consistent with natural laws. The higher they have placed themselves beyond the reach of baser passions, the further they must fall, and the more certain our conclusion. Of course, Wilde does not have to drop them far to make his point; he does not have to *show* them as animals, or bring them down to any realistic level: he can do all this and keep his scene softly comic.

The brisk pace leading to the appearance of Merriman the butler makes his entry startling. The tempo jolts to a sudden halt when he disturbs Cecily and Gwendolen. His 'Shall I lay the tea here as usual, Miss?' ensures we do not miss seeing that in the presence of the butler, the tangible reminder of their proper decorum, they are compelled ludicrously to revert to their former behaviour. They suppress their feelings beneath another surface display. The rhythmic contrast points

The Elements of Drama

the comic contrast between manners and emotions. Tempo is perhaps the prime mover of the satire.

Cecily and Gwendolen as characters are echoes and likenesses of each other. Where characters are differentiated in their persons, attitudes or motives, as are Captain Robert de Baudricourt and his Steward in the first scene of *Saint Joan*, tempo is necessarily subtler:

ROBERT, *rising*. Now listen to me, you.
STEWARD, *humbly*. Yes, sir.
ROBERT. What am I?
STEWARD. What are you, sir?
ROBERT, *coming at him*. Yes: what am I? Am I Robert, squire of Baudricourt and captain of this castle of Vaucouleurs; or am I a cowboy?
STEWARD. Oh, sir, you know you are a greater man here than the king himself.
ROBERT. Precisely. And now, do you know what you are?
STEWARD. I am nobody, sir, except that I have the honor to be your steward.
ROBERT, *driving him to the wall, adjective by adjective*. You have not only the honor of being my steward, but the privilege of being the worst, most incompetent, drivelling snivelling jibbering jabbering idiot of a steward in France.

Shaw establishes Robert as a little dictator with enough of an imposing façade to make it likely he will scare Joan when she makes her entrance. He wishes also to set the 'tone' of the scene as quickly as possible. He suggests Robert's self-importance by the sense of the words he speaks, by his aggressive rhetorical questioning, by the rich and sonorous 'Robert, squire of Baudricourt and captain of this castle of Vaucouleurs', round which the pompous little man can roll his tongue. But his most immediately effective method is to put him opposite the Steward, whom Shaw, with characteristic vividness, describes as 'a trodden worm, scanty of flesh, scanty of hair, who might be any age from 18 to 55, being the sort of man whom age cannot wither because he has never bloomed'. Such opposition, fantastic and extravagant, also serves to jolly

Tempo and Meaning

the audience into a comfortable sense of superiority so that it will laugh at either character or both as the author decides. The tempo implicit in the scene is designed to assist in both of these tasks of establishing character and 'tone'.

In general the tempo is a quickening one, but within this pattern there is a strong contrast. Robert is aggressive. Stage movements are arranged to emphasize this: Shaw has inserted the essential directions. By rising, Robert adds greater force to his first order. His first movement towards the Steward turns a question into a threat: 'What am I?' He moves on the repetition of his question and halts to pontificate, uttering his qualifications to be a bully: 'Am I Robert, squire of Baudricourt...?' After this, the threatening movement across the stage is continued. Pace in dialogue is suggested in practice chiefly by the rate at which the actor picks up his cues. Robert's straightforward character is easily communicated by the rapidity with which he raps back his speeches. He comes sharper on his cues until his object in humiliating the Steward is achieved: his are the quick cues of spontaneous, unambiguous feeling.

The Steward is more complicated: he is frightened of his master physically, and yet he has also to convey he is astute in the knowledge that at bottom Robert is weak and gullible. If the tempo rises too evenly to the crisis where the Steward is driven back to the wall, perhaps to sit ridiculously on the chest put there, it will kill some of this subtlety of relationship. Here is the problem. The Steward's slowness in his answers will indicate that he has endured this treatment on other occasions and that he knows appeasement is the safest policy. But the voice that flatters with 'Oh, sir, you know you are a greater man here than the king himself' must be accompanied by a note of calculation and a slight degree, at least, of serenity. The Steward will ostensibly communicate his growing physical fear by a greater hesitancy on his answers, the delays becoming

The Elements of Drama

more protracted: his are the slower cues of unspoken thought. But his reluctance must also suggest that he is busy framing the most satisfactory words to mollify Robert. In its general effect the scene moves forward in jerks; it might fail to reach any crisis at all were it not for Robert's commanding final speech which drives the Steward back to the wall, that is, where movement and gesture strengthen the crescendo.

With the purposeful drive of the episode, and with such authority in the central figure, effects of intonation and pause may not be enough for the Steward to convey his finer shade of meaning. He can overcome this by variety in the rhythm of his movement.

Shaw says no more of the Steward until he has him driven to the wall, when any control of the dramatic impression the Steward might have had is gone in order to give licence to the crisis. Yet before then the movements he makes in retreat can stress his ambiguous position, his fear for himself and his confidence in his own powers of flattery: this Shaw leaves to the technique of the actor after he has provided contradictory tugs within the general pull of the tempo. The Steward will not retreat evenly and steadily. He will instinctively make his step back each time *before* he makes his reply, thereby seeming to gain time and to secure a faint measure of physical security while he searches for the most honeyed words. This syncopation of the Steward's movement and speech, taken together with Robert's brusque questions, encourages an appearance of rapidly increasing pace which at the same time contains within itself an ambiguity we quickly appreciate.

A meaningful tempo, while promoting the realization of an impression, must also affect its *depth*. By this is meant that one impression is empowered to carry a greater value in relation to another. The obvious example of this is the climax in tragedy, which is often strikingly effective because it is quieter, more still and slower than the sequence which preceded it,

Tempo and Meaning

despite the fact that it is the crux of the play. So it is in *Romeo and Juliet*, in *King Lear*, in *Macbeth*. We are given a point of rest to free our minds to make their own vital contribution. Part of the unconscious task forced upon us in the theatre experience is to be constantly evaluating what we are receiving, and tempo is a cogent means of controlling our response.

It tends to be true that simpler patterns of tempo are only fully acceptable in non-realistic drama. Tempo in real life is more delicate, certainly less deliberate, more irresponsible, and where a dramatist introduces a formal rhythmic pattern, one senses theatricality in the play. On the other hand, no realistic play rejects the advantages of rhythmic control. The control may be only better disguised for purposes of realism. The exciting climax of *The Wild Duck* shows how Ibsen at his best did not neglect this aid.

The suicide of Hedvig must carry with it the cumulative meaning of the play, and from the moment earlier in Act v when the shot from the attic is heard, we are taken up with the problem of who or what has been shot, but more with the bigger but related question why the shot was fired. It was ingenious of Ibsen to insist that our answer to the first is impossible without our answer to the second. At the same time as we scrutinize the evidence after the shot, Ibsen compels us to estimate its intention and to judge the guilty. The tempo up to the discovery of Hedvig dead in the attic is deliberately contrived to drive us to the conclusions he wants.

So strong with ironic statements is the dialogue of Gregers and Hjalmar preceding the shot that the audience has the pleasure of being at least less in doubt about the cause and nature of the shot than the characters are. Hjalmar had said immediately before it was heard,

If I asked her then, 'Hedvig, are you willing to give up life for my sake?' *Laughing sarcastically*. Oh yes, I dare say! You'd soon hear what answer I got! *A pistol shot is heard in the attic.*

The Elements of Drama

The scene that follows strains to retain its irony until the discovery of the body, while sustaining the suspense that had been growing since Hedvig entered the attic. Here is the passage that includes the last of the series of thrusts and parries towards the solution of the mystery and the resolution of the tension. These thrusts and parries control the tempo of movement and speech to the climax, and this same tempo controls the drift of the imaginative argument in our minds.

HJALMAR, *going across and throwing the kitchen door open.* Hedvig, come along! Come in here to me! *Looking round.* No, she's not here.
GINA. Then she's in her own little room.
HJALMAR, *from outside.* No, she isn't here either. *Coming in.* She must have gone out.
GINA. Well, you didn't want her anywhere about the house.
HJALMAR. Ah, if only she'd come home soon—so that I can really tell her....Now all will be well, Gregers; for now I really believe we can begin life over again.
GREGERS, *quietly.* I knew it; it will all come right through the child.
Old Ekdal comes to the door of his room; he is in full uniform and is busy fastening on his sabre.
HJALMAR, *amazed.* Father! Are you there?
GINA. Were you shooting in your room, Father?
EKDAL, *indignantly, coming forward.* So you go shooting alone, do you, Hjalmar?
HJALMAR, *anxious, bewildered.* So it wasn't you who fired the shot in the attic?
EKDAL. I? Fire a shot? Hm.
GREGERS, *calling to Hjalmar.* She has shot the wild duck herself, don't you see?
HJALMAR. What is all this? *Rushes across to the door of the attic, pulls it aside, looks in and gives a scream.* Hedvig!³

As Hjalmar eliminates alternatives, by looking into the kitchen, then by looking into Hedvig's own room, the characters on the stage seem to endorse the view that Old Ekdal fired the shot on behalf of Hedvig. The quickening of the action during this search is relaxed while all three are busy with their own sentiments, Gina struggling with her maternal tears, Hjalmar

Tempo and Meaning

with his remorse and Gregers happy to put a conclusive idealistic interpretation on the issue. In the pause we have time to ventilate our own thoughts about the statements. Hjalmar's lame and inopportune optimism, 'now I really believe we can begin life over again', by this time must jar against our sense of propriety. We have respite enough to tell ourselves that neither Hedvig can begin life over again, nor Hjalmar, whose self-indulgence, even self-love, is ingrained, a view that is substantiated at the last by Dr Relling. On the other hand, Gregers's suggestion that 'it will all come right through the child', we suspect to be true in a way quite other than he thinks. Ironically, his statement points directly to the substance of the play's meaning, in which is implied a sin and an atonement. In the immensity of this crisis, now that the event is seen naked, Gregers's error suggests, not merely that he has not grasped the solution of the mystery, but that his values are hopelessly inept and sterile. This is understood, with that strangely mixed urge upon our intellect and upon our emotions this author often conjures, by our cold refusal to accept Gregers's reasoning and by our warm sympathy with an unwitting victim. A precise flexing of the tempo of this episode will permit our maximum imaginative activity. Now Ibsen can flourish his trump-card.

The entry of Old Ekdal is the final thrust, and immediately anticipates the discovery. But even with this, Ibsen keeps his finger on the pulse of the climax to its end. Hjalmar and Gina for a fraction stand in amazement: with no word from Ekdal, they are granted the pause in which to search for understanding. We, meanwhile, are many moves ahead of them, and sit in suspense. Even then Ekdal's reply is no reply to their question, and once more progress limps. He enters, a ridiculous figure, ignorant of his part in the killing of his granddaughter: 'So you go shooting alone, do you, Hjalmar?' Again we wait as Hjalmar painfully makes his next deduction.

The Elements of Drama

And again we wait while Gregers, who has had a more intricate problem to work out, offers the last possible alternative explanation: 'She has shot the wild duck herself, don't you see?'—one last restraint by which Ibsen delays Hjalmar's impulse to look in the attic, a tormented moment measuring an age of feeling, before passion is released. With a sudden access of speed in speech and movement, Hjalmar runs to the door of the attic followed by the others, and the climax is attained.

The calculated tempo of this scene is not theatrical panache: it aids meaning. Because by this time we are certain of the outcome, we are absorbed by the grossness of the mistake that Hjalmar and Gregers are making, and the size of the monstrosity engendered is measured the more precisely as we grow more certain. Each false deduction by a character makes more acute our insight into the motive for the error: each hesitation condemns. It would be true to add to this that the attic, till now a whimsical curiosity, at the most a symptom of the family's malady difficult to assimilate because so concrete, rises here to a proper dramatic status in becoming fully part of the play: it becomes at the last a symbol for tragic self-deception.

Tempo is an artificial imposition upon language. Ibsen's precision of effect suggests he has balanced the demands of psychological realism with elements that regulate tempo, reconciling as always life with dramatic necessity. Even if a particular rhythm is inseparable from a particular character, even if 'every passion has its proper pulse',[4] effects of excitement and relief, of squeeze and relax, must be shrewdly regulated to enlarge or reduce the size of the image. Ibsen's achievement is a compromise: through a character's mood, the prominence of an idea, or the duration of a speech, the actor can identify rhythm and at the same time behave realistically.

It follows that in verse drama, where the words may not obey

Tempo and Meaning

the demands of psychological realism, such effects are easier to achieve. An extreme instance of this is to be found in *As You Like It*. In the following example the dialogue is patterned and repetitive, so lending, by the tempo of its delivery, unnatural but acceptable emphasis to the meaning:

> PHEBE. Good shepherd, tell this youth what 'tis to love.
> SILVIUS. It is to be all made of sighs and tears,
>   And so am I for Phebe.
> PHEBE. And I for Ganymede.
> ORLANDO. And I for Rosalind.
> ROSALIND. And I for no woman.
> SILVIUS. It is to be all made of faith and service,
>   And so am I for Phebe.
> PHEBE. And I for Ganymede.
> ORLANDO. And I for Rosalind.
> ROSALIND. And I for no woman.[5]

Shakespeare in *As You Like It* takes us from the dark intrigues and restraints of captive life at court to a dream of freedom and fantasy in Arden, where one can fall in love at first sight, or play at being somebody else without for a moment having to consider realities. The problem for playwright and player is to point this contrast and use every trick to convert us to the new mood. Once we are truly in the Ardens of our imaginations, neither we nor Shakespeare bother much about the plausibility of the plot. The author is free to turn our values topsy-turvy, and in the change to uncover and reveal them for what they were. He dreams us into a refreshing insight into the basis of happiness. He is free, too, to stylize the dialogue for his particular purpose.

The change in the location and in the mood is reflected in the manner of the speech. So important does the way the characters speak become that, should we incline to talk Jaques's language, we should feel ourselves to be misfits as big as he. Licence is given, as in *A Midsummer Night's Dream*, for the fantastically plotted dance of lovers. The patterned

The Elements of Drama

speech marks the beat appropriate to the dance, and the dance marks the beat appropriate to the speech. The fun in the scene is in the number of the lovers, and in the similarity of their behaviour. That so many each in turn without discrimination should acknowledge unquestioningly the 'sighs and tears' and the 'faith and service', gently ridicules these notions about the content of love. The blind repetition of phrase, with each speaker picking up the tone of the other, exaggerates what is already exaggerated, and a kind of laughter must follow. Only Rosalind's probable withdrawal from the others in the procession as she half implores Orlando with 'And I for no woman', suggests that but for her own difficulties she too would succumb to their mood. But, reluctantly, she alone must keep her wits about her. The persisting impression of genuine human feeling comes of her presence in the quartet, and through her Shakespeare keeps our sentiment warm and his mixture sweet.

However this may be, sure and witty comment on romantic love arises from a single contrast in pace. Appropriate pace must accompany the contrast in tone which parrot repetition unavoidably invites. Here there is not only a contrast between how Rosalind speaks and how the others speak, but also a contrast of tempo between the two halves of the pattern. Let the voices and bodies of the characters deployed in the first half of the pattern move at the heavier pace of 'sighs and tears', let them cancel this in the second half with the eager pace and pitch of 'faith and service', and the resultant effect is one of wholehearted but kindly mockery. Where tempo tends to be unreal, drama truly aspires to the condition of music.

Thus precise and startling effects of tempo are easier in a play which moves at some distance from real life. Such another play is Sheridan's *The School for Scandal*, whose ground is a world of heightened and distorted reality. The

Tempo and Meaning

quarrel between Sir Peter and Lady Teazle illustrates the effect an artificial comedy can rapidly and expeditiously achieve by compressing time and tightening tempo:

LADY TEAZLE. ... I'm sure I don't care how soon we leave off quarrelling, provided you'll own you were tired first.

SIR PETER. Well—then let our future contest be, who shall be most obliging.

LADY TEAZLE. I assure you, Sir Peter, good nature becomes you—you look now as you did before we were married, when you used to walk with me under the elms, and tell me stories of what a gallant you were in your youth, and chuck me under the chin, you would; and ask me if I thought I could love an old fellow, who would deny me nothing—didn't you?

SIR PETER. Yes, yes, and you were as kind and attentive—

LADY TEAZLE. Aye, so I was, and would always take your part when my acquaintance used to abuse you, and turn you into ridicule.

SIR PETER. Indeed!

LADY TEAZLE. Aye, and when my cousin Sophy has called you a stiff, peevish old bachelor, and laughed at me for thinking of marrying one who might be my father, I have always defended you, and said, I didn't think you so ugly by any means, and I dared say you'd make a very good sort of a husband.

SIR PETER. And you prophesied right; and we shall now be the happiest couple—

LADY TEAZLE. And never differ again?

SIR PETER. No, never!—though at the same time, indeed, my dear Lady Teazle, you must watch your temper very seriously; for in all our little quarrels, my dear, if you recollect, my love, you always began first.

LADY TEAZLE. I beg your pardon, my dear Sir Peter: indeed, you always gave the provocation.

SIR PETER. Now see, my angel! take care—contradicting isn't the way to keep friends.

LADY TEAZLE. Then don't you begin it, my love!

SIR PETER. There, now! you—you are going on....[6]

Sheridan's object is to give us a magnified, preposterous portrait of how quarrels may come and go in married life. In particular, he wishes to pass comment on the marriage of a young lady who has tasted the freedom of town life and an older gentleman who is rather too set in his ways adequately to

The Elements of Drama

compromise with her demands. By a daring compression he paints the oscillation of a quarrel from a stage where husband and wife are petting affectionately, to the stage where they are at each other's throats. Yet suggestions of a tempestuous marriage are hardly communicated by the statements of the speeches, which are expressions of tone rather than fact. The pace of expression, aided by inflexion of voice, tells us all. It provides the chief means of telling us another quarrel is coming, while the fluctuation of the tempo of the whole presents in little the quarrel complete.

At the opening we hear the pace slowing as they sink into reminiscence, although already there is an incipient edge on what they are saying. Lady Teazle had an instant before been asking her husband for two hundred pounds, which he said he would give her as he was in a good temper. So she reminds him of their courtship when he would 'ask me if I thought I could love an old fellow, who would deny me nothing'—words that barely conceal the barb. The gentle banter continues although Sir Peter puts a slight edge upon his own reply: 'and you were as kind and attentive'. Lady Teazle pursues her advantage at Sir Peter's expense, and her next remark, spoken in the mellowest of tones, hurts a little. Sheridan gives Sir Peter an ambiguous, almost pained, 'Indeed!' which cannot be wholly spoken with the haste of an insult accepted, since the insult is softened beforehand by the suggestion that his wife had taken his part against the slanderer. Sir Peter's ejaculation is an uneasy one, but being in a good temper he inclines towards giving her the benefit of the doubt. The presence of the ambiguity reminds the actor that as yet the pace is still slow.

Lady Teazle now has the joy of being able to say to his face what she really thinks of him, by attributing her own feelings to her cousin Sophy. Here the pace has dawdled to its slowest in this longer speech, as Lady Teazle carefully weighs and calculates how far she can go in tormenting him. At the same

Tempo and Meaning

time this gives us the chance to savour the irony of what she is saying. She forestalls the burst of her husband's anger by protracting the ambiguity while she hastens to smother the blow, but still without committing herself to any unqualified approval of him: 'I didn't think you so ugly by any means, and I dared say you'd make a very good sort of a husband.' The 'so ugly', the 'by any means', the 'I dared say', and 'the sort of a husband' is the phrasing of a woman unprepared to surrender her general contention, and contains so many qualifications that it would only deceive a man who wanted to be deceived. Lady Teazle's power to tease derives from his own stupidity.

So the tempo sinks to a point of repose that is only belied by the previous ironies of their remarks to each other. Their incompatibility simmers softly while we are being prepared for the further clash to come. It is not long in coming. While Sir Peter is still caressing her, their next quarrel has already begun. Both think they have achieved a victory. In particular, Sir Peter, thinking he has made their relationship sufficiently warm, feels the time has arrived to re-establish his male and marital supremacy. Thus in a voice of infinite sweetness and patience he says the wrong thing: '...in all our little quarrels, my dear, if you recollect, my love, you always began first'. This provokes contradiction, and contradiction is provocation, and so, as if spontaneously, without the kind of calculated restraint we felt a moment before, the pace, pitch and tone mount until Sir Peter breaks away with 'There, now!' and the quarrel is on again.

This piece was written, undoubtedly, with an aural imagination controlling the pen. The rate of these exchanges is ringing in Sheridan's ears as he writes, and fluctuation in tempo is the strongest, the overall, suggestion we receive. It is the tempo that speaks to us. The image is made to expand by shrinking the time that would naturally elapse in a real quarrel.

The Elements of Drama

Telescoping time is important if a scene is to make its rhythmic statement. In his experimental *Strange Interlude*, O'Neill contrived to have characters speak 'aside' in interior monologue while carrying on normal dialogue. One reason for its failure on the stage is that in gaining one advantage, the author sacrifices another: the tempo of exchange of dialogue has largely to be neglected while characters indulge in protracted self-analysis.

Rhythm must be appropriate to content, and it is to content that producer and actor turn first to realize rhythm. Strindberg's *The Father* offers unusual problems and opportunities. As a whole, this is a play in a realistic manner, and its effects must to some degree be consistent with psychological realism. Within this boundary, Strindberg has achieved and sustained extraordinary effects of concentration. The play moves over great stretches of unrelieved tension that might seem to the casual reader to progress on one level. In the theatre one's impression is of movement at great speed, with a heat and a drive behind it that is irresistible.

Many elements conspire to create this sweep and power. It is charged by a plot which permits no side issues, which from the start submits the relationship between the Captain and his wife as a proposition which is relentlessly pursued to a conclusion. The play is dominated by the character of Laura the wife, conceived and drawn with a demoniacal passion, a character who thrusts her weapons deeper and deeper into the victim. The action is driven along by the growth of the Captain's doubt about the legitimacy of his child, until this assumes the tremendous proportions of an obsession, where every detail takes on a nightmare significance. The progress of the play is imperative, since phrase after phrase of dialogue is stamped with reference to the battle of the sexes that is Strindberg's subject. Yet the author avoids monotony and furthers his purpose by an exquisite use of tempo. The nature

Tempo and Meaning

and extent of the power of the wife over the husband is vigorously realized in this episode:

LAURA. Now I am sleepy, so if you have any more fancies, keep them till tomorrow.
CAPTAIN. A word more first about realities. Do you hate me?
LAURA. Yes, sometimes, when you are a man.
CAPTAIN. This is race-hatred. If it is true that we are descended from monkeys, it must at least be from two separate species. We are not like one another, are we?
LAURA. What do you mean by all this?
CAPTAIN. I realize that one of us must go under in this struggle.
LAURA. Which?
CAPTAIN. The weaker, of course.
LAURA. And the stronger will be in the right.
CAPTAIN. Certainly, since he has the power.
LAURA. Then I am right.
CAPTAIN. Have you the power already then?
LAURA. Yes, the power of the law, by means of which I shall put you under control tomorrow.[7]

Are these two playing a coldly cerebral game? They talk at length, and, for reasons that will appear, this is particularly characteristic of the Captain. The struggle is spun out and expressed in a verbal imagery not associated with the realism of Ibsen's *The Wild Duck*. An impression of laboured argument might easily be carried away from a bad performance. In such a performance, the Captain, painted by Strindberg as a man of intellect, could readily swamp his Laura and throw the play off balance. Revelation of her strength is of paramount importance in convincing us of the extreme outcome, the insanity of the man. The argument would indeed be cerebral and the Captain would quickly diminish the importance of Laura, were it not that the dialogue has a pervading quality of nervous intensity. The scene is governed by this feverishness, which in turn implicitly directs its tempo. The source of the scene's success lies there.

The Captain's defence rests on words alone. Laura, in

The Elements of Drama

belittling his manhood, leaves him with only his intellect by which to attempt to regain ascendancy. With a useless vanity of words, the Captain in his final struggles urges himself with unveiled despair into the battle. The more he does so, the more Laura can afford reticence. She has no need to retaliate with words: her very withdrawal marks her strength. Her repose while she listens in calm silence to his tormented rationalizing is the stance she can afford to adopt in an unequal battle, and she epitomizes an intuitive power of the female over the male. This is precisely what Strindberg wishes to communicate. Laura, quiet in the knowledge that her trump-card is yet to be played, is confronted by a man who has been driven to his wit's end, arguments exhausted. This particular opposition suggests what delicate play is to be made of the tempo of the scene.

Laura's feigned indifference to his talk, felt in 'Now I am sleepy, so if you have any more fancies, keep them till tomorrow', stresses her refusal to engage in the kind of fight he is offering, and directly personifies her detachment and strength. It also slows the speed of the action and is at the same time of a pace naturalistically suited to a character simulating sleepiness. It infuriates the Captain once more, and he is spurred to bring his argument to a head, to come down to plain terms in the effort to shock a response from her and define their relationship. He now desires 'realities' after his impassioned statement that men live their lives as 'wild dreams'. Quick with anger he says, 'Do you hate me?' A cruel joy prolongs her reply, and she curls her lips round the word that stands for the idea he had been constructing with his obsessive earnestness. She says, 'Yes, sometimes, when you are a *man*'. At this we remember the sharp poignancy of his earlier comment: 'I wanted to win you as a woman by being a man.' Thus in three speeches Strindberg achieves a rhythmic contrast in pace that is urgently felt, and a sensation of life animates them.

Tempo and Meaning

Within a moment, any feeling that this man is safe is dissipated. Laura, quick to take advantage, finally decides to return his attack. She seizes upon the weakness of his having arrived at a conclusion at all, the conclusion that 'one of us must go under in this struggle'. Once Strindberg has so explicitly made the suggestion that this was not a domestic fight, nor even a trial of strength between a man and a woman, once he has made it quite transparent in the sense of the words that this is a contest for the survival of the fittest, invoking larger issues, once he has the Captain admit that might will be in the right, then at last he can permit Laura to make her decisive thrust into the tiring adversary. Till this time, we feel the Captain to be on the attack, but to no purpose, since Laura's casual attitude is a sufficient defence: his cues had been sharp, but blunting themselves on her slow, hard replies. Now the attack is reversed, and in reply to his awful and conclusive statement that one of them 'must go under', she turns on him with a biting 'Which?' He is taken off guard, and his replies falter. His seeming assurance, felt in the words he uses, 'of course', 'certainly', is anything but assured. These words betray his new doubts, and inner uncertainty expresses itself by a hesitant cue becoming more hesitant. With the agility of a Socratic debater arguing from absolute premises, Laura presses home her quick statements, which immediately contrast with the Captain's former loquacity: 'And the stronger will be in the right—', 'Then I am right—', 'Yes, the power of the law.' She has the power to bring the whole discussion to a head with her final, unassailable reference to 'the power of the law, by means of which I shall put you under control tomorrow'. Yet in doing this, Laura has not budged from the position of mystery and strength she has been maintaining by her non-committal attitude throughout the scene. With one brilliant, neat and abrupt reversal of the rhythm of the scene as a whole, the Captain with all his feeble sophistry is cut

The Elements of Drama

down. After this he is, we remember, reduced in cold anger to throwing the lamp at her. This is the violent signal of her victory.

The twist in the tempo is carefully reserved until the crux of the dramatic argument has been reached, until the apparent protagonist is exhausted, his weapons ineffectual. The speed of the scene towards its conclusion is determined by Strindberg's conception of what his characters stand for in this situation: the man making his last struggles of brain, the woman trusting to the broad, impalpable position of her sex. Strindberg measures the length of time an audience can sustain a picture of the male bruising himself against intuitive wit. Only when we are nearly spent does he tie the knot, break the pattern of rhythm, relieve the strain and clinch the scene with an act of physical violence. That the author can make us accept ten minutes of unremitting tension is to his credit as a craftsman. He has done it by rhythmically lacing his action with conflicting statement and innuendo which keeps the spectator's interest alert throughout.

The elusive element of tempo is often taken to be a fiction of the producer's imagination, something of the theatre but not of literature. But control of tempo is more than a skill: in *The Father* it marks the depth of Strindberg's understanding of the force and nature of the issue dramatized. For tempo is conceived when the idea is conceived: they are of the same stuff. Like rhythm in poetry, tempo in itself is an index of a play's quality.

8

MANIPULATING THE CHARACTERS

In drama 'character' is not an author's raw material: it is his product. It emerges from the play; it is not put into it. It has an infinity of subtle uses, but they all serve in the orchestration of the play as a whole; and so character finds this place in the scheme. But we face probably the most difficult and confused problem, a real stumbling-block, in dramatic appreciation, and the most I can do is to offer some pointers to what seem to be the real issues for the playgoer.

Some of the dangers of falsely assessing character are obvious, but none the less awkward to avoid. We set up our own barriers to full appreciation if we take a misplaced interest in a fictional character for its own sake and out of context. Because of the peculiar sympathies a writer calls upon through character, we have a natural urge to talk about, say, Cordelia as a daughter or Edgar as a son. Because the figures do have human aspects in the play, we are encouraged to that extent to talk even of Strindberg's ghosts, Pirandello's fantasies or Yeats's masked symbols in terms of individual thoughts and feelings. We talk about what we are more sure of: human qualities and attributes.

It may be that in the frustrating task of defining a play for ourselves after seeing a performance, we take the easy way and search for a character as an absolute: we define the play *Hedda Gabler* by the qualities in Hedda the woman, *Macbeth* by the qualities in the man. Perhaps we go so far as to assume it a mark of indifferent playwriting if we cannot do this. Perhaps up to a point Ibsen and Shakespeare ask us to do so: a dramatist who works with human nature as his material is surely

The Elements of Drama

interested in character? Yet every time we look for character as something which can be neat and complete and satisfyingly objective, we are liable to blind ourselves, and judge the play by character alone, perhaps by a self-created thing. Since Aristotle, the student of drama has been led into considering character as a separate entity, without full regard for its being cause or effect.

Natural as this is, at its best it represents a slacker criticism, something of a failure to envisage the broad complexity of a character's function in a play. At its worst, for an audience to grow to love a character as if it were an old friend is to reduce its feeling for theatre to the level of the uncritical cinema audience whose appreciation of film stops short at an unhealthy interest in the actor as a person. We have to beware lest any one element like character, whether because it is a particularly striking element, or because an actor's performance has been out of proportion to his part, becomes the false centre of attention, prompting us to garner illegitimate impressions. It might lead us away from the play; it might become the play itself.

In recent years the warnings against this habit have perhaps been rather too loud. Professor Wilson Knight offered a seminal concept about Shakespeare's characters, stating that 'the persons, ultimately, are not human at all, but purely symbols of a poetic vision'.[1] But in some sense we *must* feel Lear, Macbeth, Hamlet are human. We pity or admire because we are throughout the performance in contact with humanity in human situations: the figures in the pattern are, after all, human figures in a human pattern. Lear, Macbeth, Hamlet speak for human beings; they speak for us—or what value is there in the play?

Professor L. C. Knights pursued this topic, and suggested that character was 'merely an abstraction from the total response in the mind of the reader or spectator'.[2] He was

Manipulating the Characters

rightly concerned that our proper interest in a play should not be deflected, lest we should 'impoverish the total response'; his words were more guarded. But it was noticeable that in his analysis of a play that followed this statement, he made no reference to a physical stage or to a live actor embodying a character. He demolished actor with character and substituted another abstraction in its place. When he suggested that *Macbeth* had a greater affinity with *The Waste Land* than with *A Doll's House*, it was almost a case of throwing the baby out with the bath water.

Common sense cannot accept that a character is no more than a mouth for an arrangement of words. We are bound to examine the fuller contribution we know to exist. It would be irresponsible to ignore its strangely binding quality in commanding an audience's response. And that quality is tied up with the presence of the actor on the stage.

To solve these problems we appeal to experience. The unique contribution of the living actor is his ability to fill in the author's outline, retaining whatever symbolic and universal suggestion that outline carries while representing it to an audience as alive and urgent. The key-word here is *alive*. All values in art depend upon the power of communicating them, making them a wholly felt, breathing force to the recipient. This is the limitation on the symbol: the character must be sufficiently human for the actor congruously to present it in his own person and for the spectator to recognize it. It is the test of a good morality play that it should make human where its lesson is most abstract. Tragedy depends for its intrinsic effect on keeping its hero mortal. If the gods are called in, whether in Aeschylus's *The Eumenides* or in Giraudoux's *Amphitryon 38*, they must think like people, as must ghosts and apparitions. And the test of the modern symbolic melodrama, say Betti's *The Queen and the Rebels*, like the test of classical tragedy, is whether the character can remain living while

The Elements of Drama

carrying an exceptional load of wide meanings. In this play, can Argia the self-seeking prostitute support a queenly martyrdom? The author's choice of such extremities is partly to offer unexpected hope for an abiding Christian dignity in life. To this we may wish to give consent, but not unless the character in the person of the actress can convince us of the truth in this particular human transformation. Living symbols will be judged by life.

But here is new danger. 'Judged by life': does this mean the characters must be lifelike? Is it implied that our circumspect modern audiences will not find a character adequate if they cannot find a parallel within their own experience? In the words of Mr Raymond Williams, 'we must be careful that our judgment depends not on whether the characters are lifelike, but on whether they serve to embody experience which the actor has shown to be true'.[3] It is a safer approach that does not bring preconceived, external and invalid standards from real life to the judgment of an artificial arrangement like a play. But we do.

As before, it is easy to see why we do. We find differences between speakers labelled in the way they speak: idioms, inflexions, sometimes tricks of speech distinguish them. But whether this is for the purpose of identifying the speaker in the mind of the actor as he acts, or at the other extreme, of the reader as he reads, is irrelevant: representation of life is not an end in itself. The relevant question is to ask *why* Shakespeare makes recognizable in this or that form Beatrice or Mercutio or Juliet's Nurse or Shylock, naming some most commonly discussed as 'living' individuals. Once such a question is asked, character slips into its proper place.

Another side of the same fallacy is the belief that the author who can convince the playgoer that a character has a life of its own has fulfilled a proper end of drama. The playgoer's *conviction* is held to be the mark of a good play. Such a theory

Manipulating the Characters

must be to the detriment of all the plays not written in the realistic convention—the bulk of the world's output—if the nature of the conviction is not more closely specified. Different kinds of play anticipate different kinds of conviction. We are not asked to believe, for example, that Shaw's Joan or Anouilh's Antigone or Giraudoux's Hector in *Tiger at the Gates* would have been so up-to-the-minute in their thinking. Anachronisms have always been part of the stock-in-trade of a dramatist trying to impress timeless values on a contemporary audience. Such characters convince because they are *consistent* within the little world built for them, which may be fantastic or distorted, very wide or very narrow. Theirs is a truth probable to their own world. Conviction may be important to the success of a play, but it will be determined by the organization of all the elements within it and may not be directly related to character at all.

This is not to deny that realistic characterization may be important in itself if it suggests, like the iceberg, a depth not visible on the surface. Human psychology can itself constitute a theme. Provided this depth of characterization is relevant, that is, provided the theme is dependent on this sort of conviction, common-sense would not deny it. In such a case the psychological overtones of the play may be one source for the theatre experience, and must be valued as such. Thus Strindberg in his Preface to *Miss Julie* can justifiably write,

An event in real life—and this discovery is quite recent—springs generally from a whole series of more or less deep-lying motives....
In explanation of Miss Julie's sad fate I have suggested many factors: her mother's fundamental instincts; her father's mistaken upbringing of the girl; her own nature, and the suggestive influence of her fiancé on a weak and degenerate brain; furthermore, and more directly: the festive mood of the Midsummer Eve; the absence of her father; her physical condition; her preoccupation with animals; the excitation of the dance; the dusk of the night; the strongly aphrodisiacal influence of the flowers; and lastly the chance forcing of the two of them together in a

secluded room, to which must be added the aggressiveness of the excited man.

Thus I have neither been one-sidedly physiological nor one-sidedly psychological in my procedure.[4]

In this play Strindberg wishes to stage a tragic struggle between heredity and environment. To do it he uses as a common point of reference modern understanding of psychology. In this struggle, Julie, carefully circumscribed by her background, is the author's realistic symbol for his purpose. Nevertheless, each of the factors Strindberg enumerates in explanation of Julie's behaviour plays a double part, for in addition to making this character in this situation credibly 'real', each also represents a factor in the struggle. Thus each also represents a facet of the theme. It is unwise, even in realistic drama of the best sort, to separate the character from the play, the psychology from the theme.

We must avoid begging essential questions about the source of the experience. There is a distinction to be made between the *dramatis persona* of the scene and the personality which emerges as part of the impression we derive. Character in the usual sense of 'personality' is not an agency for the writer as speech is. Even in a leading part it may indeed not exist, as many expressionistic dramas have shown; in the minor parts of even realistic drama we may not expect it. An impression of personality is more truly a by-product, a facet of the image, sometimes only an accident that happens because of the occasionally narrative turn of a play. In the weak play, we may be kept happy by the presence of personality when what that stands for cannot engross us. The author who is a cheat will tap associations from our own or typical acquaintance, till we give body to the pale shadow the author has made of his character. On the other hand, tapping our preconceived notions of character can be legitimate procedure, as in a play planned to upset those notions (we think of conventional

Manipulating the Characters

Parson Manders in Ibsen's *Ghosts*), or in the modern play using old legend (the heroes in *Tiger at the Gates*). In the latter case, Giraudoux expects us to make his Helen and his Hector familiar figures, the better to remind us of their eternal existence. Yet even here the characters remain primarily *dramatis personae*.

A rule for one type of play may not apply to another. The real test is whether a character can do what the play requires of it. The type of play that designedly breaks realistic rules thus presents a set of special problems. How do we judge a character in a farce or an extravagant comedy? Standards from life can only distract. We agree to allow half-people like Sergius and Raina from *Arms and the Man* to be the head and tail of a pantomime donkey if together they serve their purpose. The mouthpieces of a Shavian discussion-drama may be rare folk among our drawing-room acquaintance, but may be valid on Shaw's stage. What place are we to allow for the masked characters of Greek or Roman drama or of the *commedia dell'arte*? Do we think less of majestic, unearthly Electra or of fragile, insubstantial Millamant or of one-track, head-on-legs Jack Tanner because they do not display the same three-dimensional qualities of realism as Falstaff and Mme Ranevsky? We measure the adequacy of a character by the unity and completeness of the dramatic impression to which it contributes: if we can add nothing, nor wish to take anything away, the character has served.

The concept of character derives from the mask. The mask imposes a tight control upon one aspect of reality to present it simply. Basically, it dispenses with the need to 'act'; for two antithetic masks juxtaposed upon one stage provide the substance of a situation and the plan for a play. The development of drama, as Archer might have maintained, seems to have been the gradual freeing of the actor from the restrictions of the mask, but as long as the author was still writing for an

The Elements of Drama

actor on a stage, neither has been totally free. Always the basic premise of theatre has remained, that a play must concentrate and confine life within fixed limits. An author happily acknowledges these limits—even today. One can understand the usefulness to authors of what, in the jargon, are called 'types', especially in radio drama where distinctions of voice are essential to recognition by ear alone. An author frequently welcomes the readiness of a preconditioned audience to supply for him the villainy behind a pair of cruelly curling moustaches, or the innocence behind a bonnet and shawl. Moustaches may have been replaced by cleaner upper lips, bonnets and shawls by more fashionable frills, but in the eyes the seediness or the sweetness, as the case may be, is the same. The author relies upon a character to serve as a known quantity: if the audience will not furnish it, the author must establish it. From another point of view, there probably remains a preference among the acting profession for 'character' parts, because, in one way, less effort is needed to satisfy the requirements of a character with definite, that is, more limited, life.

A sequence from *Arms and the Man* may help us rethink the nature of characterization, in particular in artificial comedy. This kind of play falsifies and overstresses some aspect of human nature so that its absurdities are thrown up and tested. So in Shakespearian comedy we are encouraged to laugh at and judge the romantic excesses of Hermia and Helena, or in Restoration comedy the affectations of Lord Foppington and the mock decorums of Lady Wishfort. Sergius and Raina in this passage are of a rather more complex order:

RAINA, *very solemnly*. Sergius: I think we two have found the higher love. When I think of you, I feel that I could never do a base deed, or think an ignoble thought.
SERGIUS. My lady and my saint! *He clasps her reverently.*
RAINA, *returning his embrace*. My lord and my—
SERGIUS. Sh-sh! Let me be the worshipper, dear. You little know how unworthy the best man is of a girl's pure passion!

Manipulating the Characters

RAINA. I trust you, I love you. You will never disappoint me, Sergius. *Louka is heard singing within the house. They quickly release each other.* I cant pretend to talk indifferently before her: my heart is too full. *Louka comes from the house....* I will get my hat; and then we can go out until lunch time. Wouldnt you like that?

SERGIUS. Be quick. If you are away five minutes, it will seem five hours. *Raina runs to the top of the steps, and turns there to exchange looks with him and wave him a kiss with both hands. He looks after her with emotion for a moment; then turns slowly away, his face radiant with the loftiest exaltation. The movement shifts his field of vision, into the corner of which there now comes the tail of Louka's double apron. His attention is arrested at once. He takes a stealthy look at her, and begins to twirl his moustache mischievously, with his left hand akimbo on his hip. Finally, striking the ground with his heels in something of a cavalry swagger, he strolls over to the other side of the table, opposite her, and says* Louka: do you know what the higher love is?

LOUKA, *astonished.* No, sir.

SERGIUS. Very fatiguing thing to keep up for any length of time, Louka. One feels the need of some relief after it.[5]

In the words and actions of Shaw's puppets, every detail exemplifies his efficiency and economy in caricaturing human behaviour.

An audience seeing these words enacted does not trouble itself to entertain doubts about verisimilitude: in the theatre such a question does not arise. What then are we concerned about? Perhaps the manner in which their speech and gesture burlesque our own? This is a sophisticated reaction, which, if it occurs at all, probably does not do so during the performance. The immediate wish of the audience is to follow the 'logic' of the action, to guess by its own knowledge of human behaviour what prompts Raina or Sergius to say or do what Shaw makes them, to follow the play's general line of intention. Sergius and Raina have been so excessively applauding each other with a plethora of clichés,

You have been out in the world, on the field of battle, able to prove yourself there worthy of any woman in the world...,

Dearest: all my deeds have been yours...,

The Elements of Drama

that it is almost impossible for the actors to do anything less than 'ham' their lines. Their activity of gesture and movement—they greet each other impetuously, Raina suddenly sits demurely, Sergius kneels impulsively—suggests self-consciousness, because true emotions do not fluctuate so rapidly. Even if by this means the audience is not aware of the false romanticism that marks these characters, the downright lie from Raina, 'And you have never been absent from my thoughts for a moment', will convince it that one at least is posing. Such easy ironies are at work quite without a conscious effort of thought on our part. We come prepared to enjoy the insincerities of characters presented as distortions of human beings, misrepresentations of life.

They proceed to the limits of the line they have begun to pursue, while we know instinctively that they have forced themselves into an impossible position from which the only return must be anticlimax. We are delighted when Raina, dropping her voice and her eyes, brings to the surface the thought that she has long been privately caressing: 'I think we two have found the higher love.' It is part of the Shavian method to have a character say, not what is likely to be said in life, but what is preposterously representative of its type of mind. 'Higher love' implies a divinity which *this* representation cannot in any world exemplify. It is immediately belied by the next half-truth she utters: 'When I think of you, I feel that I could never do a base deed, or think an ignoble thought.' We are not to forget Raina's 'poor darling' of the final moment in Act I as she protects Bluntschli from Catherine, nor her tell-tale dissimulation in front of Sergius and her father a moment before in Act II.

With the mention of 'the higher love', a key has been struck, and Sergius takes the note from her in an effort to render feelings reverently in keeping with the style she has set: 'My lady and my saint!' So they vie with each other to adopt

Manipulating the Characters

the appropriate spirit for a heavenly occasion, the romantic debauch for which their sort of love stands. Unfortunately they have trouble in deciding who is saint and who is pilgrim. Their exchange grows to a stagey crescendo too embarrassing to sustain, and Shaw relieves them by the timely-untimely entrance of Louka. Divinity disperses in a flash: even the higher love must sometimes be aware of what the servants think. Raina, however, does not neglect to recover her poise with a satisfying excuse and a mollifying cliché: 'I cant pretend to talk indifferently before her: my heart is too full.' They part with gestures derived from their childhood storybooks, to all appearances convinced that this is the correct behaviour.

The audience does not care whether Raina and Sergius are deceiving themselves or each other. But we are concerned to deduce, if there is to be any continuity of interest in the scene, that their little world is a false and fickle one. As such it must be clear, for our critical pleasure, that it will rapidly become too prickly to live in. That Sergius, released from the obligation of Raina's presence, reassumes what we take to be his normal manner of treating the opposite sex when he turns to Louka, is pleasing because it satisfies half-held expectations. In addition, it comments on his behaviour with Raina, revealing him as a *poseur* and in part explaining the exaggeration of his speech and gesture. With but a little pin he is deflated. And yet our hearts are oddly warmed towards him at the same time, both because Raina deserves the treatment she gets, and because Sergius suddenly becomes understandable within his own rules of conduct. One might almost have said he becomes human. His move to flirt with Louka effectively brings down the flimsy pack of cards he and Raina have been assiduously piling up. It does not worry us that he descends so hastily from the refinement of the higher love to the crudity of his addresses to a servant: we are content to feel,

The Elements of Drama

in the play's own bold terms, that this gesture might fairly represent a certain attitude of mind, itself not unfamiliar.

To some extent this excerpt exemplifies the function of character in any play. Sergius and Raina are consistent within themselves. We give Shaw the licence, and he makes use of it to manipulate his characters for particular ends. When he has established the quality for which each stands, we look to it for confirmation of our earlier impression; but what, ironically, we see, is that quality being exposed. The continuity of the character is all-important to the author if he is to communicate with us. The gross statement of Shaw's crashing anticlimax depends for its effectiveness upon our seeing the same Sergius who talked before with Raina talking now to Louka.

It is no great step from saying that characters have only that limited existence the play requires of them, to saying that character is dependent upon the action it exists to enact. The only satisfactory way to understand character is thus to see it as a way of defining a dramatic impression. Our ultimate interest should not be in the character for itself, though this may be a way of starting interest, of separating particular impressions, often of providing a continuity of an idea through the person of one actor. But the fastidious playgoer returns to the play. D. H. Lawrence's celebrated statement belongs to drama too:

> Again I say, don't look for the development of the novel to follow the lines of certain characters: the characters fall into the form of some other rhythmic form, as when one draws a fiddle-bow across a fine tray delicately sanded, the sand takes lines unknown.[6]

As in the novel, so in the play. The form of the impressions determines and deploys the detail of characterization, shows us the perspective of the character. So before we look for consistency in a character, we look for consistency in the relationship between one and another. Just as two contiguous speeches project an image, so two characters contribute to its formation. Hamlet is not Hamlet without Claudius, without

Manipulating the Characters

Gertrude or without Ophelia. He discharges his meaning in the context of a scene.

It is true that character *discloses* itself by physical appearance, by self-exposition (if we take it at face value) and by what others think. So in Chekhov's straightforward one-act farce *The Bear*, first we see Grigory Stepanovitch Smirnov as an overbearing, middle-aged landowner. Second, he talks about himself:

Brr! How mad I feel to-day, how furious! I'm positively shaking with rage. I can hardly breathe....Ugh! my God! I'm almost fainting![7]

Third, Elena Ivanovna Popova says of him: 'You're a coarse, ill-mannered fellow! Respectable people don't talk like this to a lady.' But these technical aids offer no positive meaning apart from the particular presence of the other character—the widow with the dimples on her cheeks, Mme Popova, who resists his intrusion and makes him forget his pomposity, his misogyny and his anger, who challenges him with her husband's pistols and her charm. The play creates the simplest of impressions, constructed on the 'before-and-after' pattern. It reaches a ludicrous climax:

A duel! Yes, that's equality of rights, that's emancipation! There's equality of sexes for you! I'll pop her off just as a matter of principle!

All the processes of the play have gone to force this crisis, and reality has been left far behind. But in a moment a touch of reality is introduced, and we recognize an affectation familiar to us. The pace halts, Smirnov pauses, and the anticlimax arrives: 'But what a woman!...I'm almost sorry to have to kill her!' He capitulates. Her capitulation will follow, and, to our joy, her initial pose,

I will never go out....Why should I? My life is over. He lies in his grave—I have buried myself in these four walls....We are both dead,

is equally shattered. We do not think chiefly of Smirnov, nor of Popova, but of the sparks flying between them. Character discharges its meaning in friction and reaction.

The Elements of Drama

The reader may argue that character *develops*, which is not, he may say, something a mere 'mask' allows. But the development of character is in fact nothing but a finer definition of the features of the mask. It is properly the development of the image that deludes us into seeing a development in the character. In some plays, like *King Lear* or *A Doll's House*, the idea of change in the character can itself be a central impression, but we must not receive an effect and take it to be a cause. We oblige the author by consistently linking together this aspect and that of the mask as it appears to us. This is facilitated by the continuous presence of the actor, and we are likely to go astray only if the author has not sufficiently provided for our natural desire to complete half-formed images, or if he has left the actor with words so empty that he must fill them out from his own resources, perhaps from his own personality: the abuse of a playwright's work may be due to a fault in the play itself.

Four consecutive speeches from the beginning of Strindberg's exceptionally closely knit play *Miss Julie* suggest in little how character is created and how it develops:

JULIE. Thank you. Don't you want some yourself?
JEAN. I don't care very much for beer, but if it is a command, of course—
JULIE. Command?—I should think a polite gentleman might keep his lady company.
JEAN. Yes, that's the way it should be.[8]

Miss Julie is virtually alone with Jean her footman for the first time, since Christine the cook has fallen asleep. Thus anything said between them now takes on a meaning arising from a dramatic counterpoint: what these particular people say in private works against what a lady and her servant should say in public. Character emerges less from the seductive coyness of Julie's remarks and from Jean's reticence and embarrassment (secondary symptoms) than from the fact that this remark is made to this person in this circumstance.

Manipulating the Characters

Julie had asked for beer: 'My taste is so simple that I prefer it to wine.' She first slyly invites Jean to join her in drinking it. The seeming quibble about the social standing of beer or wine and the appropriateness of the drink to the drinker hints at the change in their relationship to come and partly prepares us to accept their perverse states of mind. Jean's reply is double-edged. He is unwilling to abandon his position of the man in the relationship, although he is still aware of his social inferiority. In the audience we await his reaction: had he replied 'Yes', we should have assumed he was asserting his masculinity; had he replied 'No', he would have been accepting his menial position. His actual reply, enhanced for us by the actor's momentary hesitation, establishes his indecision at this stage of his 'development'. But will she reduce him again to servant, or raise him to an open equality as between man and woman? Her words tell us she takes the second course: 'I should think a polite gentleman might keep his lady company.' By her voice, softer and more insinuating, she raises him to her level. They are now 'lady' and 'gentleman'. Will Jean accept this advancement? Yes, but with a degree of reluctance in the implied conditional: 'that's the way it should be'. This last remark of his is potent with a sudden new regard he has for himself. It precipitates a vision of him as the dominant partner in a sexual relationship, but one with latent abnormalities.

Character implies relationship, and development of character suggests growth towards a more precise, evolving relationship, our guided deduction. It should not confuse the argument to call this relationship the situation. Both Jean and Julie seem to develop, more especially Jean in these lines, but it is properly the situation that has meaningfully progressed. Situation is manipulated by the author; character, involved by it, appears to grow. As character grows, in turn it reveals relationship.

The Elements of Drama

'Relationship' is not being used here in the limited sense of a personal connection between people, but in the dramatic sense of a relative connection between characters, which can of course include a personal connection. We are asking not how characters affect one another, but how they affect the action. Once this is done, relationship between characters can be seen to exist even where they do not meet, as Falstaff, for example, does not meet King Henry but must by his behaviour put a construction upon what the King stands for. Neither does Macbeth 'meet' his Porter; nor the Dauphin Baudricourt's Steward. But all have their place in the pattern.

A useful concept of recent coinage is that discussed by Dr E. M. W. Tillyard as differing 'planes of reality'.[9] One character can bear a relationship to another even when it is presented at a lower or higher 'level' within the play, not necessarily a social level, but an imaginative one. We respond to a similarity or to a contrast by making the association in the sequence of impressions: so Sir Toby is imaginatively linked with Orsino, Touchstone with Jaques. Looking for so-called 'sub-plots' misleads us into falsely atomizing a play's unity of feeling. Degrees of fiction in the shape of actors are set on the same stage and related dramatically, especially in the fantasies of artificial comedy. *A Midsummer Night's Dream* uses this freedom extravagantly.

Within the magic of the moonlit wood near Athens, Shakespeare is at liberty to play dramatic variations upon his motifs of love-sickness. In the first scene the varieties of moon imagery paint the thematic setting for this wedding play: it is the moon that 'lingers desires', 'the cold fruitless moon of chastity', which is opposed to the romantic moon that,

> like to a silver bow
> New-bent in heaven, shall behold the night
> Of our solemnities.[10]

Manipulating the Characters

This moon in turn weaves the spell that 'hath witched the bosom' of Hermia. The world of *fancy* shall merge into the world of *fantasy*. Within this web of charmed love and fairy moon-madness, within this loose dialectic of verbal imagery, Shakespeare symbolizes his lovers and his fairies in the forms we know. Bottom and the mechanicals with their burlesque of Pyramus and Thisbe supply mongrel and preposterous elements that are caught up in the pattern and used to balance, criticize and complicate the luxury of sentiment the others display.

The theme is the irrationality of love, explored in the comic licence of the moonlit wood. There are five worlds of potential and actual lovers, and the formal illusion of the play is to make us wonder in which world we stand ourselves. Not in the literary world of Pyramus and Thisbe, nor in the regions of the supernatural of Titania and Oberon, nor in the grotesque circle of Bottom and his friends, nor among the tinsel passions of Lysander, Demetrius, Helena and Hermia. We can identify ourselves only with the rational onlookers Theseus and Hippolyta, who prompt us to look with the eyes of the newly-married couple for whom the play was possibly written. With their anticipation we shall speculate about romantic beliefs. Through the agency of Puck, all the lovers' sincerities are foresworn, and all their protestations of faithfulness are disputed and denied; the delicate purity of ideal fairy love is repudiated by Titania's sophisticated relationship with Oberon, and coarsely soiled by Bottom the worldly lover; and Ovid's noble story of the perfect love of Pyramus and Thisbe performed by the ignoble cannot be other than burlesqued. No sentimental sweet assumption we may have had is allowed to rest. With what quizzical judgment Theseus concludes,

> Lovers and madmen have such seething brains,
> Such shaping fantasies, that apprehend
> More than cool reason ever comprehends![11]

The Elements of Drama

Shakespeare is ironically asking whether we are prepared to acknowledge with 'cool reason' the validity of all the fancies with which unreason comforts itself.

This is the disquieting virtue of the play, to allow us no moment of easy sympathy with any kind or degree of love. We can only detach ourselves with Theseus and Hippolyta. By travesty and burlesque, all pleasing preconceptions and misconceptions are fretted and disparaged. We are quietly told of our inadequacies—'But, howsoever, strange and admirable'. This line from Theseus's lady suggests the lightness in the tone of Shakespeare's reprimand and the gentleness in the touch of his punishment.

This complexity could not have been secured had not the author felt himself free to caricature the lovers, the fairies and the clowns, free to colour each set of characters to clash with another. Laughter follows the shocks of the feather-weight irony. As each group, acting on its own plane of reality, taking its own standards of conduct so seriously, is juggled by the conjuror, romance is made an object of fun. When we examine the mechanism by which two of these caricatures, Bottom and Titania, are, at the master-stroke of Act III, scene i, thrown together, animal disporting with angel, fairy in love with ass,[12] character has become a critical term of strictly limited usefulness, or else one so wide in its application that it must embrace the whole structure of the scene. In Shakespeare's romantic comedies, like *A Midsummer Night's Dream*, *As You Like It* and *Twelfth Night*, character is more structural than individual, more general and formal than personal.

Pirandello manipulates character in a highly original way, daringly asserting the freedom of the stage. *Six Characters in Search of an Author* provides a brilliant example. 'What is true?' is Pirandello's basic question, and his play is a complex task for the analyst, especially since breaking down the play's

Manipulating the Characters

objects into neat compartments, for example (i) how an artist creates, (ii) what reality there is in art, (iii) what reality there is in life, does not help, since these three and other problems are being dramatized simultaneously. In reading the play, one may find it jerky, without an organic centre and therefore unconvincing. This, I believe, is because one tends to tease out the separate strands of the theme from without. In performance, the play is smooth and interlocking, and the ideas move centripetally by the powerful magnetism of the play's emotion. Characters that in the text seem to divide the play, in performance bind it by being precisely placed in the structural relationships enacted.

See this play as one composed of dramatized, implicit discussions between characters, some of whom have the ability to speak with more than one voice. Two of the Six Characters in particular, both by being the centre of interest and by moving freely between all the worlds of imagination the play defines, encourage us to feel the meaning of the play as a unity. The Stepdaughter and the Father speak as characters in the absent author's play, while at the same time they imply what the absent author would have said in his own defence; so the relationship author–character is demonstrated and the processes of creative art are argued. When the Stepdaughter and the Father are seen as characters the live actors are not wholly prepared to believe in, yet as characters with more life than the actors who are to play them, actor criticizes character and character criticizes actor, and the relationship character–actor is argued. Pirandello reserves his final, cumulative shock when we are persuaded that the actors are but characters, that, in the final chaos of the play when the Stepdaughter goes laughing hysterically through the auditorium, the characters are but actors, and that we are but an audience, susceptible to anything we take for granted in the theatre or in life. This hits us with the horror of a blow in one's sleep. The game is

The Elements of Drama

one of trying to find the 'right' viewpoint, the 'comfortable' attitude towards any given idea. Are we in the play or in reality? Are we looking with the eyes of the author or the character or the actor or the audience? The play does not leave us with any consolatory answer. Our final queries are about life, not about art, and Pirandello's skill is positive by being negative, serving to enlighten us by confounding us.

A particular piece of analysis will indicate the variety of forces working upon the imagination at the same time. In the following scene, Madame Pace, the repulsive milliner brothel-keeper, remaining completely the character of the absent author's fiction, speaks a broken English, which amuses the watching group of actors and actresses and pleases the Producer:

PRODUCER.... Yes, speak like that, Madame! It'll bring the house down! We couldn't ask for anything better. It'll bring a little comic relief into the crudity of the situation. Yes, you talk like that! It's absolutely wonderful!

STEPDAUGHTER. Wonderful! And why not? When you hear a certain sort of suggestion made to you in a lingo like that...There's not much doubt about what your answer's going to be...Because it almost seems like a joke. You feel inclined to laugh when you hear there's an 'old señor' who wants to 'amuse himself with me'. An 'old señor', eh, Madame?

MADAME PACE. Not so very old...Not quite so young, yes? And if he does not please to you...Well, he has...*prudencia*.

MOTHER. *Absorbed as they are in the scene the Actors have been paying no attention to her. Now, to their amazement and consternation, she leaps up and attacks Madame Pace. At her cry they jump, then hasten smilingly to restrain her, for she, meanwhile has snatched off Madame Pace's wig and thrown it to the ground.* You old devil! You old witch! You murderess! Oh, my daughter!

STEPDAUGHTER, *rushing over to restrain her Mother.* No, Mummy, no! Please![13]

What is the audience thinking as it listens to this? To make each remark carry meaning, it must first have decided where the character speaking stands in relation to the character commented upon. The spectator will also be trying to assess

Manipulating the Characters

where the character stands in relation to himself. When the Producer says, 'Yes, speak like that, Madame! It'll bring the house down! We couldn't ask for anything better', we know he is speaking from a position *outside* the play-within-the-play in which we take Madame Pace to be, and in part speaking for us in the audience, since, like the choric group of actors and actresses on the stage, we are also watching the rehearsal he is conducting. But when he adds, 'Yes, you talk like that! It's absolutely wonderful!' there is a shift of understanding and we take up a position outside *him*, because now he has started talking to a 'character' as if she were an 'actress', and we recognize that he is being deluded by the degree of reality Madame Pace possesses. From our superior position we criticize the inadequacy of his vision, and reflect momentarily upon our own former limitation when we joined him in his approval of the cheap theatrical titillation of the broken English. The art of the theatre is under the microscope whenever the Producer speaks. Nor is the Producer's shortsightedness allowed to appear a human shortcoming, an understandable weakness. Because the situation of Madame Pace and the Stepdaughter is melodramatically emotional, it colours all attitudes not in keeping with melodramatic feeling, and we involuntarily condemn the Producer and his company as culpable monsters whenever they speak for the theatrical profession.

We are thus prepared for the Stepdaughter's criticism of the Producer, 'Wonderful! And why not?' with which we now agree. We assume she is with us *outside* the rehearsal, as if in the audience looking on. We quite forget that the passion with which she turns on the Producer comes not wholly of a desire to criticize the ways of the theatre, but more of her own passionate concern with the part she must perform in the play-within-the-play, whose reality she never questions. The venom of her sarcasms should have passed the warning that she is only half outside the rehearsal. In giving her our sympathy we find ourselves making the mistake we have made already many times, as the author intends: the mistake of taking the Six Characters as real and the Producer and his company as unreal. The emotions of the play-within-the-play are again made deliberately harrowing by the ugly euphemisms in the Stepdaughter's mimicry of Madame Pace. As soon as the Stepdaughter recreates the scene in her mind, her position shifts as if by the impulsion of her bitter thoughts. She addresses Madame Pace directly: 'An "old señor", eh, Madame?' Immediately we recognize that she is *inside* the play again, suffering in a second capacity.

When Madame Pace replies, her callous 'Not so very old... Not quite so young, yes?' can only be spoken completely 'in character'. It is spoken directly to the Stepdaughter, showing she is quite oblivious of the critics around her in the persons of the actors and the characters and of us, the true audience. By her very obliviousness Madame Pace's reality comes in question. Yet because of the sincerity of the scene she is enacting, against which the Producer and his actors seem petty, we tend unconsciously to question the substantiality of the others too. The play modulates through a discussion of the shams of the theatre to one of the relationship between character and reality.

The Mother, who has been looking at the scene as if it were the past resurrected, suddenly by the force of her emotion takes the past to be the present and the play to be reality. In a flash we are startled, as we were when Madame Pace made her supernatural entrance, into the illusion that the exchange between the Mother and Madame Pace is the only truth. This effect is enhanced by the credibility of Madame Pace's horror when her wig is thrown off. The Stepdaughter, deceiving us by her double role inside and outside the play-within-the-play, for a space suggests that her attempts to calm

Manipulating the Characters

her mother are the attempts of a child to appease a parent, until we reflect this might also be the behaviour of a daughter conscious of her mother's making a *faux pas* in public, the public being the Producer and his company. This impression, that the Stepdaughter is farther outside the play than the Mother, is stressed when the Father's advice to the Mother follows: 'Calm yourself, my dear!' This reaffirms that she is moved by the presence of Madame Pace to the exclusion of all else. In performance, the half-existence of the Mother by contrast makes the Stepdaughter more 'alive' than the play's structure would suggest.

The modulations of the action are easy. The audience turns its feeling and its critical intelligence elastically on this, then on that, aspect of the subject, because it is led through the play uncertain of the level at which it must feel and of what it is free to criticize. Through the vacillation of response to this or that character Pirandello is able to dramatize his abstract discussions.

The complexity of the play's suggestions increases rapidly. The ambiguities become bewildering in the scene of Madame Pace's shop which the Stepdaughter and the Father enact for the Producer:

FATHER, *coming forward, a new note in his voice.* Good afternoon, Miss.
STEPDAUGHTER, *her head bowed, speaking with restrained disgust.* Good afternoon!

How are we to see these characters now? Are they merely representing the spectator's point of view, criticizing the professionals and showing them how it should be done? If this make-believe is a further comment on theatrecraft, then they are acting acting. But Pirandello means us to accept their performance as truth, for his direction to the Father is that he must at first look troubled and very pale,

But as he approaches from the back of the stage he smiles, already absorbed in the reality of his created life. He smiles as if the drama which is about to break upon him is as yet unknown to him.

The Elements of Drama

As the sequence develops, we are to be moved by a more realistic style of acting: actors of Pirandello must be 'plastic' according to the distance of their speech and movement from the author's conception of the 'true' reality. In 1925, the author wrote:

> The six characters must not appear as phantoms, but as 'created realities', immutable creatures of fantasy. They are more real and consistent than the voluble actors.[14]

And the play itself has provided for a subtle changeover by which the Stepdaughter and the Father are more convincing than the actors. We are to take the brothel scene as reality, so that when the Ingénue interrupts with 'Oh, I say! Those are *our* hats!' we are shocked into recognizing that we are being deluded, and the discussion of our awareness of degrees of reality is successfully dramatized. This aspect of the play is later emphasized when the Stepdaughter criticizes the Father's *performance:* and then again when the Leading Man and the Leading Lady attempt to re-enact the performance they have seen. They act now with a lesser realism, though Pirandello makes it clear that their acting must be near enough to accepted standards to make us consider it seriously as a possible interpretation:

> *The playing of this scene by the Actors will appear from the very first words as something completely different from what was played before, without its having, even in the slightest degree, the air of a parody.*

The Father's immediate reaction is to cry, 'No!', and the Stepdaughter cannot restrain a burst of laughter. By this process of refining our standards of reality in dramatic statement and counter-statement, we are forced to argue about probability and credibility. Our thoughts are set wrangling with our feelings.

It would be unlike Pirandello to leave us complacent. Before we are allowed to go, he arranges it that the climax of the play-within-the-play coincides with the climax of our

Manipulating the Characters

experience, and that the fictional reality of the characters becomes inextricably confused with the comparative reality of the Producer and the Actors. The end of the play introduces a revolver shot which is perhaps the most effective shot in drama. It effects a conjunction of the real and the unreal, hits off the climax of our emotions and sums up the play's puzzle. By this shot, shadow is made solid, and the spectator dizzy with a terror of the unknown.

Then first from one side, then from the other, the Actors re-enter.
LEADING LADY, *re-entering right, very much moved.* He's dead, poor boy! He's dead! Oh what a terrible thing to happen!
LEADING MAN, *re-entering left, laughing.* What do you mean, dead? It's all make-believe! It's all just a pretence! Don't get taken in by it!
OTHER ACTORS, *entering from the right*, Make-believe? Pretence? Reality! Reality! He's dead!
OTHERS, *from the left.* No! Make-believe! It's all a pretence!

These contradictory extremes compel our silence, not our laughter: they mark the subtlety with which the characters have been manipulated, and our absorption in the play.

To stifle *Six Characters in Search of an Author* with preconceived notions of what character may do in a play, or what degree of conviction it must carry, is to treat character as something external, hopelessly making nonsense of the experience. The playgoer can finally admit character only as a mask in its meaning and a puppet in its action, and judge it only by standards of reality and conviction which the orchestration and total purpose of the play demand.

9
BREAKING THE CONTINUITY

All drama, like any fiction, works by make-believe. The author takes it that his audience will accept, for the time being, something as plausible or possible when all parties know it is unreal: he asks us to ignore improbabilities or impossibilities for the sake of some specially concentrated illustration of a human situation. He gets us to consent to stretch our beliefs in order to exercise our imagination, even in the most realistic of plays. He assumes we will forget the existence of the theatre as soon as the curtain has risen. All audiences have disregarded the form of the play to enjoy its substance: 'convention' is only serviceable when it is taken for granted.

But a number of modern dramatists have been anxious to make the audience aware it is in a theatre. As a way of making us question our beliefs and certainties, Pirandello, as we have seen in *Six Characters in Search of an Author*, reveals sharply to us that we have been accepting a convention falsely. *Each in his Own Way* seems to have reached the limits of what convention will stand, by tormenting reason with a play-within-a-play-within-a-play. The author reminds us that imagination has been roving too far from reality, but only after it is too late for us to revoke a false emotional conviction. He compels a keener imaginative activity by taking liberties with our generosity of mind.

So for a particular purpose a dramatist may today call attention to the convention within which he is working. Mr Hesketh Pearson has told how Shaw in rehearsal turned *Androcles and the Lion* from a comedy into an extravaganza.[1] Bertolt Brecht cultivated in a play like *Mother Courage* what

Breaking the Continuity

he called an 'effect of estrangement' (*Verfremdungseffekt*), breaking down the audience's readiness to accept illusion to induce a critical attitude towards his events. Mr Sean O'Casey and M. Jean Anouilh mix contrasting moods within a scene to shock the audience into an acuter perception. We recall the startling effect of the colloquial address of the Knights in *Murder in the Cathedral* by which we suddenly leap on into the present day. Mr Thornton Wilder, particularly in *Our Town*, puts naturalistic dialogue on to an unlocalized stage: the trick serves to sharpen the edges of words and situations blunted by over-familiarity.

It seems that in the modern theatre the dramatist can explore to the limits of what a convention will allow; acting on a great variety of precedents, he is more free today to choose what style is suited to his subject. But nevertheless no dramatist can work outside a channel of convention, since only this permits continuity of attention. Even when it is his object to break this continuity, he must begin by moving along one of these channels. It must be an already flowing train of feeling that he interrupts if after the break he is to secure that exciting renewal of attention. Such interruptions suggest a true dramatic wit.

This wit is kin to, perhaps indistinguishable from, any shattering of the image. In literary criticism a 'conceit' ordinarily denotes verbal imagery which brings together two ideas by the perception of an unexpected relationship between them. There is a conceit in the theatre too, one that falls naturally within its province: it lies in relating suggestions by ingenious juxtapositions, the dramatist linking together two ideas or emotions which seem mutually to contradict and confound each other. Always provided the correspondence between them is purposeful and eventually apparent, by such means the spectator can be powerfully moved, have his imagination set alive, be started on an urgent chase of thoughts. The work

The Elements of Drama

of Pirandello and M. Anouilh has proved a play need not collapse under the shock of such a technique if the author can precisely calculate the audience's sense of congruity. It may be that the balance in a play by M. Anouilh is so delicate that its impact is lost to a London audience, while in Paris the play is a complete success.

It will help to look at a few of these effects in more detail. A purposeful shock may arise with the switch from a comic to a tragic mood, or vice versa, felt within the continuity of a scene. In the plays of Mr O'Casey the mood undergoes internal changes without breaking the convention. Of course in the run of ordinary experience one passes from one state of feeling to another without thinking it unusual. But there are forces at work in the theatre which can make such a transition a disturbing sensation. First, the unnatural compression of time will make the jump between the two states so abrupt their effect must impinge upon the spectator's consciousness. Second, the planned intensity of the feelings will make the gap to be bridged between them wide and excitingly dangerous. Realism, deliberately avoiding obvious exaggeration, had all but denied the dramatist his freedom to effect such juxtapositions. The modern author is forced to arrange his action in new ways if tragic and comic elements in experience are to compel attention. In his early plays, Mr O'Casey's was a Dickensian, melodramatic kind of mind that shocked his audience, harshly juxtaposing apparently irreconcilable feelings.

Juno and the Paycock is a lesser play than *The Plough and the Stars* because its effects suggest contrivance; the method does not lift the pseudo-tragic elements from melodrama; and the play's momentum does not carry us through the transitions with assurance. In Act II, Mary's rejection by Bentham while bearing his child; Juno's awareness of poverty, emphasized by the removal of Boyle's suit, the furniture and the gramophone,

Breaking the Continuity

that sign of luxury; the killing of Johnny after the votive light flickered and went out; the heroic figure of Juno left in distress —all this mixes uneasily with the comedy of Joxer and Boyle, good as this is. The anticlimax of their drunken entry would have been a bitter irony had the tragic elements previously been more delicate, had they stamped less than they did. The play is not wholly acceptable because the comic and the tragic do not spring from the same root.

The Plough and the Stars is more subtle, not because the mixture is any less incongruous, but because the tragic implications flow more smoothly from a source itself potentially comic. In *Juno and the Paycock* the author tried to conjure comedy out of tragedy; in *The Plough and the Stars* he conjures tragedy out of comedy. Here the tragic elements are as stock, and yet, when the comic comment scratches away their flakes of sentiment, they achieve a dignity. Above all, the incongruities of mood which permeate the play grow from the same situation. What seem to be episodes loosely joined are actually a series of selected emotions meticulously interwoven. The conceits are effective. A short example makes this clear:

ROSIE. It's no joke thryin' to make up fifty-five shillin's a week for your keep and laundhry, an' then taxin' you a quid for your own room if you bring home a friend for th' night.... If I could only put by a couple of quid for a swankier outfit, everythin' in th' garden ud look lovely—
BARMAN. Whisht, till we hear what he's sayin'.

Through the window is silhouetted the figure of a tall man who is speaking to the crowd. The Barman and Rosie look out of the window and listen.

THE VOICE OF THE MAN. It is a glorious thing to see arms in the hands of Irishmen. We must accustom ourselves to the thought of arms, we must accustom ourselves to the sight of arms, we must accustom ourselves to the use of arms.... Bloodshed is a cleansing and sanctifying thing, and the nation that regards it as the final horror has lost its manhood.... There are many things more horrible than bloodshed, and slavery is one of them!

The figure moves away towards the right, and is lost to sight and hearing.

The Elements of Drama

ROSIE. It's th' sacred thruth, mind you, what that man's afther sayin'.
BARMAN. If I was only a little younger, I'd be plungin' mad into th' middle of it!
ROSIE, *who is still looking out of the window.* Oh, here's the two gems runnin' over again for their oil!

Peter and Fluther enter tumultuously. They are hot, and full and hasty with the things they have seen and heard....

PETER, *splutteringly to Barman.* Two halves.... *To Fluther.* A meetin' like this always makes me feel as if I could dhrink Loch Erinn dhry![2]

Rosie the street-walker is indifferent to the revolutionary talk outside the bar, though at times she is belligerent because politics are interfering with her trade. Her self-centred comments preceding the Voice already provide an implicit criticism of what he is about to say. And what he says is a comment on her. Their speeches give firm impressions of the material and the spiritual, the two conditions the author interweaves through the play. Rosie is bothered by money, and money only—except in so far as she is also bothered by what money can fetch. The Leader of the Easter Rebellion is no materialist, for all his practical talk of 'arms' and the repetition of his operative word 'accustom'. His thinking is in clichés, and he is docketed an idealist. The juxtaposition of his stylistic rhetoric with Rosie's references to concrete and familiar things, the 'laundhry', the 'swankier outfit', wrapped up untidily in her colloquialisms, 'It's no joke...', '...everythin' in th' garden ud look lovely', makes an immediate contrast. It throws up the Leader's verbal flights, yet his speech rouses emotion, and we must in some measure respond to a tone belonging to a higher world of feeling. This is because we see him only dimly: his figure avoids particularity like his speech, and he affects us impersonally like a chorus. His rhythmic and patterned speech, and his reference to matters that cannot be taken as comic, have only one effect at the time of speaking: one of serious and heightened sympathy.

Breaking the Continuity

But our after-response to the Voice is, if not critical, nevertheless not purely emotional. Can low comedy and high sentiment be so joined in the imagination to create definite meaning? The playgoer will know an uneasiness remains, a lack of direction for feeling. This is precisely what the author wished the sequence to yield. It is an achievement to make a chaos to some purpose. With the clash of this discord in our ears, we realize that both Rosie and the Voice, seemingly moving in spheres at variance with one another, are talking of the same thing, the urge to rise above the frustration of the human spirit, to the vivid presentation of which Mr O'Casey devoted his first act. There is an imaginative logic in the apparently loose associative links in his action. Rosie and the Voice are symptomatic of the incongruous elements in the Irish character, and in us all.

The author saw the mixture of our greatness and littleness, and the Easter Rebellion provided him with a vehicle to express this. Mr Denis Johnston describes an incident that he says 'has not been included in the lore of those Homeric times':

A very brave and romantic young man, by name Joseph Plunkett, stepped out of the rebel stronghold in the General Post Office and began to read the Proclamation of the Irish Republic to the assembled citizens at the base of the Nelson Pillar. He had not gone very far with the news when there was a crash of broken glass from nearby, and the cry went up, 'They're looting Noblett's Toffee Shop'. With a whoop of delight that far exceeded their enthusiasm for the Republic, the sovereign people departed, leaving young Plunkett to finish his proclamation to the empty air.[3]

This external reference may clarify the effect which passes subtly between the stage and the auditorium. In later scenes, the form of the response we give to Rosie and the Voice is repeated, and in particular the incongruity of the heroics with the looting is precisely reproduced in Act III:

WOMAN.... I wonder, would you kind men come some of the way and see me safe?

The Elements of Drama

FLUTHER. I have to go away, ma'am, to thry an' save a few things from th' burnin' buildin's.

THE COVEY. Come on, then, or there won't be anything left to save.

The comedy of Fluther and the Covey rasps on the pathos inherent in the event.

To return to the scene in the bar. Rosie earlier referred to the men outside the window in these terms:

You'd think they were th' glorious company of th' saints, an' th' noble army of martyrs thrampin' through th' sthreets of paradise. They're all thinkin' of higher things than a girl's garthers.

Her sarcasm tells us she certainly does not believe her customers are 'saints' and 'martyrs'; nor do we. This grotesquely ambivalent view of the characters overlies all our reactions. Setting the scene in the bar to which the characters retire between revolutionary sentiments is ingeniously symbolic of their contradictions. We cannot reconcile statements about deeds to be done on behalf of the Republic with the actual behaviour of the characters. The two facts of the Rosie way of life and the Leader's sentiments summarize private and public man. Enlightenment comes when we recognize that it is the same man who embraces this incongruity. The entrance of Peter and Fluther at the height of the fever is designed to press this point home later. They come in bellicose, but they have not forgotten their thirst.

As the scene proceeds, the incongruities become insistent. The comedy in Rosie's comment on the Speaker, 'It's th' sacred thruth, mind you, what that man's afther sayin'', and in the Barman's 'If I was only a little younger, I'd be plungin' mad into th' middle of it', arises because they speak in the shallow, easy tone which indicates a complete indifference to what they are saying. Business is slack, and they are partners in disappointment. Their phlegmatic nonchalance prepares us for the 'tumultuous' entrance of the 'two gems'. Their physical appearance, Peter sad and thin, Fluther small but

Breaking the Continuity

alive like a little cock, their riotous manner of entering, the fury of their drinking, the pitch and pace at which they speak, can only contrast with the sentiments of the Speaker. When we heard words alone inciting a crowd to action, our imagination was free to put the normal, appropriate construction on them; now that we hear the same sentiments expressed by Peter and Fluther, whom we see for what they are, we are directed to respond as to a burlesque of patriotic soldiery. The particularities of what we see, set against the generalities of the rhetoric, control the image. We cannot fit together what we heard with what we see, so we laugh. Even then what they say is at odds with what they do: 'A meetin' like this always makes me feel as if I could dhrink Loch Erinn dhry!' says Peter. Any excuse for a drink, thinks Rosie, think we. So Peter and Fluther play the buffoon to confirm the dual quality in man proposed initially by public-house prostitute and rebel hero, Rosie and the Voice. The chaos of the conceit is for the present resolved and meaningful. The oscillations of our feelings die down, but only until the next dissonance discomforts us.

The shock of breaking convention is an effect that quiescent traditions in the modern English theatre have made easy to achieve. Shakespeare and the Elizabethans freely jumped from rhetorical poetry to colloquial prose, but the device fell within the general manner of their plays. Mr Eliot attempted a shock of the modern kind in *Murder in the Cathedral* when the Knights address the audience after the climax of the murder of Thomas the Archbishop. It is not their direct address that disturbs us since we have been prepared for this by the intimacy of the Chorus and by the sermon from the pulpit, both forms of direct address which are in keeping with the general presentation of the play within a church building. It is the surprise of colloquial modern prose after we were tuned to the poetry of the Chorus, of hearing the Knights

The Elements of Drama

come out of period, of receiving realistic distinctions between their characters after we had accepted them almost as an impersonal chorus. We are not to take their reasoning at face value: the intention is to startle us out of the turmoil of emotion, to make us alert to the significance of the event, to release us temporarily for a cooler reassessment of the state of our beliefs.

Mr Eliot does not repeat his effect. In *The Family Reunion*, the convention is so uncertain throughout the play that even the physical appearance of the Furies or the ritual of the birthday cake cannot disturb us. Again in *The Cocktail Party*, suggestions built up through two acts that the Guardians, agencies of our destiny, are among us though we may not know it, prepare us subtly for the explicit revelation of the libation scene. In neither of these plays does the author truly break convention.

On the other hand, Mr Thornton Wilder's revolt against realistic presentation in *Our Town* is designed to gain what the author calls our 'acknowledgment of artifice and make-believe'.[4] A bare stage quickly permits the introduction of a representative range of people, and a significance is curiously added to details of ordinary life and commonplace conversation. Realistic miming on a stage without properties draws attention to the minutest of details. Perhaps too much of the play is devoted either to a capricious use of this kind of effect, or to exploiting its comic possibilities: the rattling of unseen milk-bottles punctuates the entrances and exits of Howie Newsome the milkman until it becomes frivolous. However, the imagination is made unusually receptive by such a method and very trivial details can be emphasized with extraordinary effect. To choose one of the tiniest: George receives some advice from his future father-in-law about the conduct of married life. Slowly round the bare stage he wanders home. As he does so he avoids stepping in an imaginary puddle in the

Breaking the Continuity

road. The actor's movement across the stage enables him to express something of his bewildered state of mind, but the puddle suddenly sharpens in a vivid flash the effect of the utter normality of George's situation.

The accumulation of such effects permits the author to take the most commonplace of situations and see it freshly. It is an experiment in making the typical particular and the particular typical. But reinvigorating technique is not enough: we may have legitimate doubts whether these commonplaces have value in themselves. The situation must be informed with the kind of particularity a new insight brings. Having forced upon us a special awareness of the qualities of everyday routine, it is poorly employed to set off uninspired sentiment about life and death. Nevertheless Mr Wilder gives us a rare evening of exciting, if unfulfilled, possibilities in the theatre, by disturbing our complacency towards convention.

With less justification Mr J. B. Priestley unsettles our apprehension of reality at the end of *An Inspector Calls*. This play is written ostensibly in the realistic manner and striving explicitly to make its particularities universal in reference. Unhappily they become merely typical. It is enough that his sample of modern sinners exemplifies a variety of vices, which we can hardly fail to notice after the opening scene has played many minutes. Nor can the figure of the Inspector, a strong judge and stronger priest, do other than impress upon us that we must receive a message. But the author is not confident we will take his meaning, for all the punctilious construction of the play; perhaps he suspected that it would not involve us emotionally. It does not call upon us to re-experience a living situation, nor can it, while his characters must serve as a portmanteau for text-book evils. So the author startles us immediately before the final curtain by jogging our memory, giving his message a spurious emphasis irrelevant to the substance of the play.

The Elements of Drama

At the end of the play, the telephone rings again and the announcement is made that 'a Police Inspector is on his way here—to ask some—questions—'. A hint at retribution for those members of the family who fail to heed the Inspector's lesson? This does not warrant a check in continuity. A new inspector, the second of an infinite series destined to plague the guilty to the end of time? That is, another trick to shake our renewed confidence in the reality of appearances? The play's coincidences did not claim a full response before. It can only confirm the feeling of the insubstantiality of the situation and cheapen its meaning. As a device it destroys validity in the realistic action, and undermines sympathy for Eva Smith and what she represents. There was only one way to communicate the theme of the brotherhood of man, and that was to move us to understanding. To make us question reality at this stage is to kill our feeling for the proper subject of the play. There is probably no way of making a morality play out of realistic detail without destroying the specific virtues of realism. A realistic morality play may be a contradiction in terms, but making a joke of its realistic elements will only make a joke of its morality.

Making a switchback of the spectator's readiness to accept a convention is a practice to be indulged with care. It can be fatal to an emotion: its characteristic is to trick our intellect into activity. However, the jerk back to consciousness has been put to striking use by M. Anouilh in his play *Ardèle*.

M. Anouilh's practice in this play is to disturb not only our thoughts, but our ways of thinking. He is not ashamed of overstatement and sensation, which he thinks proper to the theatre: we are entitled to judge his sensationalism, of course, but only by the end to which it is put. It is not of the kind associated with the blood-and-sex cinema and novel, the easily evoked emotions of the general run of melodrama, or the frivolous

Breaking the Continuity

laughter of farce. When it serves him, he presents a violent and astringent mixture of extreme farce and extreme melodrama, insisting that our feelings fluctuate to such an extent that we are never sure of our state of mind. The one extreme balances the other. It may be, as has happened, that some audiences will not suffer this treatment: in many plays he tries our acceptance of make-believe to the utmost. But if we can sustain his attack, its total effect can be a new and satisfying theatrical experience. However, since his method is calculated to work upon an audience in the conditions of the theatre his drama hardly takes effect in reading. Just as the warm mixture of feeling met in Chekhov is for want of words frequently described as a blend of laughter and tears, so in M. Anouilh we resort to saying that his laughter is colder and his tears are bitterer, being equally at a loss to identify a flavour savoured only in the play performed.

His mixture in *Ardèle* is composed of a deliberate contrariety of ingredients: a conceit fertilized the play in its conception. Through the length of the play the spectator is thrown back and forth, uncertain when to smile and when to surrender to emotion. The farce of General Léon Saintpé's affair with the maid is made grotesque by the mimicry of the children Toto and Marie-Christine, and by the screeching of his demented wife Emily. The comedy of manners played by the Count, the Countess and her lover Villardieu (the stage direction reads, 'Nothing must distinguish the Count from Villardieu—same moustaches, same high collars, same monocles, same air of distinction, and probably same club') is countered by the adulterous love of realistic Nicholas and Nathalie. Various as these attitudes to the sexual relationship are, they in turn are criticized by the 'pure' love felt by the General's sister Ardèle. Yet even here we may not immediately set them up as our working standard: Ardèle is a hunchback, and in love with another hunchback. In this assortment of

The Elements of Drama

apparent contradictions, the play employs its freedom to invert, jumble and perplex the continuity of feeling. Driven by the disgust the family express for their love, Ardèle and her lover take their own lives, and in an artificial world we are brought up painfully by a sting of reality.

This is the text of the episode that follows the wife's demonstration of her obsession, an admixture of appalling jealousy, hate and prurience:

EMILY, *now a drooping, pathetic creature, murmurs as she is led to her room.*
I know—I know everything. I'm watching—watching—

As the door is reached, two shots ring out close by. Everyone stops dead, but the madwoman, who appears not to have heard, continues her wailing chant.

EMILY. I'm watching! I'm watching! I'm watching!
GENERAL. My God! What's that? See to her, will you? This time I'm breaking down that door!

The Count, the General and Villardieu throw themselves against the door, puffing and blowing and getting into one another's way. They make a ridiculous, wholly ineffectual trio. This must almost be a clown act, despite the anguish of the situation. Finally, Villardieu pushes them aside, takes a run at the door and breaks it in, falling with it. The General steps over him into the room. Villardieu gets to his feet, rubbing his shoulder. There is a pause. The General comes out again and says quietly,

The fools. They've killed themselves. Run for a doctor, someone. I think Ardèle's still breathing.

Villardieu runs out. The Count and the Countess follow the General back into the room. Below, Nicholas and Nathalie, who have not moved all this time, stand looking at each other.

NATHALIE, *softly.* You see, we don't even have to kill ourselves now. These two who were made for the world's laughter, they have done it for us. Good-bye, Nicholas. Never think of me again. Never think of love again, ever.

Nathalie goes quickly up to her room. Nicholas stays a moment motionless, then goes out into the garden. A door opens and Toto's head appears. Seeing the coast is clear, he and Marie-Christine come out of the room. They are

Breaking the Continuity

dressed up.... They look all of a sudden like two grotesque little dwarfs strutting down the stairs, striking poses and making ridiculous melodramatic gestures. A spotlight is trained on the darkened stage.

TOTO, *rolling his 'r's to make it really passionate.* My dearest!
MARIE-CHRISTINE. My beloved one.[5]

So much in this confounds traditional modes of directing our feeling. The comic figure of the General has now been brought to seriousness by the crazed exhibition of the wife. Our repugnance for her obsession is equalled now by our repugnance for the old man. Merely a figure of fun before, when his wife was an invisible harridan, he is shown in the cold sour light of her personal accusations. Yet so fantastic is her obsession, so grotesque the picture of the bumbling General, the scene so broken with the peacock's cries of 'Leon! Leon!' echoing Emily's cries to her husband, so eccentric the chanting of the catalogue of his crimes, we are never intended to be moved to any kind of compassion for them. Our only relief from the pressure might have been laughter, but at this moment the shots are heard.

We are suspended in the theatrical state of fantasy, and these shots strike the incongruous note of the shot at the end of *Six Characters in Search of an Author*. How real are they? Our minds jump to interpret their meaning. Death is shocking in fantasy. Suddenly we realize how serious are the implications of what we have seen, and our former views are subjected to a brutal criticism. M. Anouilh, with his remarkable sense of an audience's response, leaves the wailing of the wife to linger in our ears while all other life on the stage is motionless: 'I'm watching! I'm watching! I'm watching!' We are caught by the first of a compact series of hoaxes. It is a persuasive ironic wit which suggests that hypocritical lust pollutes all in the family except Ardèle, casting it in two shapes, one farcical and the other tragic. The common factor in the farce and in the tragedy is ugliness, and it is suddenly exhibited by uniting

The Elements of Drama

at a stroke the two responses. We hurriedly review our summary judgments.

No sooner are we about to adopt an attitude than the author produces his second stratagem. As if answering to our wish, the stage leaps into activity, but in quite an unexpected way. The Count, the General and Villardieu rush to the focal point of interest, Ardèle's door on the balcony; but these three are again the characters of farcical comedy. The author is not to allow us the satisfaction of sympathy. His stage direction states specifically: 'This must almost be a clown act, despite the anguish of the situation.' What twist of mind has made the author want this?, the reader may well ask in the cold light of the text. The action before Ardèle's bedroom door must be prolonged until the audience is laughing again. Why? To make us again critical of our emotion, by reminding us that the unfeeling commit a crime against human dignity. We fill the vacuum between the extremes of the tragic and the farcical by taking a fresh view of the human condition that has produced them.

The farce ceases abruptly. Attention is trained upon Nathalie and Nicholas, left alone on the lower stage, a motionless centre in and after the bustle of activity. These two, playing in the realistic manner, now concentrate in themselves our judgment on the rest. It was Nathalie who had said a few minutes earlier, 'Those two upstairs, they are touching each other, they are in each other's arms! Oh, how hideous love is!' and 'if we loved each other furtively, in secret, it would be ugly and horrible like theirs'. But after the suicide she can say with simple clarity, 'You see, we don't even have to kill ourselves now. These two who were made for the world's laughter, they have done it for us.' Nathalie is finally sure of herself. In one spare statement she condemns herself and Nicholas, she elevates the hunchbacks to a symbolic authority, makes them an immutable point of reference, sets them up as

Breaking the Continuity

our standard of purity. By their tremendous but repellent love we are to measure the quality of all other forms that have gone before. More than this, she marks and identifies the larger irony of the play. Her statement, 'These two who were made for the world's laughter, they have done it for us', epitomizes the uneasy mixture of feelings we suffer in this act: while Ardèle and her lover are physically deformed, they are the only ones spiritually untainted. The earlier view that love between two such people is inconceivable is now under an icy inquisition. M. Anouilh draws the distinction between the carnal and the spiritual by first showing us the carnal in the distorting mirror of social forms, and the spiritual distorted by our own carnal prejudices. Then he lets us see the truth simply by removing the mirrors. The carnal lovers had thought only in terms of their own limited understanding of love; we with Nathalie now see other and better standards, ones noble to the point of death. Where incredulity and laughter went before, belief and understanding enter now: the play's final image reveals the grossness of our error. This is no pessimistic finale: the suicide has been used to put a case, not to pronounce sentence.

The author reserves his master stroke: he will remain in control of our feeling. The children Toto and Marie-Christine enter, playing in a mimic world of their own, horribly reminiscent of the adult world we damn. They too are making game of human relationships: but as children they are real. This is M. Anouilh's last conceit. Laughter is too dry and painful to voice. We reason at once that the General and his wife and his 'ripe, juicy peach' Ada, the Count and the Countess, the one with his little seamstress and the other with her aristocratic lover, Nathalie turning in disgust both from her husband Maxim and from her lover Nicholas—they all in their several ways have been as children playing a game with emotions too precious for them to handle. In addition to this,

this youngest generation is not only aping its elders, but also foreshadowing the pretences of later life. Perhaps these will remain in kind a mockery, as casually turning to deceit and to hate as their game does now: 'if you loved me less one day I'd kill you!...I'll show you who loves you most, you little half-wit!' So Toto, a little caricature of human indignity, rains blows on his cousin, but to the last we do not know if they are genuine or sham.

Ardèle is a play erecting its own framework to prompt feelings otherwise dormant and to shock a callous modern sensibility.

10

THE MEANING OF THE PLAY AS A WHOLE

We judge a play by its sufficiency as a whole. We can usually spot the writer who writes without saying anything: too many plays are not a formula for a 'particular emotion', but only a formula. Other writers often lose sight of the target and become obsessed simply with the need to make a loud enough bang to 'satisfy' the stage with a cheap laugh or a quick thrill. The action then includes theatrical padding, and no other literary form seems more open to this error. In better plays occasional padding is a woolly substitute for experience that has not been suffered, like the sketchy treatment of the Jewish problem in John Van Druten's *I Am a Camera*, or of the unfaithful wife in Mr Terence Rattigan's *The Browning Version*. Because a play demands that the writer project his thoughts into an artificial world of which he may never have been in its proper sense a witness, because it is easier to remain unreal about an insubstantial feeling, even the good writer often finds himself in parts of his play repeating well-worn patterns of stage action which lead him away from the particularity he wants. The dramatizer, as distinct from the dramatist, betrays himself in his momentary misfires.

The playwright expects to be judged by his total effect, but all of us are shy of it. The playgoer gives way to the habit of finding, say, a first act good, a last act bad, and so on. Examples spring to mind readily: some of us do not approve of the Epilogue to *Saint Joan;* Bridie is regularly accused of writing bad third acts, as in *Daphne Laureola;* the second act of *The Confidential Clerk* was praised at the expense of the rest of the

The Elements of Drama

play; the impressive moments were singled out from Mr John Whiting's *Marching Song*, a play composed for the cumulative effect of its motifs. Likewise the actor looks to his 'big' scene, trusting this to carry him through. Perhaps here is a reflection on the deadening exigencies of weekly repertory, or, among amateurs, the lack of interest in plays as distinct from playing. The student works on sequences and scenes, even on individual speeches, as apparent entities. The days of the purple passage are over, but it is still unfortunately true that the student, in the need to discipline his subject, makes it conform to rules not its own. There are no words to define what it has fairly taken the play itself in its own medium to define.

Stanislavsky boldly insists that the actor should look for a 'super-objective' which 'the whole stream of individual, minor objectives, all the imaginative thoughts, feelings and actions of an actor should converge to carry out'.[1] He implies that the actor can epitomize a main theme for himself by a tag: Molière's *Le Malade imaginaire* carries the idea 'I wish to be thought sick', and Goldoni's *La locandiera* carries 'I wish to do my courting on the sly'. This is no different from Sir Laurence Olivier's putting a restringent stamp on the meaning of *Hamlet* by telling his cinema audience initially that it is the story of a man who could not make up his mind. It is wise to be conscious of a play's theme, but it is another thing to accept either as feasible or workable the abstraction of any idea so compact that it can be summed up in a few words.

The changes taking place in the mind of the audience during performance, and what it feels as the result of the impact of a play, cannot be discovered by any straightforward adding up of the sum of its parts. If the audience is affected by a growing unity, in which the parts gather added meaning from their place in the pattern, one cannot make a decision about a play's effect on the evidence of a single, even a final, suggestion. Thus the effect of Chekhov's *The Three Sisters* is not to be

The Meaning of the Play as a Whole

judged, even if the author wished it to be, solely by the sentiments expressed by Masha, Irena and Olga at the final curtain. The sisters say, as if in conclusive chorus, that they must go on living and working and trying to find out why they are suffering, expressing a desperate hope that life will be better for others. This is an example of an impression apparently working at odds with the trend of the scene. The accumulating impressions delineate people who cannot escape the consequences of their own natures. This is not a reference simply to the pointless death of Irena's suitor Baron Tuzenbach, to the unlucky departure of the regiment commanded by Masha's admirer Colonel Vershinin, to the fact that brother Andrey's Natasha has a child by another man, or to the other painful events that serve as milestones in the last act. These events, followed by the apparently heartening conclusion from the sisters, are not to signify that fate *is* playing the characters unkind tricks which they will rise above. If this were so, the ending would surely supply a false close.

This is a play about time, time that the sisters cannot restrain; their life is a dream that deludes them into inertia; they represent people searching for answers they will never hear because they are asking the wrong questions. Chekhov is too gentle to have them appear stupid, but at the end of the play time is still slipping through their fingers; even if Moscow has faded, they still hug their dream; do they not still ask the same questions as at the beginning? To define our final sensations by the final words of the sisters, simply because they speak, is to treat fictions as truths, characters as mouthpieces, and to disregard the contribution of the whole series of impressions. Is this a play of hope? Rather, of resignation and endurance. Is not Chebutykin *also on the stage*? The following is a hint at the kind of inspection this play should get if we wish to arrive at its composite meaning.

In the last five or ten minutes, it is as if Chekhov is writing

The Elements of Drama

terse dramatic footnotes to the previous scenes. He does not let the image rest. The pathos of Vershinin's parting from Masha is enhanced, while Masha herself is almost belittled, by the pathetic comedy of Kulyghin, her dull schoolmaster husband, whose insufficiency as a man is likely to make her future even drearier.

> KULYGHIN, *embarrassed*. Never mind, let her cry, let her.... My dear Masha, my dear, sweet Masha.... You're my wife, and I'm happy in spite of everything.... I'm not complaining, I've no reproach to make—not a single one.... Olga here is my witness.... We'll start our life over again in the same old way, and you won't hear a word from me...not a hint....[2]

As Kulyghin gropes for comforting words, and, quite unable to fathom the realities of his own position and hers, finds comfortless ones, what is the audience thinking? That Masha is unlucky? That dear, kind Kulyghin is a fool? Neither of these suggestions stands alone. We conjure a composite picture, of the woman who has never taken the first step towards understanding her husband starting life over again 'in the same old way', with a man who has never shown a real understanding of his wife, only an inadequate sympathy. We cannot be wholly uncritical towards them. The characters have not heard Chekhov's gently insinuating whisper; but we have.

Heard offstage is the shot that reminds us Irena's love-affair is over. Love-affair? In that shot we hear the echo of the stunted marriage Irena would have made. We remember her words:

> I'll be your wife, I'll be loyal and obedient to you, but I can't love you... What's to be done? *Weeps.* I've never loved anyone in my life. Oh, I've had such dreams about being in love! I've been dreaming about it for ever so long, day and night....

Her romantic ideas will now never suffer the test of experience: Irena will go the way of Olga. All this we feel as she herself

The Meaning of the Play as a Whole

enters in a state of wishful happiness, and says with undisguised joy in her voice, persisting in her error, 'Let's sit down together for a moment, and not talk about anything. I'm going away tomorrow, you know...'. We know better. Then Kulyghin for the moment condenses all their stupidities in his vain attempt to amuse his distracted wife with a comic antic:

Yesterday I took away a false beard and a moustache from a boy in the third form. I've got them here. *Puts them on.* Do I look like our German teacher?... *Laughs.* I do, don't I? The boys are funny.

Olga laughs, responding to the need of the situation. Masha struggles, but bursts into tears again. Poor, lovable Kulyghin. A little aggrieved, he adds, 'Very much like him, I think!' Irena's thoughts are far away.

So the impressions accumulate. Natasha enters, the little-minded wife of Andrey, and she flashes about the stage, reminding the sisters by her manner that she is now the mistress of the house. Her apparently positive qualities, sinister though they may be, have won her this position, and we here see them concisely enacted. At the same time she retraces in her behaviour what she was and what she has become. The children are to be tended by their respective fathers, and in arranging this she is conscious of playing the virtuous mother: 'What a lot of work these children make!' The irony is unmistakable. She comments as if sympathetically on Irena's going away: 'What a pity! Do stay just another week, won't you?'—but she has already made plans for Andrey to have Irena's room and for illegitimate Sofochka to have her husband's, this with no sense of his humiliation. This closely woven speech shows her mind in its fully 'developed' state, insincere, vicious, opportunist. She even contrives to introduce a sarcastic cut at Andrey and his violin. And she will have the trees cut down, the very trees upon which the Baron commented, 'What beautiful trees—and how beautiful, when you

The Elements of Drama

think of it, life ought to be with trees like these!' She marks her assumption of a 'superior' taste by unconsciously returning Olga's criticism of her dress when she first entered the house, only it is Irena who is the victim:

My dear, that belt you're wearing doesn't suit you at all. Not at all good taste. You want something brighter to go with that dress....

Having attacked all she can within a few seconds, she flings back into the house with a scream of abuse at the maid. This is the calculating little coquette who felt 'dreadfully shy' at Irena's party in Act I. Her speech summarizes a creeping evil, not to be exorcised by the ineffectual and the lamely hopeful, however warm-hearted they are.

Chekhov does not hesitate, as in *The Cherry Orchard*, to call upon a sound effect to provide a further emotional epitome of the situation, every adjunct to the image defining it more precisely. The remainder of the scene is coloured by the music of a military band growing fainter and fainter. The sisters think it jaunty; for us it at once suggests the incongruity permeating the action, the spirited music of a brassy military band taking its high spirits with it as it goes. Against this sound, boisterous at its height, Irena is told her Baron has been killed. And against the sound of her tears the stagnant doctor Chebutykin, indifferent to life or death, passive and growing numb where Natasha was active and malevolent, takes out his newspaper once again and sings to himself: 'Let them cry for a bit.... Tarara-boom-di-ay....'

With all this as their setting, the sisters finally offer the chorus of their feelings: they will live and work. They sing their slow song, voices rising to a crescendo as the music of the band fades in diminuendo. They realize Moscow has gone for good: they complete their cycle and return to their sterile beginning. What they say we cannot now accept at face value for we are still assimilating and fashioning our impressions of Masha and Kulyghin, of Irena and Natasha, and of Chebuty-

The Meaning of the Play as a Whole

kin. But we, 'the people who come after', learn from their experience; and we shall remember them kindly. We know it is only the limitation of time, the time we have been made so well aware of in the play, that will prevent such another cycle recurring for these particular people. In 1902 Chekhov added a new touch in a revised stage direction.[3] Kulyghin, all smiles, enters to fetch his Masha, and Andrey is seen pushing Bobik in his pram. After the intense and statuesque pose of the sisters, motionless in a way strikingly at odds with the realistic manner of the rest of the play, suddenly the stage bustles into activity again. This is the last comment: life goes on. Kulyghin and Andrey are in thrall to normality, and Masha, Irena and Olga know they will be dragged back there too. This microcosm of life sways between the forces of indifference and the painful urge to understand, between Chebutykin and Olga:

> CHEBUTYKIN.... What does it matter? Nothing matters!
> OLGA. If only we knew, if only we knew!

I do not see how we can agree with Mr David Magarshack's evaluation of this scene. It would be the greatest mistake to interpret it, he writes,

> as an instance of what is so generally assumed to be the expression of 'Chekhovian' frustration and gloom. Mary [Masha], indeed, says in the bitterness of her heart that her life is a failure and that there is nothing more she wants, but as her little speech in the chorus of the three sisters shows, she soon recovers from her feeling of desolation. Parting is such sweet sorrow—and Chekhov makes it quite clear that it is not by any means the end.
>
> The other great themes of the play—the theme of the illusion of happiness, the theme of mankind's future, and, above all, the theme of the regenerative powers of work—all are carefully interwoven with the action and find a *gay* affirmation of life in the final chorus of the three sisters to the accompaniment of an invigorating march by the band of the departing regiment.[4]

The illogicality of Masha's quick 'recovery' after her loss, of the 'gay' affirmation of life, of the 'invigorating' march, and

The Elements of Drama

so on, does not need insistence. The alternative to frustration and gloom is not necessarily gaiety. Yet curiously, perhaps by contrast with Natasha and Chebutykin, the sisters do not present us with negative values: their sensitiveness, their warmth and love, their buoyancy, their refusal to become callous in the face of adversity, is a reassurance. The play therefore leaves an incisive question. Chebutykin's and Olga's last two lines are the dying notes that suffuse the large complex image we carry away. Are we to join in Olga's desperate search for consolation? Do we know what matters?

With Chekhov, as with all good dramatists, the clustering of the impressions does its own work. The playgoer likes to know what the writer is 'saying', but drama is the literary form least likely to tell him directly. There can be no final asking what the experience *is*: one can only see the piece played over again. Wagner asserted that when you create, you do not explain;[5] Henry James went a step further and suggested that a work of art one has to explain fails of its mission.[6] As a poet thinks with words, so a playwright weaves his fabric by thinking directly in terms of the materials he manipulates.

Stanislavsky demanded of serious drama what he called 'perspective', a distinctive path through the play. It is

> the calculated, harmonious inter-relationship and distribution of the parts in a play or role.
>
> This means further that there can be no acting, no movement, no gestures, thoughts, speech, no word, feeling, etc., etc., without its appropriate perspective. The simplest entrance or exit on the stage, any action taken to carry out a scene, to pronounce a phrase, words, soliloquy and so on, must have a perspective and an ultimate purpose.... Without those an actor may not so much as say 'yes' or 'no'.[7]

If we assert that it is not enough for a playwright to explode a loose series of brilliant fireworks, but that they must set each other off in a chain reaction, then we must agree that one damp squib can extinguish the whole display.

A case of this kind arises in the presentation of Mr Denis

The Meaning of the Play as a Whole

Johnston's *The Moon in the Yellow River*. This is a courageous but unsatisfactory play because one extraneous impression, that of the girl Blanaid, pulls against its general tenor. The author waggishly calls the play 'a quiet little exercise in character-drawing', a dry understatement about a play which depends for its very real and fruitful interest upon the amazing combinations of incongruity among the events, the characters and their attitudes. All are seen through the objective eyes of the German Herr Tausch, part character, part chorus, whose presence at once invites the audience to Gulliver it with him among the Irish, and to some degree throws us into sympathy with those he naturally distrusts, Blake and Lanigan.

But for the most part his bewilderment is ours as intelligence is torn between the whimsically altercating turns of mind and mood represented in the play. The belief in fairies jostles with the trade in pigs. We are made, for example, to balance this discordant mixture in one sparkling speech of Agnes to Willie the gunman:

Military business! Indeed! And what sort of military business gives him the right to come trapesing into my clean living-room with the mud of three counties on his boots, I'd like to know.[8]

This quotation suggests the dappled background made up of Aunt Columba's relevantly irrelevant love affair, of Captain Potts who in grief drank too much to carry his deceased wife's flowers to the cemetery, of a grotesque interest in ballistics and the making of a cannon, a quirk which suddenly assumes an earnest importance, and, with special force, of the birth of Mrs Mulpeter's baby. Against this background we entertain the arguments of a philosophy which reads 'If you don't like the Government you deny its existence'. Thus far the wit is effective because the interweaving in the structure is finely executed. Immersed in fantasies close enough to life for the needs of conviction, we willingly fantasticate upon the theme of the lawlessness of the law and the lawfulness of the lawless

The Elements of Drama

which runs through the play until it explodes, literally, in the climax of the third act.

But the author does not settle how we are to admit into his scheme the pathetic, lonely character of Blanaid. The cool satire excludes the realistic portrayal of Blanaid's troubles to the point where her mere entrance is mawkish, if only because we exercise the critical faculty so feverishly upon the incongruities of the rest of the action. In the play's extraordinary cacophony her symbolic isolation has no place that is emotionally congruous. Mrs Mulpeter's baby fits: this birth tallies with the birth of an Irish national policy which, one takes it, is the core of the discussion. Blanaid annexes our attention at the end with a disproportionately personal problem and a facile solution that rocks the fine equilibrium of the rest.

The first, perhaps the last, step towards understanding the meaning of a play as a whole is to sense where its weight and balance is felt. Dr I. A. Richards offered a strong hint when discussing in *Practical Criticism* how an author's intention manifests itself. He suggested there were plenty of cases especially in drama, in dramatic lyrics, in fiction which has a dramatic structure, 'where conjecture, or the weight of what is left unsaid, is the writer's weapon'. Meaning may be due 'not to anything the writer has said or to any feelings he has expressed, but merely *to the order and degree of prominence* that he has given to various parts of his composition'.[9] It is a fair comment upon this speculation, that, if we believe a play should demonstrate and not tell, invite experience and not impose belief, then the weight of what is left unsaid is *always* the playwright's weapon. The spectator is incessantly making adjustments of imaginative assessment to the new experience he is undergoing. In plays as different as *Heartbreak House* and *Antony and Cleopatra*, the spectator is incessantly weighing unspoken values.

The excitement in the battle scenes in Shakespeare's *Antony*

The Meaning of the Play as a Whole

and *Cleopatra* is due to a simple alternation made possible by the fluid Elizabethan stage. It is not simply the alternation of Antony's and then of Octavius Caesar's situation, like the editing of a cops-and-robbers sequence in the silent cinema. Impressions of Antony's elation and uncertainty, with interpolated reminders of Caesar's confidence, are arranged to suggest the fortunes of war. The sequence is cinematic in that the *order* of the impressions is doing the work, and the poetry enforces the contrasts. This is not the awkward workmanship that was not so long ago held against the author,[10] but a neat economy in building to a vivid visual and aural crisis. Shakespeare is not only portraying a battle: he is demonstrating a mood.

Fluctuations of strength and weakness, a prelude to fluctuations of success and failure to come, are felt long before the battle begins. Antony's spirits before the battle move between the extremes of,

> Alack our terrene moon is now eclips'd,
> And it portends alone the fall of Antony[11]

and,

> The next time I do fight
> I'll make death love me: for I will contend
> Even with his pestilent scythe.

Our sensation of a pendulum motion grows as the significance of the impending battle is clarified. We respond to the quiet note of the solitary Enobarbus: 'I will seek / Some way to leave him', and this calm impression of controlled disaffection is followed promptly by Caesar in a rage, the single figure replaced by an 'army': 'He calls me boy...!' With such an agitated image of disquiet strongly in mind, we hear the 'music i' th' air' and 'under the earth' with more misgiving than the soldiers, because we have been prepared emotionally for the tense pause of this episode.

The battle scenes lead us buffeted to the moment when

The Elements of Drama

Antony's lieutenant Scarus confirms our experience. The oscillating of the words in his brief breathless statement makes the image precise:

> Antony
> Is valiant, and dejected, and by starts
> His fretted fortunes give him hope and fear
> Of what he has, and has not.

A forlorn Antony enters with the decisive monosyllables of his conclusive 'All is lost...'. Neither Scarus's nor Antony's words have dramatic validity outside this finely calculated context. The battle scenes induce a crescendo of feeling which rises to meet the death of the hero. These scenes, part only of a larger pattern, suggest how the spectator responds to the swaying action to experience their meaning.

The ebb and flow of the battle scenes reflect in little the ebb and flow by which the whole play advances. The play swings between Rome and Egypt, between cold politics and warm human relationships. Even the little tragedies of Octavia and Enobarbus reflect on Antony's problem. We swing between the responsible comments of Demetrius, Philo, Caesar, and the irresponsible comments of Charmian, Iras, Alexas, between policy and the female principle, between the soldier and the sensualist in Antony, between the queen and the sensualist in Cleopatra. It is hardly possible to exhaust the catalogue of the discords by which the dilemma of the play expresses itself. The fluctuation of idea works itself out on the sensibility of the audience, until the death of Cleopatra itself unties the 'knot intrinsicate'. But it leaves the audience with a powerful, subtle and complex first-hand insight into some of the ambiguities of life.

The play which does not fully dramatize its subject is the play which does not speak through the ordering of its impressions and the imaginative activity of the spectator. Many plays found to be unsatisfactory stress, and are liable to overstress,

The Meaning of the Play as a Whole

their point by direct exposition, since even a very strong verbal statement in a play will not determine its effect. There are lapses of this kind in the more unambiguous moralities of Mr J. B. Priestley and Ernst Toller. One distrusts the play that hammers its theme before it evinces it.

A final example of a play which has suffered from contradictory judgments because, it seems to me, audiences isolate one impression and then use it as a stick to beat the dramatist: this play is M. Anouilh's *Eurydice*, known in English as *Point of Departure*. Some are not disposed to recognize this play as an oblique statement of which the symbolic figure of death, M. Henri, forms one element. Unaccountably they look upon this figure as the author's mouthpiece. Ignoring, as it seems, the structure of the play, critics have dwelt at length upon its pursuit of a 'cult of death'. Interpreting the play as an essay in the realistic manner, they have complained of its 'lack of vitality'. As in any play which makes itself felt by the order in which it presents its impressions, meaning is elusive.

The play is an animated pattern of satirical and tragic ironies. Act I orients the map of the play preparatory to our moving over M. Anouilh's territory. This act criticizes the apparent inevitability of pretence about life as one grows older. The antithesis between age and youth and between experience and innocence is quickly proposed in two vivid sequences, one establishing Orpheus in his situation, the other establishing Eurydice in hers.

To encourage his son Orpheus to throw off his melancholy, the Father offers him 'love': 'What about love? Did it ever occur to you there is such a thing as love?'[12] But while he says this both we and Orpheus reduce his suggestion to that of a mere physical stimulation. This the author compels us to do because as the Father utters the words he belches over the rabbit he is eating and makes an obscene grimace at the plump Cashier of the station buffet. This degradation of the man in the presence of an aloof Orpheus forcibly initiates the irony to be developed.

The next sequence suggests its refinement and elaboration. We pass to the female attitude to the same subject and receive a corroboration through Eurydice. Her Mother is an actress on the stage and in life: 'In feather boa and plumed hat, [she] makes a triumphal entry. Ever since 1920 she has never stopped growing younger.' She also encourages a base course of action to her daughter by intimations of her own experience: 'I could have got myself kept by anyone I wanted....' At the same time she is reprimanding Eurydice for neglecting a lover, Matthew. The Mother largely resembles, but is a more complex character than, the Father because she is torn between the teachings of her own ugly experience: exploit your sex, accept a lover when you can, but keep up appearances till the last. And as she chatters on to an indifferent Eurydice, she intersperses her thoughts with talk of immediate and material vulgarities: of the tour, the waiting-room, of peppermint, of fly dirt in the sugar. Nor is this Eurydice quite like the Orpheus who protests: her innocence was lost to Matthew—and others, as we learn. Within a few minutes of the rise of the curtain, the parallelism of the Father and the Mother urges a likeness between the son and the daughter. But is it Eurydice's greater experience that makes her different from him? Are we to lend her our sympathy as readily as we lent it to Orpheus? How far is she worthy of blame? These questions in the mind of the audience indicate immediately that the play is not simply about the physical degradation of age and the loss of innocence.

The Mother is joined by her ageing lover Vincent, an actor from the repertory company. He is a man whom M. Anouilh paints colourfully by granting him the superb clichés of the theatrical world. But the stage direction suggests that his eyes are 'without expression': his sensibility is dulled by a life of

The Meaning of the Play as a Whole

imitation. It is this man who chooses to reminisce romantically with the Mother about their first meeting in the Grand Casino at Ostend. While they speak, we begin to loathe them from the details of the sordid meeting. To the sentimental tune of Orpheus's violin, they talk of the sensations of first love:

VINCENT. Oh, that first uncertain, disturbing day! You explore, you sense, you guess, you don't know each other yet, but already you feel sure it will last your whole life long.

While these sentiments are heard, degraded by the pathetically ridiculous picture presented, Eurydice is seen looking for Orpheus, and then, as if moving to the rhythm of these words, approaches him. They stand motionless face to face: this too is first love, and we are suddenly aware that Vincent's words, like the commentary of a chorus, may apply to them too. Does the shadow of his repulsive suggestions fall upon Orpheus and Eurydice; do the contaminated infect the pure? But when Orpheus and Eurydice speak, the gentle simplicity of their words, and the physical presence of youth, strongly felt on the stage, contrasts with the flamboyant bombast of Vincent, and their comparative innocence reasserts itself.

In the struggle of sensations for precedence, the tension in the theme comes alive, and it is not allowed to flag. A repeated call to Eurydice disturbs their intimacy before it can become too sure: 'GIRL. Don't forget Matthew!' and we are reminded of our doubt about her. Even in the beginning is felt the hostile presence of the past.

The forces the author is employing spin together in a sharp juxtaposition. Hints of the pressure of the past still strong in the present, queries as to the source of guilt, doubt about the inevitability of corruption, compelling suggestions that the great issues of life are treated only as play-acting, all converge upon this scene. All are set in the atmosphere of the sordid buffet and accompanied by the echoes of the nostalgic violin.

The Elements of Drama

Having thus prepared his ground, M. Anouilh can make his first dramatic statement, working fully within his medium.

> EURYDICE. A nice fix we're in, standing here face to face, the pair of us, with everything that's going to happen to us all lined up already behind us....
> ORPHEUS. You think a lot of things will happen to us?
> EURYDICE, *gravely*. Absolutely everything. All the things that happen to a man and a woman on earth, one by one.
> ORPHEUS. The amusing, the gentle, the dreadful things?
> EURYDICE. The shameful and the sordid ones, too. We are going to be very unhappy.
> ORPHEUS, *taking her in his arms*. What bliss!
> *Vincent and the Mother, who have been dreaming with their heads close together, begin to speak gently.*
> VINCENT. Oh, love, love! You see, my sweet, on this earth where everything crushes us, where all things deceive and hurt, what a wonderful comfort to think there still remains to us—love....
> MOTHER. My great big pussy-cat....
> VINCENT. Men are liars, Lucienne. Hypocrites, fickle, false...babblers, bombastic and base, vile or filled with lust; the women—inquisitive, treacherous, artificial, vain or depraved. The world is an unplumbed cess-pool, its formless, crawling creatures wriggling over mountains of filth. But in this world there is one thing holy, sublime—two beings, loathsome, imperfect, merging into one.
> MOTHER. Yes darling, that's from *Perdican*.
> VINCENT. Is it really? I've played the part so often.
> . . . .
> *Orpheus and Eurydice have been listening, holding on to one another in horror.*
> EURYDICE, *whispering*. Make them stop, please. Do make them stop.

What, first, do we take from the exchange between the young lovers? We hear the deliberate simplicity with which they in their innocence or ignorance comment on their own future. M. Anouilh keeps his actors still and statuesque, using the stylized manner of the play to force upon the attention Eurydice's obtrusive remark about fate. They stand there 'with everything that's going to happen to us all lined up already behind us'. Nothing has yet justified a pronouncement like

The Meaning of the Play as a Whole

this, but it is as if the author has now decided that the visual and aural juxtaposition of the old and the young shall be given limited definition. Eurydice momentarily ceases to be a character in the story and speaks impersonally. She has not the experience of the Father or of the Mother and Vincent, but the author has given his puppet a perceptive moment of wisdom in the instinct of a woman. Quiet and grave, Eurydice, in the one almost restful moment, offers her new lover a future of mixed blessings. She speaks in words so simple in style as to be ambiguous, and they invite us to fill them out with the stuff of the impressions we have been storing against such an opportunity as this. As they stand grouped with their *backs* to the older characters, Eurydice's words point decisively to the Mother and Vincent.

This moment of rest from the urgencies of irony is shattered immediately as we hear Eurydice understate the kind of nightmare they are calling upon themselves by accepting each other. But we are not allowed to forget that Eurydice is the agent, and that Orpheus is the patient. She offers, he accepts. She is aware of the meaning of experience, he is aware only of their innocence. 'ORPHEUS, *taking her in his arms*. What bliss!' Because of this, the difference between them is stressed again. It is again Orpheus's story as much as Eurydice's. From this moment he does much more than accept unhappiness. His desire to engage his spirit sets in motion what is 'all lined up already behind' them, as the Chorus in the same author's *Antigone* described in overt terms a year later: 'The spring is wound up tight. It will uncoil of itself.'[13] This echoes the Prologue to M. Jean Cocteau's *The Infernal Machine* which defined this kind of tragic inevitability more closely:

Spectator, this machine you see here wound up to the full, in such a way that the spring will slowly unwind the whole length of a human life, is one of the most perfect constructed by the infernal gods for the mathematical destruction of a mortal.[14]

The Elements of Drama

Both M. Cocteau in *The Infernal Machine* and M. Anouilh in *Antigone* use the 'fate' of Greek myth arbitrarily, and without the weight of theistic reference found in classical tragedy. It can become a cliché if all that is gained is a merely sensational tension towards the last act. In *Eurydice* the theme, essentially concerned with the pressures of the past and the future on the present, sufficiently justifies the play's use of myth as a theatrical device.

Upon this declaration by the young lovers, his action becomes more acid, more hysterical in its incongruity. The divided stage of the station buffet permits attention to pass again to Vincent and the Mother. Their next exchange is not a repetition of what has gone before. The new comparison between young and old is sharper because our view of Orpheus and Eurydice has been modified and clarified. The cruellest stroke is to have Vincent reiterating in his own terms Eurydice's own sentiments. Another double irony.

'Men are liars, Lucienne. Hypocrites, fickle, false....' Is the nobility Eurydice and Orpheus acquired by accepting the human condition enhanced, or is it ridiculed? We are not to be sure, and because of this kind of uncertainty, can an accusation of sentimentality apply to this play? The sentimental play gives comfort, eases pain, settles notions, indulging a romantic impulse to accept or reject life; the unaffected play keeps us alert, uneasy, making us question and probe our motives. There is a world of difference between M. Anouilh and Barrie, in spite of the dash of vinegar in *Mary Rose* and *Dear Brutus*. Vincent is hardly conscious whether he is on stage or off stage. His words, calculated in style for a theatrical effect, reflect upon himself: he calls himself 'hypocrite' without meaning it, a gesture of rhetoric which contrasts with Orpheus's honesty. Yet because Eurydice implied his substance in what she said, she invites us to accept his statement as truth. What are we to believe? That, in one sense, truth is lost to the experienced because its real implications have become obscured in self-

The Meaning of the Play as a Whole

deceit. That, in another, the truth to the young and innocent becomes obscured in a haze, a haze due to their romantic lack of concern with their environment. But the truth emerges for us because we stand between the two extremes: we judge the old and the young equally. The image becomes startlingly clear when the love the young people thought would overcome the degradations promised for the future is given expression by the hypocrite: 'But in this world there is one thing holy, sublime—two beings, loathsome, imperfect, merging into one.' When the Mother indulgently reminds him that he is quoting de Musset, and when Vincent flattens his exalted tone for the shock of the anticlimax: 'Is it really? I've played the part so often', any sense of his sincerity is effectively killed. We withdraw to criticize again.

The author achieves an effect of fine theatre during this passage. Our ears attend to the Mother and Vincent, but our eyes are taken by Orpheus and Eurydice. As we hear Vincent damn himself, as any suggestion of purity in the relationship between the sexes is relentlessly smeared by the character of his liaison with the Mother, we are painfully conscious that the young lovers are listening, and that all that is said colours their own possible future. Will they be able to accept 'All the things that happen to a man and a woman on earth, one by one?' As they cling to each other in horror, we question their strength because it is evident that they do themselves. Equally revolted, we anticipate Eurydice when she says, 'Make them stop, please. Do make them stop.' Orpheus and Eurydice have to find a different way.

From this beginning, the course of the play becomes plainer. Briefly, Orpheus and Eurydice in their intimacies make it clear that the view of impurity they have will not deter them. But from now on events are arranged to test their resistance, especially that of Orpheus. He survives the knowledge of her former lovers. They survive the suicide of Matthew. They

The Elements of Drama

survive the gentle threats of the death figure, M. Henri. In his words, they are 'Ready to play the game without cheating, right to the end'. We, however, have other suspicions. With M. Henri we are omniscient. We would be beyond shocks, but suddenly at the fall of the first curtain their position becomes frighteningly critical:

ORPHEUS. Now the story is beginning...
EURYDICE. I am feeling a little afraid...Are you good? Are you bad? What is your name?
ORPHEUS. Orpheus. And yours?
EURYDICE. Eurydice.
Curtain.

For one act we forget that these two in unassuming modern dress have a story to tell that is determined and inexorable. We are gently reminded.

In the rest of the play the attack upon sentimental affectation is maintained. Orpheus's doubts about his mistress grow. Eurydice tries to face and control experience by reconstructing its ugliness: 'Just suppose you have seen a whole lot of ugly things in your life, do they all remain with you?',[15] but through fear she prevaricates. Orpheus insists that the 'ugly things' must remain unless there is 'confession', but she cannot confess since she already doubts his power to resist the truth. Her anxiety is increased by the Waiter in the dirty provincial hotel where they are spending the night:

The people I've seen in this room, lying on that bed, as you were just now! And not all beauties, either. Some too fat, some too skinny, some hideous, but all of them slobbering about 'our love'. Sometimes, on an evening like this, I seem to see the whole lot of them together. It's crawling with them. Ah, there's nothing nice about love.

The plot moves on until Eurydice is killed by accident. Dulac, the manager of the repertory company, horrifies Orpheus by telling him of his own former relations with her. When M. Henri presents Orpheus with another chance to have his

The Meaning of the Play as a Whole

Eurydice, it is inevitable in every sense that he should kill her finally. He cries,

> To live, to live! Like your mother and her lover, maybe, with their cooing and their simpering and self-indulgence; then the fine meals, and afterwards they make love and everything is all right. Oh no. I love you too much to live.[16]

Is the audience to assume that his 'killing' her and his own eventual suicide, this submission to death, is advocated as the easy and the only way out? If the death of Eurydice and Orpheus's suicide are seen as realistic, it might be possible to assume that death is M. Anouilh's answer to the problem of evil. But in the nature of the myth and its manner of presentation, how can they be realistic? The intricate preparation of Acts I and II, the protracted struggles of Eurydice in Act III and of Orpheus in Act IV, convey their belief in an ideal, in a way of life which is real and worth suffering and dying for. Their symbolic deaths are but to emphasize their determination to make the tragic sacrifice to preserve this inviolate. A fictitious impression of the impossibility of purity in human relations is a real statement of the desirability of it. That M. Anouilh is concerned to present us with a sympathetic Orpheus and Eurydice in spite of their errors of behaviour and judgment seems to me a proof that the author's meaning is a challenging and a positive one.

It might be argued that the older generation in the play have the dice loaded against them too heavily. But it is not their presence that decides the result of the game. They are the dark background against which the painter sets his bright angels. Dr Ivor Brown put the extreme view at the time of the London production:

> His play does, indeed, contain the lusty figure of Orpheus's father: he is another wandering minstrel, shabby and squalid, but he has Dickensian vitality and the 'guts' to go on living and laughing and enjoying his meals. and he is held up to us as a bad example because of his vitality! Could any

doctrine be more pusillanimous than that of M. Anouilh, who seems to share with the philosopher Novalis the notion that man's only salvation lies in universal suicide.[17]

Does not the use of the word 'doctrine' suggest a failure to recognize the processes by which we arrive at the composite meaning of a play? Does this see the Father as a piece in the pattern?—it refuses to accept the Father's 'vitality' at the valuation of the author of the character. The vitality is sham, and the Father and Vincent are two of a kind, though Vincent is not selected as an example. Has the play been allowed to slip into and establish its twilight fantasy?—this review looks for Ibsen's depth of characterization, when these characters are designed to be representative puppets as in Greek drama. M. Anouilh's own answer to this kind of criticism was made in an interview with the press in one of his few public pronouncements:

In 1936 I discovered that a subject did not necessarily have to be treated in a rigid form, in the natural simplicity or even crudity it has at first. I realized that the dramatist could and should *play with* his characters, with their passions and their actions. *Le Voyageur sans bagage* was the first of my works in which I 'played' in this way.... To 'play' with a subject is to create a new world of conventions and surround it with spells and a magic all your own.[18]

The playgoer must go about understanding a play within the terms by which it invites that understanding. The magic world of *Eurydice* is fabricated by style and statement, myth and symbol. Within it, it states its first premise that pretence grows proportionately with age and experience; the second premise states that the past is irredeemable and the future inevitable; from this syllogism, Orpheus and Eurydice infer that death is the sole purification. The whole pattern is an invention to move us to an imaginative perception. Hero and heroine suggest a recognizable and human ideal, the rest corruption; this being so, we are asked to accept what the play insists, that the two are incompatible. We are asked to build

The Meaning of the Play as a Whole

the total experience with the dramatist's materials, not our own.

The play asks us to do these things, but the ordinary playgoer, who enjoys a good meal, pays his income-tax with reluctance, and does not think too hard about sin and salvation, is likely to regard *Eurydice*, and plays like it, as a blasphemy against nature. He may refuse to go into what seems to be M. Anouilh's never-never-land of pessimism. Yet the first problem is how to put this refusal into effect. For it is possible to detest M. Anouilh's kind of drama, and yet find oneself moved by it in the theatre. The dramatist has every right to express his point of view (and must have if drama is to survive), provided he does not corrupt us. He owes established attitudes no moral allegiance, though this does not necessarily mean he is amoral. Nor is M. Anouilh likely to corrupt us; he is as severe a moralist, as fanatical in his own way as the optimist who wrote *The Tempest*. 'Pessimistic', any more than 'optimistic', should not be a critical pejorative.

The real question is whether, when we are moved in the theatre, we feel that the artist has been oversimplifying the issues raised. We can only ask whether the play's emotionality is justified by the situation as presented and is appropriate to the stimulus, whether that situation is sufficiently defined and concrete or whether it suppresses any experience essential to the true completion of the picture. In *Eurydice*, in effect, only ideal happiness is suppressed—because the nature of this happiness is the subject under discussion. We the audience are invited to supply what is missing. We suffer the emotions that M. Anouilh's symbolic creatures of fantasy have temporarily forced upon us, hate them as we may. The theatre demands that for the moment we submit to the imaginative world of the play, and the author rightly does all he can to ensure that the meaning of the play as a whole shall at least be received by us before we rub him out, if we will.

PART III
VALUES

11

AUDIENCE PARTICIPATION

A play is to be judged by its value to those who watch it. Not only the experience, but also the degree to which we re-create it is the measure of its worth. 'Audience participation' is a loose and difficult concept, and it needs first to be defined, and then to be seen as it is affected by the kind of play presented. For it is not another branch of stage technique: it is a force in the nature of drama.

Perhaps because of some interesting experiments conducted in this century to 'reclaim' the intimacy of the spectator with the actor, we tend today to think of audience participation as contingent upon the shape of the theatre building, or upon the actor's manner of address. The early and later work in Moscow of experimental producers like Vakhtangov and Meyerhold, of which a great deal has been written with enthusiasm,[1] has its place. But productions arranged so that we do not forget we are in a theatre, do not for that reason touch the nervous core of drama. On the contrary, actors who are not allowed to get under the skin of their parts, who mix with their audience, who use the auditorium as an acting area indiscriminately, have a strictly limited usefulness. These methods are more likely to exclude the spectator than to involve him, more likely to make him aware of the mechanics of the theatre at the expense of the theatre's own emotional persuasiveness.

How far are more recent experiments in Germany more solidly based? Bertolt Brecht's theory of 'alienation' or 'estrangement' is, as he explained it in a post-war statement, 'to induce an enquiring, critical attitude on the part of the spectators towards the events shown'.[2]

The Elements of Drama

The stage and the auditorium must be cleared of all 'magic' elements, and no 'hypnotic fields' are to be set up by atmospheric settings. The actor should openly play to the audience and not identify himself completely with the character he represents. He should no longer speak his text 'like an improvisation, but like a quotation', playing the incidents 'as historical events'. Brecht then suggested what effect this procedure would have upon an audience. Since the actor, he said,

> does not identify himself with the person he represents, he can choose a particular point of view regarding him, reveal his own opinion of him, and even invite the spectator (who also was not asked to identify himself with the character) to criticize the person represented.... A critical attitude on the part of the spectator is a thoroughly artistic attitude.

This is not the place to examine the Epic Theatre, but simply to point out that a critical attitude on the part of the spectator has always been possible to achieve through the traditional methods of selection and arrangement from Aristophanes to Pirandello; comedy has always made the stage a laboratory. But these methods do not in addition deny the spectator, as Brecht's theory does, the freedom to re-create emotional subtleties of imagination as he would expect to do less actively in the normal intercourse of life.

A more plausible case can be made for the fuller use of the auditorium, such as we have seen in recent years in productions of *Murder in the Cathedral*, *Cockpit* and *A Sleep of Prisoners*. This seems profitable in *Murder in the Cathedral*, where church ritual, in itself a near-dramatic form, is used as a medium of expression for the ideas and emotions of the play itself. The church makes a natural theatre, with its congregation in the nave like the audience in the auditorium, its priest and choir the actor and chorus. Its fixed setting and décor supplies an almost non-representational background which frees the play from realistic limitations. As a congregation we celebrate Thomas à Becket's martyrdom; as an audience we

Audience Participation

identify ourselves with the Women of Canterbury and their emotions. In our first capacity as audience, we are captured by the movement of the Chorus through the nave, and by the approach of the Knights to the chancel steps from behind us, as we have seen, without relinquishing the advantages of our second capacity as congregation. But such a play must be an exception. In Miss Dorothy Sayers's *The Zeal of Thy House*, where monks file in and file out and pilgrims come to gape, or in *A Sleep of Prisoners*, where the chancel is freely used as Adam's jungle, the pulpit as Abraham's mountain or as Absalom's tree, a looser use of the church setting has so dispensed with the church as church that the imagination must be tricked into action by other means, means traditional to drama.

The use of theatre-in-the-round, where scenery must be supplied by suggestion and where the audience is drawn into the circle of the action, makes for exciting theatre. But there are two elements in this kind of playing that should be separated: participation and intimacy. Participation does not necessarily need an absence of scenery or a performance in an arena. Intimacy does not necessarily imply participation, though it may help it. The intimacy of theatre-in-the-round is not unlike that of the Elizabethan playhouse, or indeed of any kind of theatre where the stage and the auditorium are close enough. The force of the aside, the soliloquy and varieties of indirect address to the audience, which we associate with this theatre, lies more in its invitation to participate than in its special intimacy. But a great deal of Elizabethan speech is effective for embracing both. Thus,

> ROMEO. What lady's that which doth enrich the hand
>   Of yonder knight?
> SERVANT. I know not, sir.
> ROMEO. O she doth teach the torches to burn bright:
>   It seems she hangs upon the cheek of night,

The Elements of Drama

> As a rich jewel in an Ethiop's ear:
> Beauty too rich for use, for earth too dear:
> So shows a snowy dove trooping with crows,
> As yonder lady o'er her fellows shows.[3]

Here Romeo, almost certainly downstage on the platform in the centre of the auditorium, is looking upstage towards the boy Juliet dancing. He is looking where the spectator in the Elizabethan theatre is looking, and he is speaking into his ear. In this intimate position, and with these illustrative and decorative words, Romeo not only suggests warmly that he has fallen in love, he also supplies in the most suitable language Shakespeare could devise a verbal commentary to make the boy actor seem a rare and beautiful girl. Shakespeare takes advantage of his theatre and has her pointed out visually and adorned verbally. Shakespeare assumes that the Elizabethan audience will not be passing its time examining the back of Romeo's costume, or straining to see his features. The spectator accepts the presence of Romeo near him, so that the words he speaks may direct the spectator's eyes. His eyes follow the movements of Juliet in the dance. His mind, meanwhile, would be constructing a basic impression of Juliet's brilliance which is to suffer the bombardment by a thousand other impressions through the play. Only this activity can properly be thought of as *participation*.

But so much more depends on the writing than on the technical requirements of the stage or the physical circumstances of the audience that to think of participation in terms of things external to the drama itself can only distract. A play maps out its own country. One method of drawing a response from us is to make its people and its laws as like our own as possible. Even if the play introduces us to strangers who talk as we shall never hear people talk in life, they will be consistent within their own boundaries. Both types of play are working by a common and fundamental assumption, that it is indispens-

Audience Participation

able to have a measure of departure from, yet a likeness to, a real standard of behaviour that we, the contemporary audience, set. There can never be a complete departure from it, nor a complete likeness. The conclusion is rightly drawn that there is no essential difference between an artificial and a realistic play. In both types the audience is continuously busy, whether consciously or not, making personal comparisons with what it sees and hears on the stage. The social basis of comedy or the moral basis of tragedy is founded on such comparisons.

Now the invitation to the audience to make all such comparisons is an invitation to bridge a gap, not the physical gap between audience and actor, but the dramatic gap between audience and character. To span it requires all the most delicate judgment of the writer, for it is the theatre's most fragile instrument.

Every dramatist knowingly or unknowingly proceeds from Dr Johnson's cardinal tenets, 'that the spectators are always in their senses', but that 'delusion, if delusion be admitted, has no certain limitation',[4] and from Coleridge's subtler suggestion that 'the true stage-illusion in this and in all other things consists—not in the mind's judging it to be a forest, but in its remission of the judgment that it is not a forest'.[5] It is debatable whether the spectator is always in his senses, that he is always conscious of the form of his experience: consciousness in the theatre I do not take to be absolute. There can be persuasive moments of strong emotion and interest when the audience is so in sympathy with a character, or following his reasoning so intently, that there is no theatrical gap. But for the most part we do not suffer complete emotional identification with, for example, Shakespeare's tragic heroes. Most of the time the author is working to narrow or widen the gap as the play demands. If delusion be admitted, it consists in the spectator's readiness to make a bridge by his imaginative co-operation and to submit to the persuasion of the suggestions showering across the footlights. The good dramatist may be able to stretch it so wide that we give a roar of laughter or a cry of horror and protest.

So the good play must first be one to which an audience thus makes a positive response, irrespective of the dramatic genre. The play which captures us, whether at the level of full-blooded emotional melodrama or in the intellectual way of Shaw's *Getting Married*, is at least capable of further valuation. But how is it we fail or refuse to respond and participate? We look in two apparently different directions for the solution, towards the two ends of the line of communication: the stage action and the audience reaction. Either or both can be at fault, but in practice they are not distinguishable. For the thoughts and feelings of the audience with all its particular limitations are not only the target for the play, but also the materials from which the author has to fashion his drama. Mr Somerset Maugham has said that 'the nature of the audience is for the dramatist the most important convention within which he must work'.[6] To whatever extent the spectator is limited, to that extent the drama will be limited. The dramatist will always be asking himself how far imaginatively, emotionally or intellectually he can take him, and to what depth he dare explore. Audience participation is a problem envisaged in the play's inception.

How does a dramatist envisage his audience? Perhaps only as the body of people who previously made a play a success. Some undoubtedly write down to their audience when they rely on safe but threadbare materials and methods. But what can the sincere artist who desires a fresh expression *assume*? He is torn in countless ways between the dramatic need for a sure response and his quest for an original expression. Thus one set of problems may turn on how far the play is to be set in a particularized locality and using particularized symbols,

Audience Participation

like the Irish of Synge's *In the Shadow of the Glen* or of Yeats's *The Land of Heart's Desire*. Can these be sure of representing universal values to, say, an English audience who may narrow them by identifying them only with their source?

How far must the dramatist clarify the issue in a 'problem' play? Many plays, especially since the war, have chosen to debate a topic still fresh in the mind of the audience, topics from wartime evacuation to homosexuality. With these, topicality has ensured success, as well as some easy solutions. But what special work of exposition is wanted in a play fighting acknowledged opposition? In the case of *A Doll's House*, almost the whole play had to be given over to the preparation of the point of argument, which Ibsen expertly arranged to coincide with the climax of the play. The incompletely dramatized Freudian symbolism in *The Ascent of F6* spoils the play for the audience it might well have captured. The dramatist may not assume a body of knowledge, especially if it is central to the play, unless that knowledge itself is translated into dramatic terms.

Again, the sensitivity of an audience to psychological truth may do battle with the aims of the dramatist. If he draws a melodramatic villain for an audience familiar with stage villains, perhaps he can trust them to boo to order. But supposing he wishes to break with a decaying tradition and suggest a subtler, a sympathetic villain, like Willie Loman in Mr Arthur Miller's *Death of a Salesman*? Is the character certain of acceptance? From another point of view, a black and white depiction of the bad and the good is today suspect, and has made many well-constructed melodramas of the last century, like Zola's *Thérèse Raquin*, fit for salvage only as burlesques. And audiences are prepared to make only meagre concessions to the unfounded sentiment in plays like Pinero's *The Second Mrs Tanqueray* and Barrie's *Mary Rose* where an unreal psychology is called upon to establish the validity of the

The Elements of Drama

play. More recently, Mr Graham Greene's *The Living Room* was a play which repelled some for religious reasons, but many more for an unequal psychology which unhappily sapped its strength and betrayed it as insufficiently realized.

Obstacles in a play's 'style' and convention may destroy its effect. *The Way of the World* presents difficulties because the intrigues of its plot are beyond deciphering in performance, but, for all its graces of wit and phrasing, the radiance of Millamant and those scenes which, in their acutely representative quality, stand on their own, the level of its fantasy does not seem remote enough to encourage that detached attitude to sexual matters which is necessary for full appreciation. *Major Barbara*, in spite of its masterly argument, does not persuade us to the unwelcome conclusion of the last act, and we resist Barbara's conversion to the extent of questioning the play's foundations; overshadowed by Undershaft and Cusins, perhaps she so loses emphasis that the change seems too quick. But the real trouble is deeper: it is a failure in Shaw the artist that he has led us to ask for Ibsen's depth of character in a play which leans structurally towards extravaganza. In Mr J. B. Priestley's *They Came to a City*, a non-realistic structure becomes uncomfortably prominent when clothed in realistic speech and behaviour. Two opposed standards of judgment thwart each other, and as a result the play seems to shout its theme too loudly and deter our participation.

One misjudgment of the audience's imaginative licence, in fact, can damage the strongest dramatic statement. *The Firstborn* urgently involves the spectator by making him question personal suffering in contemporary terms; but the curt expression of hope which Mr Fry seems to provide as a loose afterthought to the play's main idea must fail to satisfy him imaginatively. One element in *Ardèle*, that of physical deformity, an element essential to the projection of its meaning, has repulsed many tolerant playgoers, and consequently

Audience Participation

blunted the impact of the play. But who can say that, in earnest drama of this kind, the deficiency lies with the author and not with the audience? All that is certain is that it is a failure which affects primary dramatic value.

What can be assumed of an audience by a playwright deliberately proposing his play in philosophical terms unfamiliar to it? Existentialist drama of recent years has made this an acute problem of audience participation. M. Jean-Paul Sartre's *Les Mains sales*, played in English as *Crime Passionnel*, a title hardly chosen to guide the playgoer, seems to have succeeded for the wrong reasons. Existentialism has taken well to the theatre in some forms, as it has to the novel, since it is expressly concerned with the quality of the individual. In life, as in existentialist drama, there are no final answers to conduct: we make choices by one standard or another, uncertain of the outcome. For the Sartrian existentialist, however, the conscious choice, taken as a means of asserting his natural freedom and dignity, taken to prove to himself he is not a cabbage, is important *in itself*, and in this he is at variance with his uninitiated audiences. It is in human nature, as the tradition of dramatic practice has confirmed, for the ordinary playgoer to be intensely interested in the external consequences of a decision also. This divergence of theory from practice makes complete participation in a play like *Crime Passionel* a special problem for the author. In so far as its situation grips us—and M. Sartre is skilled in fostering interest and building tension—and in so far as its emotional momentum impels us, we accept the play in the usual way. But there comes the point when the hero must face his destiny in the cold light of Sartrian existentialism, and here forces other than dramatic are brought to bear. As soon as M. Sartre solicits a view of the issue based on a thesis outside our own experience, the play begins to disintegrate. It cannot persuade us over the last, the intellectual, fence. M. Sartre has therefore

The Elements of Drama

to employ special methods to challenge us with *his* interpretation of the action in the face of our own.

In *Crime Passionnel*, Hugo, the existentialist hero, chooses to disprove his cowardice by killing Hoederer, a man he takes to be a party traitor. Carefully drawn as a weakling, Hugo knows that he will only find confidence in himself and be able to relieve his *angst* if he performs this task coolly. It is a play of doubts, hesitations and delays, in which the hero's self-questioning is skilfully dramatized. He is uncertain whether what he is doing is not all a game—an insinuation which recurs through the play in various guises. He discovers, moreover, that not only does he like the man he has to kill, but that this man trusts him, thereby partly weakening his motive for action. Opposed to this is the confirmation in Hugo's mind after a visit of the enemy party that Hoederer is a traitor, and, further, his discovery that Hoederer is making love to his wife Jessica. It becomes clearer that the author is pressing us to attend to the motive for the killing, as in *Hamlet* and *Crime and Punishment*, by drawing attention away from the killing itself.

Hugo finally shoots Hoederer in Jessica's presence. Before he does so, Hugo says to her, 'I'm not angry with you, and I'm not jealous either, we're not in love'.[7] In spite of the fact that his primary motives are selfish, in that he wished to prove his manhood to himself to dispel his despair, it now seems he wishes to rid his deed of all taint of selfish interest. It is not to be a crime of jealousy, neither of Jessica for stealing Hoederer's affection, nor of Hoederer for stealing his wife's. But all that happens is that one selfish motive is substituted for another. Hugo turns on Hoederer:

But he, he very nearly caught me in his trap. 'I'll help you, I'll help you become a man.' What a fool I was! He didn't give a damn for me.

His motive, not jealousy, not politics, comes very close to being one of personal pique. He cries, 'You have set me free!' Does this mean that he is free from personal obligation towards

Audience Participation

the man he undertook to kill for political reasons, or is it merely freedom to act in the interests of self-realization? In thus understandably confining our attention to the motive and not the deed, the author has given us one too many alternatives, and the non-existentialist will not take the one expected. Had the play been written merely at the level of modern political melodrama, we could have accepted this as a political killing, and we might have been satisfied. Is it possible to accept that, all other motives removed, the man we have identified ourselves with has killed for a selfish reason? An innocent spectator might be forgiven for assuming that the claims of common decency must condemn a man consciously responsible for the ultimate crime.

Confusion arises after the killing, when we have ceased to follow the author's argument. Further statements are made which only emphasize the miscarriage of the play's theme. Hoederer in his dying moment tells his bodyguard that it was a *crime passionnel*: 'Don't hurt him, any of you...He was jealous.' Why does he say this? It can be argued that Hoederer feels now that Hugo is a man fit to live; but our feelings remain ambiguous enough for us to apply a non-existentialist interpretation, that, say, Hoederer had begun to look upon Hugo with a paternal sympathy. Again, in the Epilogue we are told that Hoederer's assassination was a mistake, and that, because of a reshuffle of political affiliations, he may even have a statue raised to his memory. Evidently this is to re-emphasize that the mere killing was of no consequence. But it will strike the non-existentialist as a peculiarly bitter dramatic irony. So it happens that Hugo is asked to disown the crime—which might have provided a superbly cerebral anticlimax. Yet, again our experience finds no direction, and we automatically put a Christian valuation upon this outcome: that a man's death is relevant to what it shall do to the soul of the man who kills him. It would be interesting to discover how many playgoers saw Hugo's suicidal final exit as a mark of his acceptance of guilt for his crime, as a sign of fitting remorse, rather than as that of an existentialist openly claiming his 'freedom' and happily accepting his destiny as a man who has found himself.

It is noticeable that M. Sartre indicates that he is unsure of our response, as well he might be, since by a twist of argument which now has little dramatic weight in the total meaning of the play, he gives Hugo these last lines:

A man like Hoederer doesn't die by accident. He dies for his ideals, for his policy, he is responsible for his own death. If I recognize my crime before you all, if I reclaim my name of Raskolnikov, if I agree to pay the necessary price, then he will have the death he deserved.

I would deny that this can mean anything to an audience not already converted to the philosophy. We may have been willing to accept Hoederer's death as a noble one by normal standards, and we may see Hugo's decision to make it a worthy one as giving credit to Hoederer and not to Hugo. Yet the focus of the action to the end is properly on Hugo and his fate. We see him give himself over with an ironical bow to what he knows to be death. The ironical bow could be the gesture of the traditional villain making his surrender to the forces of justice. Does he thereby redeem his existentialist manhood or his Christian soul? After only a light struggle, the audience is likely to choose the latter. There is no harm in M. Sartre's offering unusual circumstances to demonstrate his principles, but they must be fully realized in terms neither sensational nor arbitrary if the play is to avoid being simply melodramatic.

The breakdown occurs when the audience constructs an image other than the one intended. In his anxiety to demolish the obvious reasons for the assassination, M. Sartre neglects to give his audience a positive lead. He trusts it will supply Hugo's state of mind which he defines by the negation of all other recognizable causes for it, and which he hopes to go on

Audience Participation

to expound in the subsequent discussion of the Epilogue. He forgets that the imagination abhors a vacuum, and that not only is human motive, as an audience might apprehend it from its own experience, a diverse and subtle thing, but that he has not, in the play itself, adequately countered the one that would come to an uninitiated audience most readily. The Epilogue cannot in the time allowed bridge the gap the audience has bridged already by making a moral judgment customary to it. Like many dramatists, Aeschylus, Marlowe, Chapman, Goethe, Pirandello, M. Sartre has used a philosophy to justify writing his play, but unlike these writers, his philosophy ceases to *inform* the play when a strain is put upon its validity. A failure in technique is a failure in value; where a distortion of experience cannot be disguised by the skill of the playwright, perhaps a failure in value is also a failure in technique.

Thus a writer must make many finely balanced decisions concerning his audience. He may seek to win sympathy, but he must stop before it becomes sentimentality, else his play may cloy and repel. He may seek to win laughter for serious ends, but not at the expense of making his characters grotesque and his play farcical, else his meaning may be dismissed out of hand. He may seek to interest by satire, but his satire must not become sarcasm, or cynicism. He may hit upon a contemporary problem, relying upon an interest already present, but he will be wise to dramatize the problem in terms of qualities permanent in human nature and behaviour, else it will have no authenticity. He may legitimately employ spectacle and sensation, but with the moderation that will ensure that feelings are not glutted and denied the power of response to the theme these effects serve. The dramatist has no wish to make us laugh until we cry, or cry until we laugh. Such problems as these are familiar, and common to all the arts.

They all raise questions of the appropriateness of the

impressions. The better writer does not let his effects run loose: he retains control. We are familiar with the release of the audience by emotional anticlimax or 'comic relief' before the next strain is to be felt, in order that we surrender to it the more energetically. Diversionary tactics of delay and digression are used to increase the tension preceding a crisis: we think of the distracting stabbing of Roderigo during the time that Othello goes to Desdemona's chamber, and of Edgar's painfully limping confession while we wait news of Lear and Cordelia imprisoned. And the strong curtain is, after all, only the projection of an impression strong enough to carry us over to the next scene. There is a great variety of such tricks of control. But there are no rules where a writer's talent in one direction overrides his play's deficiencies in another. The lavishly overcrowded scene of comedies as different as *Bartholomew Fayre* and *Under Milk Wood* impresses its sense of life by sheer weight of numbers, though there is a hidden arrangement of character and vocal contrasts in the latter which obliquely stresses Llaregyb's 'variety in identity'. And we forgive excesses of speech when fresh and vivid, whether in an early Shakespeare like *Love's Labour's Lost* or in a later O'Casey like *Red Roses for Me*.

Many of the expressionist dramas of the 1920's are open to charges of poverty of image control. It is because these plays largely refuse to present particularized people, with the kind of specific interest these can claim, that what their audience will accept is less calculable than usual, and more liable to be arbitrary. This may account for the distemper in a striking theatrical movement and the subsequent deflection of its technical achievements into other, hardier channels. Dr Ivor Brown said these plays executed a mass attack on the emotional system;[8] full participation may have been the intention: it was rarely the result. Georg Simmel provides a clue to the source of failure when he says in definition of

Audience Participation

expressionism that it attempts to seize life in its essence, but without its content.[9] In the act of abstracting representational properties from a social situation, other no less important properties of conviction and connection may disappear. The character which becomes an impersonal label for a state of feeling, like Zero in *The Adding Machine*, may become so impersonal it is denied sufficient life to evoke that state of feeling. Shakespeare used characters as symbols, but he did not rely on a thin, flat speech to fatten his outline. And language that eschews conversation without achieving a poetic quality may be devoid of the feeling necessary to carry a serious theme. The shock-tactics and staccato scene construction tend to prohibit the persuasive continuity of thought and feeling the 'well-made play' legitimately depended upon. The attempt to make a fuller use of the stage is to be praised; its lack of success in creating a new non-realistic form is to be regretted.

Eugene O'Neill's play *The Hairy Ape* serves as an impressive example. The author declared the play to be 'a symbol of man, who has lost his old harmony with nature, the harmony he used to have as an animal and has not yet acquired in a spiritual way'.[10] That is a fair statement of intention; but as a theatrical experience the play cannot strictly be said to 'mean' anything. Yank is intentionally a sketch of a character. In that he rises to a state of self-awareness, he is superior to his mates, but he is otherwise established as one among others, a symbol of industrialized man, an illiterate, bestial ship's stoker. Visually, he and the other stokers are not to have a wholly human appearance:

The men themselves should resemble those pictures in which the appearance of Neanderthal Man is guessed at. All are hairy-chested, with long arms of tremendous power, and low, receding brows above their small, fierce, resentful eyes. All the civilized white races are represented, but except for the slight differentiation in colour of hair, skin, eyes, all these men are alike.[11]

The Elements of Drama

We are not expected to respond to Yank as a person. Suited well enough to the world of the stokehold, he leaves the ship for a world of fantasy which is distorted to suggest it is seen through the eyes of Yank, but which remains recognizable to us. Neither in Fifth Avenue nor among 'The Industrial Workers of the World' does he 'belong'. Finally he goes to the zoo, where in a long soliloquy he finds more sympathy and talks more comfortably with a gorilla in a cage than with his own kind, until the gorilla crushes him to death. The author explains the meaning of the scene:

Yank can't go forward, and so he tries to go backward. That is the significance of his shaking hands with the gorilla. But not when he goes backward either can he find a place where he belongs. The gorilla kills him. The subject is the same as it has always been, and always will be for drama, man and his struggle against destiny. The fight used to be waged against the Gods, now it is against man's own self, his past, and his attempt to find where he belongs.

It is necessary to read this first, because the actual experience in the theatre conveys little of it. O'Neill's statement measures the play's failure.

The scene in which Yank addresses the gorilla would in reading seem explicit. This gives the gist of the last soliloquy:

Welcome to your city, huh? Hail, hail, de gang's all here! Say, yuh're some hard-lookin' guy, ain't yuh?....Ain't we both members of de same club—de Hairy Apes?...I was in a cage, too—worser'n yours—sure—a damn sight—'cause you got some chanct to bust loose....Say, how d'yuh feel sittin' in dat pen all de time, havin' to stand for 'em comin' and starin' at yuh...! On'y yuh're lucky, see? Yuh don't belong wit 'em and yuh know it. But me, I belong wit' em—but I don't, see?...Youse can sit and dope dream in de past, green woods, de jungle, and de rest of it. Den yuh belong and dey don't....Yuh're re'lar! Yuh'll stick to de finish! Me'n you, huh?—bot' members of this club! *Yank...forces the lock on the cage door. He throws this open....*Shake—de secret grip of our order.... *With a spring the animal wraps his huge arms around Yank in a murderous hug....*Christ, where do I get off at? Where do I fit in?[12]

Audience Participation

Growls and roars from the gorilla are interspersed through this speech: the intention is to suggest an approximation to a conversation between man and beast.

Objections to the clipped, uneven phrasing of Yank's words are here irrelevant, since it must be granted that by their agency the author does supply a clear sequence of suggestions. Yank with his dull irony reasons his way to his conclusion: he feels sympathy with the animal because he resembles it and because his own sense of being inescapably caged alive becomes suddenly recognizable when he looks at it. His cage, unlike the gorilla's, is one into which he was born; he nevertheless hopes the rough affinity between them is capable of development. But his sympathy is not reciprocated, and he dies without knowing his place. O'Neill adds the ironic comment, 'And, perhaps, the Hairy Ape at last belongs', implying a ghost of tragic intention in the *dénouement*, though we may doubt whether one belongs anywhere away from one's natural habitat; to compare the gorilla in his cage with Yank in society is to mix two symbols somewhat confusedly.

In effect, how much of the author's intention is fulfilled in the theatre? The symbol of Yank as an ape receives increasing emphasis through the previous scenes. It runs perilously close to the ludicrous, but its seriousness is saved because there is still room for our imagination to trim it to measurably human proportions. We restrict its meaning to Yank himself: his presence controls it. But in the last scene of the play, the symbol is visually particularized in the shape of the gorilla itself. As a symbol, it now suffers any aberrant meanings the inarticulate animal itself suggests. It would not be unfair to say that among the strongest of these are Darwinian associations which are quite distracting. It is an error of judgment on the part of the writer: to feel with Yank in his perplexity now as we did before, we must also feel sympathy and respect for the animal, and this is hardly possible. During this scene

The Elements of Drama

we stand outside the play; we spend our time supplying connections other than those intended. The danger of a comic effect is due to some sympathy with Yank clashing with our knowledge that an animal really would be indifferent to brotherly understanding. We hear every remark as a *double entendre* because we hear it without feeling. The emotional crisis of the opening of the cage in this atmosphere arrives as bathos. We make an image, but of our volition, not O'Neill's. That Yank can go neither forward nor backward is a remote idea that might well defy a delicate poetic elucidation, which here the author cannot give it because of the restrictions in the dialogue of his illiterate characters. Are we to see the cage as a destiny for society, and ourselves as Yank, just as Yank sees himself as the gorilla? None of this is dramatized. O'Neill's earlier play *The Emperor Jones*, though a more successful attempt to communicate a similar theme, nevertheless fails for the same lack of sensitivity to the independent imagination of the audience.

It is another matter to estimate how far a play remains alive when it rests on conventions within the writing remote from the audience's experience. Virginia Woolf declared that the Elizabethan play sets us free to wander

> among dukes and grandees, Gonzaloes and Bellimperias, who spend their lives in murder and intrigue, dress up as men if they are women, as women if they are men, see ghosts, run mad, and die in the greatest profusion on the slightest provocation, uttering as they fall imprecations of superb vigour or elegies of the wildest despair.[13]

But does it? These people may not become dramatically substantial for us today at all. A modern audience may lack the means within itself to accept that freedom. It would be exhilarating to think that future dramatists truly had at their command the resources of all the conventions from the Greek chorus to the telephone. But the catalogue increases of partial failures and moribund attempts to revive the dead. However

Audience Participation

this may be, one may be sure that those basic conventions, notably the chorus and the soliloquy, which are used primarily to encourage an audience to participate, must find some substitute. For drama is a shared activity *to an extent* which the novel, for example, is not. It is in the nature of the theatre, for the most part, that the author is forgotten more than in the novel, and the kind of activity the theatre expects of the spectator, far from detracting from its value, must increase it.

Seeing that modern realistic drama does not use choric, soliloquized and other forms of lyrical and rhetorical speech, nor the imagery and rhythms which 'serve in various ways to overcome the disadvantages of that brevity which is essential to the concentration and immediacy of drama',[14] we are perhaps too ready to point out the limitations of the stage. We may think of the novel as the form of expression most able to persuade us as the early dramatic conventions did. For the novel has the power to guide and control the understanding of the reader and to concentrate attention on thought, motive, mental reaction, the subtleties of unspoken feeling with all its rhythms—all, in fact, that is *not* said in realistic dialogue, all that might invite a really full collaboration between stage and auditorium. Can thought and introspection, and that inarticulate region we call human relationship, be *dramatized* with precision in today's objective, perceptual speech? That is, can these matters be presented without falling back upon largely unaccepted conventions and without inviting a tame assent?

When Ibsen is not straining his dialogue to carry heavily symbolic implications, as in *The Master Builder*, or to make us work out a rather analytical psychology, as at the end of *Rosmersholm*, he supplies in his work a wealth of satisfying answers to these questions, and to understand Ibsen's way of working is to comprehend the distinctive virtues of audience participation common to all drama. Ibsen gives his characters a memory, as it were, and as a result we spend the time

The Elements of Drama

reconstructing the past for ourselves. In this way we begin to feel after a very short time that his characters have their roots in a real situation: it is real to us because we admit it only through the sieve of our own efforts and experience. The past becomes an event in the present, as it does in the good modern novel. Where suggestions about the past can be controlled by the author through his actors, and assimilated by us in the unique deductive processes of drama this book has been insisting upon, a well-wrought dialogue between two characters can offer a deep and immediate experience which we share, and can supply some substitute for the participatory function of the older conventions.

If we pursue the opening scene of *Rosmersholm* a little further, to the initial exchange between Rebecca and Kroll, this play usefully demonstrates an as yet undeveloped relationship, one hardly depending on the little that has gone before, and one which seems deceptively simple.

KROLL, *sits down and looks about him.* How charmingly pretty you have made the old room look! Flowers everywhere!
REBECCA. Mr Rosmer is so fond of having fresh flowers about him.
KROLL. And so are you, I should say.
REBECCA. Yes, I am. I think their scent has such a delicious effect on one—and till lately we had to deny ourselves that pleasure, you know.
KROLL, *nodding slowly.* Poor Beata could not stand the scent of them.
REBECCA. Nor their colours either. They made her feel dazed.
KROLL. Yes, I remember. *Continues in a more cheerful tone of voice.* Well, and how are things going here?[15]

The relationship begins to grow from this greeting, though a snatch of Rebecca's uneasy feeling about Kroll, Beata's brother, had been suggested in her previous mention of him. We must be especially careful to exclude anything as definite as the suspicion that has entered Kroll's mind by the time he leaves the room at the end of the act. In spite of this, the insistent process of delicately touching in thoughts and feelings through apparently flat and colourless dialogue begins.

Audience Participation

By the words he is given to speak, Kroll is shown to feel a strong reaction to the room decorated with flowers. Why should this be? We tell ourselves, without consciously thinking about it, that the appearance of the room must seem unusual to him, that it represents a change since he was here last, and that it surprises him. We are interested to decide the nature of this surprise: is it one of pleasure or is it one of regret? There is nothing in the politeness of his comment to tell us. His surprise is singled out and unadulterated so that it should be received by us unmistakably. On the other hand, Rebecca significantly feels the need to supply an explanation: 'Mr Rosmer is so fond of having fresh flowers about him.' But we wonder why this remark needs to be made, since Kroll is obviously on intimate terms with Rosmer, having addressed him as 'John' just before. We strain to make a possible connection between the mention of death by Mrs Helseth and the flowers newly displayed, but as funeral garlands they can only be incongruous. The explanation of Kroll's surprise begins to emerge. Beneath his polite address his surprise is a shade puzzled and alarmed, while Rebecca's curious explanation is an inadequate gesture towards an apology. So when Kroll adds, 'And so are you, I should say', we are now bound to interpret this as something more than a charming but casual compliment. It suggests that Kroll, in looking for an explanation for the incongruity which he felt as we did, does not expect that Rosmer himself would have decorated the room like this. Kroll has observed Rebecca's implication that she has done it for him, and her 'Mr Rosmer' will later gain significance.

Rebecca makes a bold reply that now has in it little hint of apology: the best form of defence is attack. Her choice of words, 'such a delicious effect on one...', suggests that she is being a fraction brazen. When she goes on to add '...till lately we had to deny ourselves that pleasure, you know', we

The Elements of Drama

assume that not only are these Rebecca's flowers, her defiant contribution to the room hung with old family portraits, but that whatever death has occurred in this house was possibly for her a welcome departure. We note, too, that her use of 'we' for 'I' suggests that she is again implicating Rosmer in her action. Through Rebecca's manner, her fresh flowers, coupled with her earlier comment on 'the dead', which is now recalled as a comment tinged with a criticism, we begin to create her attitude. Now the shadow of a revulsion against whoever has died adds another stroke to fill out Rebecca's feelings.

Only her relationship with Kroll requires finer definition, and this is demonstrated through a similarly oblique revelation of his thoughts and feelings. Kroll nods slowly: 'Poor Beata could not stand the scent of them.' What does this nod mean, with the weighted reply? The nod may signify agreement and understanding, but as a gesture it is ambiguous enough to mean, too, sympathy with Beata. Again, the spectator's curiosity is excited and suspended, and the producer will supply the slightest of pauses with the nodding sufficient to evoke this response. The opposition of the terms by which the scent of flowers is referred to, first Rebecca's 'such a delicious effect' and now Kroll's 'could not stand the scent of them', makes us specially alert. A double judgment by Kroll is implied by the ambiguity of his words: does he judge Beata as in error or Rebecca as callous? Ibsen does not resolve the ambiguity. As an ambiguity it appears convincing, for Kroll cannot speak ill of the dead, cannot in the interest of good manners criticize Rebecca. The remark is careful, hesitant, and receives an extra emphasis because in itself it contains the first explicit reference to the name and sex of the dead, emphasizing her who cannot appear.

In Rebecca's reply we receive another bare indication of the cause of Beata's death, a subject about which we have been growing steadily more inquisitive: 'Nor their colours either.

Audience Participation

They made her feel dazed.' We begin to link this with the millstream Mrs Helseth mentioned. But this kind of exposition works upon us in a manner different from the direct statement of classical drama. We do not calculate as we listen that the author is supplying expository detail. It was a brilliant stroke to use in Kroll a *confidant* to whom the truth could not be spoken outright, and thus to stress an embarrassment an actress can display, so that certain half-formed questions niggle us: why, if both parties know the cause of the death and knew the dead woman intimately, does Rebecca have to remind her visitor of the effect of colour upon Beata? Is it not that she is making sure that the evidence is complete and completely understood? That therefore she doubts Kroll's complete understanding? That she is not certain where Kroll's sympathy lies? That she needs to prompt him to commit himself and declare his sympathies? And why does she distrust him? Has Rebecca any feelings of guilt? Does Kroll have some information that is denied her? But Kroll's reply denies us, as well as her, the satisfaction of a definite answer: 'Yes, I remember.... Well, and how are things going here?' With the change in the tone of his voice, we are again left in suspense. Some part of the explanation does follow in a line or two, when Rebecca pursues her purpose and asks the deliberate question,

After a short pause, sitting down in an easy-chair near the sofa. Why have you never once been near us during the whole of your holidays?

Ibsen prepares this vital question with the pause, and it is as if Rebecca contrives to take the edge off its pointedness by sitting at ease near to Kroll, but it raises again all our suspicions about her feelings and her relationship with Kroll. His subsequent evasiveness sharpens the point still further.

In this way, Ibsen gives his audience a dramatized version of a human relationship, one that quickly becomes a relationship in some depth and ambiguity though this is by no means the central relationship in the play. Indeed, it is principally

The Elements of Drama

created to throw light on Rebecca's relations with Rosmer, who is soon to enter. The play has the power to concentrate attention on thought and motive; the understanding of the spectator is directed, and directed without the intrusion of the author and as an effect of immediate experience. Realistic dialogue makes us see, offering us concrete detail, but it also leads us to think and feel: its language is perceptual, but its implications may be conceptual.[16] At least it guarantees the active contribution of the spectator as neatly as could the Greek chorus, the Shakespearian soliloquy and the realistic modern novel.

In the theatre the spectator has to re-experience the situation in order to respond; and the response in turn is an experience. His own intelligence and quality of feeling lend meaning to the action, while in the good play the action leads his intelligence and develops the quality of his feeling. Sitting beside the spectator in the audience is, so to speak, the author himself, who spends the evening pointing out the evidence to his associate in the artistic endeavour. This is true participation in a very real sense, since it is prerequisite. The playwright speaks through moving and talking pictures in the faith that those who see them will re-create his idea.[17] Every new attempt to speak is a new trial of faith; every new play, every new performance, is an experiment with an audience. It is logical to add that the greater the spectator's contribution, and the more the play entails, the greater its worth is likely to be.

A final point: today a play is not fixed by a religious or social context, and we can no more judge a modern tragedy by the standards we might apply to Greek tragedy than we could comfortably wear a suit of armour in an underground railway. A classification of plays by types is today supremely unhelpful; to stamp a play as a tragedy or comedy, a melodrama or farce, is to bind it by rules external to itself and illegitimately borrowed. The practice began when *Measure for Measure* was

Audience Participation

pigeon-holed a comedy, *Troilus and Cressida* a tragedy and *Henry IV* a history, and continues today in abortive and distracting controversy over the nature of plays like *Saint Joan*, a 'chronicle', *Ring Round the Moon*, a 'charade', and *Waiting for Godot*, a 'tragi-comedy'. The contemporary playgoer must think of distinctions of quality, not of kind: he cannot anticipate his response, but must submit to the guidance of the play.

Perhaps it is because modern plays depend upon a greater degree of realistic motivation that the majority of them shun the extremities and freely blend elements of tragedy and melodrama with elements of comedy and farce into mixtures that can be called by none of these names. Each is a 'play of ideas', and subject only to the particular attitude of the author to his theme and his audience, the attitude which gives it its predominant tone. The modern dramatist exults in his freedom to play over an audience's whole emotional scale, and those who are most up-to-date are those dramatists like Chekhov, Strindberg in his later plays, Pirandello, Mr O'Casey, M. Anouilh and Mr Samuel Beckett, who vigorously explore new territories of feeling.

At least we can say that today's playwright can no longer forecast the kind of response his play will receive by trusting to any traditional form or to the nature of the subject. Modern plays are often to be judged only by the shade of feeling and the sort of laughter experienced. They attempt less to offer solutions than to pose problems based on the vitality, variety and anarchy of human sensations, helping us towards a personal understanding of our complexity through their fusion of impressions. The best drama of the future may not be recognizably tragic or comic, psychological or social, but of a subtler, mixed form, capable of ranging musically over our feelings, persuading us of human riches and touching us wholly.

12

PASSING JUDGMENT

Too great an insistence on methods and techniques may lead us to think of playwriting as a skill whose finest achievement is sheer cunning. There is a place for control over the medium, but too great a stress on it will probably lead us back to the circus. From another point of view, to approach a play simply as a piece of craftsmanship must reduce our playgoing experience to a jigsaw-puzzle enthusiasm. The mystery of the play's quality remains, because drama cannot be reduced to rule, nor a spectator's participation be measured by quantity. The last task is the most difficult: to ask to what extent the play is good. It is the final move in our encounter with the playwright.

Perhaps the question should not be posed in this form at all. Asking it would seem to call for four progressive decisions, none of them simple. First, why is the play different from life in the way it is? Second, what is the quality of the play's impressions and the ordering of them? The third is the decision the playgoer makes about himself: what is the quality of my own interest? And last, how valuable is the play in its fulfilled intention?

A play's organization is not always apparent in its externals. To take two farcical comedies, an excellent case could be put up for promoting Pinero's *The Magistrate* above M. Anouilh's *Ring Round the Moon*. The former is deft in the extreme, and very funny. But it pleases as a feather tickles. Its success is due solely to Pinero's flair for devising a ridiculous situation, and slickly arranging it for its shocks and surprises. *Ring Round the Moon*, for all its Cinderella-fairy-story lightness of touch and its surface gaiety, is a serious play, as light but as serious as a slip with a razor can be. It is a play with which one tingles long after leaving the theatre. This is because the play with all its fantastic characters is evolved from within, evolved round the theme 'all is vanity', were it possible to wrap so heavy a burden in so delicate a fabric. It is a play that, like M. Anouilh's *Thieves' Carnival* and Ugo Betti's *Summertime*, hits precisely the balance between extravagance and buoyancy, and slyly insinuates its comments on life by the slightest of cuts and glances at our civilized habits of matchmaking, of belief in true love, of spending money; our general behaviour as social animals is gently ridiculed. With Hugo and his aunt Madame Desmermortes, we softly animate the puppets and watch the contortions of their dancing.

Assessment of value must be made on a wide basis. When we look for final criteria, we look perhaps to the play's broad and elusive quality of 'style'. We look to the play's kind of intention before the fulfilment of it: its style alone may make its intention felt, but defy analysis. So it is with all plays of felt authority, plays as different as *Riders to the Sea* and *Peer Gynt*. When Aristotle offered his view of how drama operates by suggesting it imitates life, we know from the plays he must have seen that he was not asking to be taken literally, not asking us to think of *mimesis* as an end in itself. He was implying that life in its presentation on the stage is to be apprehended in the imagination and recognized within its self-begotten and self-evident style.

For in its style dramatic life sets up its own values. If we can be enthusiastic about highly mannered forms like ballet and opera, we should not be distracted by the style of high tragedy. Playgoers are often worried because in *King Oedipus* or in the *Agamemnon* of Aeschylus the heroes ought by realistic standards to have seen their danger coming. Others are disturbed because in Synge's *Deirdre of the Sorrows* it is too unlikely that Deirdre would have returned to Ireland, thereby falling into King Conchubor's snare; they are even doubtful whether she would have so contrived her death as to drop into Naisi's open grave. The whole of *Deirdre of the Sorrows* is arranged so that we may match the quality of our own lives against Deirdre's, and test the significance of our own imagined love and death by Deirdre's standards—not by direct comparison, but by allowing her temporarily to impersonate our finest desires within the world of the play. Her last speech over Naisi's grave is nothing if not grandiloquent, and so it must be in order that ideal behaviour may be portrayed, though it is none the less sincere in its context.

A quick examination of this speech should demonstrate how a play proposes the standards by which it invites judgment. Deirdre 'stands up and sees the light from Emain', and says, 'Draw a little back with the squabbling of fools when I am broken up with misery'.[1] Thus she begins by invoking the full pathos of her personal situation, rising to stress the weight of her pronouncement. But, more important, she firmly compels us to repudiate the commonplace, and to measure the worth of her feelings against the petty tactics of Conchubor. These we readily dismiss, together with everything in ourselves not comparable with the elemental emotions in Deirdre. Then, having blazoned her heroic stature, she becomes prophetic of the future, because she has assumed that we have admitted her actions to be transcendent: 'because of me there will be weasels and wild cats crying on a lonely wall where there were queens and armies and red gold, the way there will be a story told of a ruined city and a raving king and a woman will be young for ever'. In her prophecy she links Conchubor with the meanest of animal life, thus in a vivid picture raising herself far above him, while in turn the spirit of the comparison suggests that she is herself a creature of nature, elemental, artless, as the play's verbal imagery has reiterated.

Passing Judgment

Exalted, she calls nature into sympathy with her and recalls her supreme happiness with Naisi as a background to her death: 'Little moon, little moon of Alban, it's lonesome you'll be this night, and to-morrow night, and long nights after.' She grows before our eyes as she sees herself, a myth stretching across time. She sees herself, ideal and immaculate, in the tragic story of Deirdre and Naisi: '...and you pacing the woods beyond Glen Laoi, looking every place for Deirdre and Naisi, the two lovers who slept so sweetly with each other.' Her feelings for herself, and ours for her, mature to impersonality. The author now brings into full harmony the rhythms and repetitions of the language he has devised, and in a speech that sings its way to a crescendo, Deirdre gathers her tentative feelings into one rare impression which embraces the purity of her love:

> I have put away sorrow like a shoe that is worn out and muddy, for it is I have had a life that will be envied by great companies. It was not by a low birth I made kings uneasy, and they sitting in the halls of Emain. It was not a low thing to be chosen by Conchubor, who was wise, and Naisi had no match for bravery. It is not a small thing to be rid of grey hairs, and the loosening of teeth. *With a sort of triumph.* It was the choice of lives we had in the clear woods, and in the grave we're safe, surely....

Even the mention of senility exalts her, for the play has constantly stressed the regret that youth and love pass, and now she in her death, in a sense, preserves them for ever. Her wish to recognize God's intervention in her story raises her still higher: 'Keep back, Conchubor; for the High King who is your master has put his hands between us.' And as she shows Naisi's knife, she prepares to commit the decisive act that is to establish finally the size and importance of her death. Synge is perhaps troubled by the thought that her death arises from a base treachery as much as from her own choice, but he allows the cumulative impact of the words to override a theoretical doubt, and sustains the tragic elevation: 'It's a

The Elements of Drama

pitiful thing, Conchubor, you have done this night in Emain; yet a thing will be a joy and triumph to the ends of life and time.'

In the course of a play like this we willingly reject familiar realities, the better to apprehend the source of greatness in human behaviour. Human behaviour is the starting point for the excursion into unusual states of feeling, and to this beginning we return enriched.

Perhaps because we have so much realistic dialogue and presentation today, judgments upon farce and artificial comedy inappropriate to these forms are easily made. *The Importance of Being Earnest* does not offer a realistic portrait of the upper class in the 1890's. The Restoration comedy of manners does not photographically report the Caroline audience. Nor, because M. Anouilh's *pièces roses* and *pièces brillantes* uncompromisingly exaggerate to satirize contemporary aspects of human frailty, ought we to assume their author's outlook is jaundiced.

In judging such plays we must of course look for the link between the stage and the spectator. But we must allow them some selection and emphasis, even distortion, in order to make us think, to break down our resistance and to incite comparison with our own reality. We find it difficult to judge a play like Sir John Vanbrugh's *The Relapse, or Virtue in Danger*, or Farquhar's *Beaux' Stratagem*, to name plays recently revived. Some prefer to hide their heads in the sand with Charles Lamb, who wrote in defence of Restoration comedy

> I could never connect those sports of a witty fancy in any shape with any result to be drawn from them to imitation in real life. They are a world of themselves almost as much as fairyland.... They seem engaged in their proper element. They break through no laws, or conscientious restraints. They know of none.... It is altogether a speculative scene of things, which has no reference whatever to the world that is.[2]

Lamb's excuses do not approach half the truth. Perhaps it was necessary for him in his own time to express himself in

Passing Judgment

this way, but if this drama has 'no reference whatever to the world that is', how is it to be judged? With modern realistic drama one can at least say, 'This is like life, so I know from my own experience that such a man is a bad man'. Or one can say with an aesthetic reasoning, 'This is presuming to be true, but in fact it is not; it is false, and therefore it is a bad play'. But how are we to judge fairyland? The answer is that there are good and bad fairies. The conduct of fairies is based upon the conduct of the human beings who invent them. We can judge Vanbrugh's play, for example, by deciding two things: first, has it effectively made us accept its fairyland for the time being? Second, has it exploited our acceptance of its fairyland in any valuable way? As for the morals of this kind of play, it was not simply that the institution of marriage was being ridiculed, or that sexual wickedness was being made the subject for entertainment. The truth is that sex was laughable, and still is: it makes rational men and women behave irrationally. And in this period the playwrights had a rare freedom to deal with this their most promising source of comic material, and to hit hard at the biggest target that that or any other audience could provide them with. This is not to say that these writers, like those in any age, did not frequently lose sight of their object in the joy of their freedom: they are of course to be judged by their intentions like any other playwrights.

To take Lord Foppington as he is in *The Relapse*, effeminate, fantastic, and to see him as representative of the gentlemen of the period, is to underestimate human wit in that or any period. Vanbrugh wanted his audience to view Lord Foppington's attitude to life, as it appears in his personal foibles and in his larger vices, as much by contrast as by comparison with its own. It is striking, as many recent playgoers have discovered, that there are in Lord Foppington sufficient permanent qualities representative of all men to make the play one of strict relevance to our time as well as to Vanbrugh's. The

The Elements of Drama

important thing is to estimate the difference between ourselves and the characters, just as the Restoration audience had to do. If we recognize the key signature accurately, we may find that the notes themselves are the same. By the laws of comic theatre and of any comic art, perhaps the more incisively and vigorously the writer wishes to probe, the farther into a Ruritania must he transport the spectator first.

So a first step towards judgment is not to ask how far it is like life, but why it is different from life. But in asking 'why?', we come close to looking for that tiresome, misleading, ungainly phantom, the play's 'message'. The common assumption that the more the playwright teaches a tidy lesson, the more considerable it is, is a dangerous fallacy. Though we may consciously disavow it, it is an assumption we hold unwittingly. Drama does not tell what it has to say, but shows it. The good mother does not say to her child, 'Go away and play'; she says specifically, 'See if you can find the cotton-reel in my basket'. The playwright owes it to his audience to find particular and concrete action for the general and abstract idea, so that the playgoer can move across common ground with him. Because the stage expects concrete detail of behaviour for its living actors, no other literary form is more objective, less moralizing. When Bridie wishes to tell us Tobit is old and blind and devout, he makes him say,

Tut, tut. Clumsy old fellow. Tottering about like a sturdied sheep. My stick. My stick. Now where did I leave my stick? Dear, dear, I'll be forgetting my prayers next...,[3]

translating a general, bare statement vividly. So a play may not give immediate satisfaction to our casuistical instincts.

Without losing one's sense of the complexity of the whole, the discussion must become one about the ordering and emphasis of the play and the relation of its parts, not immediately about its content or message. Injustice has been done to the work of Bernard Shaw, though he invited it

Passing Judgment

himself, by a general refusal to give him credit as an artist before assessing him as a thinker. This is somewhat true of Molière, is still largely true of Strindberg and Pirandello, for years was true of Shakespeare, and may yet blight the fortunes of M. Anouilh today. Shaw's own attitude to Ibsen, as seen in *The Quintessence of Ibsenism*, showed a similar error of judgment. Should the spectator become aware of the preacher in the playwright, aware that a view of life is being thrust upon him, the play will destroy itself.

A poem can make a deep and broad meaning out of a tiny subject, and what is true of poetry is true of drama. The meaning that matters emerges from the way the subject is treated. The family of *The Cherry Orchard* makes a departure, the family of *The Three Sisters* does not, but there the seminal ideas end: the rest is growth and fruition. The satisfaction of drama arises from no logical consistency in the events, nor from their magnitude. The power of the play comes of its consistency within itself, and its content achieves magnitude by the quality of its exploration, its width of view and its sense of proportion.

In arriving at a judgment, the second step is therefore one inseparable from our decision about the quality of the texture and the ordering of the impressions, together with decisions about the delicacy and precision by which the author and his agents originate and project them. Brief instances from two uncertain comic fantasies, *The Lady's Not For Burning* and *Tobias and the Angel*, may illustrate this second step. Neither of these plays is in the front rank, but there is a recognizable distinction in quality between them.

Mr Fry's play is one of opposites and paradoxes freely permitted by its fantasy. Briefly, the subject concerns a medieval Thomas Mendip who wishes to die,

> To make an example of himself to all
> Erring mankind.[4]

The Elements of Drama

We are not expected to take his death-wish too seriously, even if we could, because of its featherweight context. Nevertheless, he wishes to die, but may not. At the same time, Jennet Jourdemayne, a beautiful materialist enamoured of life, is taken to be a witch: she has no wish to die, but she must. They fall in love by degrees, she jealous of his wish to die, he captured by her own 'damnable mystery'. A long scene between Thomas and Jennet establishes their temperamental differences and their disposition towards each other. In the light of this, the sentence of burning upon Jennet begins to mean a little more than a miscarriage of justice: it becomes a persecution of the joy of life she holds dear. Justice Tappercoom sentences her to the stake, whereupon she faints. He then discloses a decision which echoes the Chaplain's happy suggestion that Thomas

> · might be wooed
> From his aptitude for death by being happier.

This is the sentence he passes on Thomas:

> TAPPERCOOM. Found guilty
> Of jaundice, misanthropy, suicidal tendencies
> And spreading gloom and despondency. You will spend
> The evening joyously, sociably, taking part
> In the pleasures of your fellow men.
> THOMAS. Not
> Until you've hanged me. I'll be amenable then.
> JENNET. Have I come back to consciousness to hear
> That still?—Richard, help me to stand.—You see,
> Preacher to the caddis-fly, I return
> To live my allotted span of insect hours.
> But if you batter my wings with talk of death
> I'll drop to the ground again.
> THOMAS. Ah! One
> Concession to your courage and then no more.
> Gentlemen, I'll accept your most inhuman
> Sentence. I'll not disturb the indolence
> Of your gallows yet. But on one condition:
> That this lady shall take her share to-night
> Of awful festivity. She shall suffer too.[5]

Passing Judgment

This moves on two levels of ironic suggestion. At a first level, it seems to a degree empty. Thus the idea of curing misanthropy by enforcing sociability is an incongruity which marks Tappercoom as an unimaginative bumble. It might be little more than a contrivance of plot and to cause laughter: it allows a third act and amuses as oddity amuses. Nor is there anything in Thomas's reply to force us at once to measure seriously the implications of Tappercoom's sentence. I think it unlikely that we digest his 'Not / Until you've hanged me' at any level deeper than a verbal witticism, for the possible argument that Thomas thinks he will find joy, sociability and pleasure in death is denied by the comment that follows: 'I'll be amenable then.' Mr Fry does not, from his choice of the word 'amenable', wish to enforce such an interpretation: it is a sharp reply in character, and laughable at a trivial level. The ironies to this point are loose and unimpressive, of no real consequence in carrying forward the meaning of the play.

Jennet's recovery from her fainting fit, at the particular moment when Thomas is declaring his determination to die apparently as warmly as ever, is to remind us of their new intimacy. It gives the actor in the part of Thomas an opportunity to respond to her feeling for him, in order to make it evident that the concession he is about to offer is because of her. It is not made clear through anything in the dialogue what precise form his response to her must take. His 'Ah!' communicates nothing in itself, is indeed nearly impossible to speak, but the complete reversal of his views in making his 'one concession' gives us a deal to think upon. We know that Jennet's interest in him as a man and her reluctance to have him talk of death have increased her desire to live. Can we accept his argument that it is her 'courage' alone that has influenced him to withhold his pert demands for a hanging? He is still obstinately deceiving himself about the nature of his own cynicism. He says that it is for the sake of her courage that he will undertake to join the festivities of the evening, but by now we more than suspect his own deeper interest in her, though he will not admit it. One can feel the quality of the dramatic excitement changing.

Then he makes his condition:

> That this lady shall take her share to-night
> Of awful festivity.

In a moment the intention behind Mr Fry's situation floods our understanding. Apparently giving himself a lease of life in order to allow Jennet a lease of life, Thomas unwittingly puts on trial what each stands for. We anticipate and relish the prospect of a breezy trial of a pessimist: for how will Thomas with his attitude to life suffer one such evening when he knows that the first person for whom he has felt altruistic feelings must die next morning? Will the evening lend them a greater urge for life? Will Thomas be granted a new vitality now that Jennet's one-day caddis-fly life is to become a sharp reality? The cynic must be brought up hard against Mr Fry's cheerful version of the life force. The play's crisis is prepared and grows briskly in the mind.

The irony that seemed pale takes on in retrospect a sudden intenser colouring. The foolhardy plan of the Chaplain and Tapercoom to restore Thomas to happiness has possibilities they did not dream of. And Mr Fry has the wit gently to drop the pebble that will start the landslide. Thomas, in saying 'She shall suffer too', is not so capricious as he would seem to be. Jennet too is involved. Beneath the bravado of their language, the irony of this impudent situation leads us to hear this low comment as a jaunty threat that will echo through the next act. Jennet will ache from a luxury of life she will know to be all too brief. Thomas's ordeal, that of a man compelled to think twice about his purpose in life, is to be a surprise to him, for in testing her courage, he will test the sincerity of his own bluff cynicism.

Passing Judgment

Even within this short passage it is possible to feel the quality of the play varying within itself and, in its general tone, striking an unequal note, largely due to a tendency to write at times a catchpenny line which modifies the total effect. Mr Fry regularly explodes his serious comment, in this play as in *A Phoenix Too Frequent*, with a less serious; alternatively, he drops a telling remark among the frivolities. This may not be objectionable as a way of keeping the touch light and fantastic, but it puts a tongue in Thomas's cheek in a way that the meanest actor of comedy would not dare to do. Thus his confident flippancies prevent our giving much weight to his death-wish; the play permits us to argue audaciously but without feeling.

By contrast, Bridie's *Tobias and the Angel* stands up less well to this kind of irresponsibility. The following well-remembered passage represents the play's best qualities. Sara, the spoilt girl-princess, is in conversation with Raphael, the Archangel with a sense of humour:

RAPHAEL. What is going on in your mind, woman?

SARA. 'The sons of God saw the daughters of men that they were fair.'

RAPHAEL, *standing up*. Sara, you have the mind of a child and the instincts of an animal. You have a smooth, weak, meaningless face. When your face moves prettily it is play-acting. When it is moved by emotion it is ugly beyond speaking about. When you take off your shoes you walk like a duck. Your whole body is a compound of absurdities and irrelevancies. Your only admirable feature is the magnificent impudence that impels you to make sheep's eyes at an Archangel six thousand years your senior.

SARA, *begins to weep, silently.*

RAPHAEL. Don't snivel. You can't hope to make any impression upon *me* by that wretched exercise.[6]

Bridie set out to write a morality play, perhaps over-conscious of the difficulty of doing this for a modern audience. His tone of condescension is felt uneasily when he chooses to write with the kind of speech thought to be acceptable to us. The author did not wholly trust the vivacity of his chosen

The Elements of Drama

situation, for much of the real fun comes without sugaring the pill, from the simple irony whereby the characters do not know that the servant Azarias is the Archangel Raphael. Thus, immediately preceding our quotation, Raphael reveals his identity to Sara. The outcome provides an excuse for this charmingly bizarre scene in which Sara's feminine coquetry tempts her to try to attract him.

To what end? Later, it is true, Raphael is enabled to tell of Tobias's virtues, and this is the beginning of Sara's change of mind towards her betrothed. But it is difficult to say what this extract contributes to the play beyond possibly stressing Sara's stupidity and Raphael's humanity, both of which had been enlarged upon. Both characters are left dramatically unaffected by the exchange. With a theatrical irresponsibility typical of this author, the scene tends to detract further from the uncertain meaning of the play, for the sake of a bright but irrelevant joke. The author spends his verbal talent prodigally. We see Sara's intention immediately, and we anticipate Raphael's rejection of her with glee. He is provided with a neatly modulated speech, which, as it builds up, prepares us for the witticism at the conclusion. The danger of the lightly secured joke is that it reduces the rest of the scene, which is concerned with the declaration of Sara's and Tobias's love for each other, to a certain anticlimax. Play-writing is not spasmodic fooling: it must exert its own discipline from within. The pill is sugared until there are no medicinal properties left.

The textural comparison of quality between Mr Fry's extract and this of Bridie's is unavoidable. The force of Bridie's joke is in effect expended upon reducing Sara to tears. All we are likely to take away from this is either that it takes an Archangel to manage a spoilt child like Sara, or, since she is simply revealed for what she is, and for what we perhaps guessed her to be, that even an Archangel can make

Passing Judgment

little impression upon her. Such contradictory meanings are hardly intended by the author. Mr Fry's verbal tinsel in his early comedies is not quite of this order.

We may expect to find a more subtle dramatic texture in a good farce than in a bad tragedy. It bears no relation to the *genre* of the play. The kind of question we ask at the next stage of making a judgment on a play is not whether, for example, tragedy is a higher form than farce, but rather, if the play is taken for what it is, what *quality of interest* is it stimulating? The spectator's decision about himself must constitute the third step in evaluation. He may, after all, be quite satisfied with a music-hall joke.

The playgoer has to be honest with himself. Any play that satisfies something, whether a strong need or a passing whim, can fall within a definition of entertainment: this is too arbitrary a concept, and must be abandoned. A playgoer's satisfaction will reflect the kind and quality of the imaginative life he is living: it is as urgent a matter as that. If the play offers to help him to make any sense out of his private chaos; if the play illuminates any side of his life which was dim before; if the play encourages him to discover for himself where his true satisfaction lies; if it does not falsely engage his interest by excluding another equally deserving aspect of experience; if he feels that the play is serving any of these ends while at the same time treating him as an honest man, then he can say that there is quality in the interest stimulated.

Honesty might seem a strange requirement in the theatre, the very home of pretences, and perhaps needs a quick gloss. It does not refer to methods, but to aims. The methods of the theatre may be legitimately bold or cunning without incurring the stigma of dishonesty. The aims of a particular play, however, are always suspect, and it is important to ask whether they treat one's intelligence and feeling with respect or contempt, and whether one's integrity as a sensitive playgoer

The Elements of Drama

is being underestimated or even flouted. Only if they are honest can two minds meet.

It is difficult to be sure the playwright is being strictly honest even when the interest stimulated appears to be profound. Mr Terence Rattigan's one-act play *Table Number Seven*, in the double-bill entitled *Separate Tables*, for example, has been generally acclaimed one of his best pieces of work. In this play all Mr Rattigan's skill as a craftsman is used to present an impostor, Major Pollock. This man is cutting a figure as an army major with a famous public school and regiment behind him. In fact, his school is a council school, and the rank and regiment he boasts are false. He is in despair when, after being found guilty of improper behaviour in a cinema, he suffers the indignity of being exposed in the local newspaper. During the play we consider, and sympathize with, the reasons for his pretension. His early environmental frustration is acceptable to an audience learned in pseudo-psychology, and we agree that Major Pollock's case might have been anyone's. The character is drawn as a pathetic result of modern civilization, and is a well-documented and fully human creation, like Crocker-Harris in *The Browning Version*. So far there is no quarrel: Mr Rattigan writes with his customary finesse which can command only respect.

But the play does not rest on this character alone. Major Pollock is set upon in his absence and judged by the others who live in the private hotel. They are led by Mrs Railton-Bell, the type of snob with whom no dramatist has ever asked for sympathy: the trial of the Major is therefore dramatically rigged from the start. He then receives the sympathy of another pathetic creature, the repressed daughter of the same Mrs Railton-Bell, whose rebellion against her mother is designed to secure another certain response. He survives the ordeal of facing public opinion and he assumes a truer dignity. Thus the play ends on a note of hope for the future. As a play

Passing Judgment

it is less a psychological study of the quality of Mr Rattigan's *The Deep Blue Sea* than a morality, well constructed, decisive, but essentially comfortable, sentimental and dishonest. All decisions are made for us, when the author ought to make a real provision for free discussion. We sit accepting the development of the play, exuding the tolerance we are gratified to think is right for our times. It may be, but we are as comfortable in our seats as Mrs Railton-Bell is comfortable in her hotel. I submit that a morality play should challenge. *Table Number Seven* falsely engages our attention, and its dishonesty is strictly comparable with that of a play of propaganda. Some themes are too important to be treated by dramatic clichés.

The problem of easy sentiment is allied to that of sensationalism. Sensation, we suggested, is the trade-mark of the theatre. The whole impulse of an actor on a raised platform is to shout: the form that drama takes lends itself to the shout; the dramatist in the nature of his work is one who wishes to sway his audience. It is small wonder that sensation of eye or ear, of thought or emotion, is traditional in the theatre. Classical tragedy is in one sense a particularly sensational form. Aeschylus's *Agamemnon*, Sophocles's *King Oedipus*, Euripides's *The Trojan Women* are compact of sensations. None of these dramatists hesitates to exploit the emotions. *The Trojan Women*, for example, relies upon a wide range of such effects: a mother weeping over her son condemned to die a cruel death, the son then carried to his death by his grandmother, the violent quarrel between Hecuba and Helen, the thrilling climax of the fire. *Hamlet* employs a ghost, introduces displays of madness, a duel over an open grave, death by drowning and by poisoning, death through an arras, and so on. And yet we think of Mr Tennessee Williams's *A Streetcar Named Desire* and even the English kitchen comedy as plays of sensation, not these. Why?

The Elements of Drama

Neither *The Trojan Women* nor *Hamlet* leaves the spectator with the residual impression of the sensational, and therefore neither is properly to be defined as sensational drama. Without shame, they are using our susceptible feelings to further the end of the play. The subject of *The Trojan Women* is not war, but regret for war. *Hamlet* is not a revenge play, it is an exploration of personality faced with some of the antitheses of life. But *A Streetcar Named Desire*, otherwise a play with a deeply arresting theme, in its over-anxiety to stress the cruelty and pathos of life, swamps itself with a superflux of emotionalism. Likewise, domestic comedies, revolving chiefly round courtship and marriage, are not criticized for their subject, which offers material as solemn and as fruitful as comedy could want, but only for the facility with which they secure laughter without real concern for the distortions that result. In such plays there is no hint of an attempt to redress the balance.

Sensationalism is thus not confined to tragedy and 'straight' drama. Comedy has its own sensational unbalance. A severe emphasis is an intrinsic method in comedy, but how great may the exaggeration be before the audience jibs? Incongruity is the trusted method of ridicule, but how incongruous dare the writer be without exploding the subject of it? Such effects become sensational as soon as they are felt to be either out of tune with the rest of the play or inserted irrelevantly. Each character who is an object of attack in Ben Jonson's *The Alchemist* is grossly simplified for the purposes of the satire, but equally so, and the play has unity. But so many modern family comedies are to be seen in which comic success rests upon a sniffing servant-girl with a love problem or upon a maiden aunt with a grudge. Such characters enter the scene as specially created figures of fun: they are often betrayed by the style of the other characters, and may blur the total impression of the play. They are essentially sensational. Much

Passing Judgment

as Sheridan's burlesque *The Critic*, to take another type of drama, is to be admired for its ingenuity, it exemplifies how this form too easily falls into the bad ways of the sensational: burlesque being in itself an exaggeration, its author must minutely judge how far he may stretch his incongruity if laughter is not to be abused and the play as a whole received as merely ingenious. The piecemeal construction of this play, where it is not part of the burlesque, betrays a lack of control and direction.

The play that has to redeem itself with sensations, trusting it can deceive by working upon the vulgar feelings, lays itself open to charges of poverty. The play that can confidently risk using the power of the sensational and yet keep its balance has found a way of speaking naturally within the medium. Unhappily, it is easy to submit to the dramatist who bullies the spectator with cheap tears or laughter, to the cheat who makes him feel virtuous while indulging his vices. Step three therefore is as much a judgment upon the audience as upon the play. The residual impression is ours: if the quality of it matters to us, we are in a position to find it worthy.

The fallacy of the play with wide appeal has grown up in an age of journalism. To pronounce greatness on a play for this reason is to lump together by the same error *Macbeth*, say, with Gilbert and Sullivan on equal terms. Conversely, it is unwise to dismiss *Troilus and Cressida*, say, with Mr Ronald Duncan's *This Way to the Tomb* on grounds of a narrower appeal. Playgoers are individual enough to enjoy the same play for a multiplicity of reasons, but it is wrong to assume that range of appeal bears any relation to the value of the theme.

Dr I. A. Richards cited *Macbeth* as a play that seems to be enjoyed at more than one level:

Its very wide popularity is due to the fact that crude responses to its situations integrate with one another, not so well as more refined responses, but still in something of the same fashion. At one end of the scale is

The Elements of Drama

a highly successful, easily apprehended, two-colour melodrama, at the other a peculiarly enigmatic and subtle tragedy, and in between there are various stages which give fairly satisfactory results. Thus people of very different capacities for discrimination and with their attitudes developed in very different degrees can join in admiring it.[7]

Were it possible to prove this, the results would be meaningless for criticism. The playgoer with a limited capacity for discrimination can be assured he will not enjoy *Macbeth*. We can deceive ourselves about this. The partial understanding that may come at a first visit to the play may be enjoyable, but this is because the playgoer is already getting a stimulating insight into its full complexity. The *Macbeth* that is the 'two-colour melodrama' does not exist. Shakespeare's *Macbeth* is another play, touching the opposition of the public and the private world and the consequent horrors of the divided mind, a play so controlled it does not admit a division between a merely sensational and a tragic response.

The implication has been that judgment is a disciplined and moral act, involving an ethical valuation of an author's motives and our own, the play providing the common evidence. Going to a play can be an earnest adventure. There is no need to be ashamed of treating the theatre with such dedicated fervour, though good intentions are not enough. Sutton Vane's *Outward Bound*, with its complacent sentiments, Galsworthy's *Strife*, with its mechanically balanced equation, are both dedicated plays. There must be a last step. The question has still to be asked, 'To what extent is the play's theme of value?' This is a comparative question: it implies comparison with a play that has gone before, or more often with the play that might have been. As a way of estimating the size of this problem, it is fitting to conclude with an examination of the values in a play which has, through its intentions, made most other post-war plays seem puny. That play is *The Cocktail Party*.

Passing Judgment

The Cocktail Party is a play about happiness, happiness to be conceived at the highest spiritual level that each of Mr Eliot's samples from contemporary sophisticated humanity is capable of. Mr Eliot's non-technical problems have been two: to make his central enigma of the mind representative enough to include in its scope the modern heterogeneous, uncertain audience, and yet definite enough within its limits of belief and understanding to touch it positively. Because to a large extent he succeeds, as I feel, in affecting us, because many of his poetic statements have the weight of realized feeling, and because the issue of happiness is necessarily a nebulous and complex one, we may be encouraged to find values in this play that do not in fact exist there. Since the requirements of dramatic form must restrict the action to a manageable number of situations, it attempts to embrace its mongrel audience by stressing only two recognizable enough to typify the extremities of the human problem, that of Celia and that of the Chamberlaynes. Because it cannot chronicle all the human gradations existing between a Lavinia and a Celia, the play opens enough windows for its audience to flirt with its subject in vague terms. We happily admit a facet of Celia and a facet of the Chamberlaynes as belonging to ourselves, but we inadvertently add facets of our own perhaps irrelevant troubles and do not wholly surrender to the influence of the play. In addition, the author is compelled to provide unequivocal and realistic answers to persuade us to a dramatic conviction of the Celia-condition and of the Chamberlayne-condition: Celia dies and the Chamberlaynes make their compromise explicitly. But this necessary lucidity may lead the audience to take these symbolic solutions at face value without regard for the overtones of meaning Mr Eliot was working for. This scarcely makes for authoritative drama. Again, if Mr Eliot carefully avoids Christian terminology, as he feels he must in order not to prejudice his dramatic reasoning, is there not a danger that those who possess a background of

The Elements of Drama

Christian belief—or any other for that matter—will begin to give the action the specific values he avoids? In sum, Mr Eliot sets himself the formidable task of making a play propose and control values so typical that their evocation would in any case be fortuitous. The important critical object in dealing with a play of this calibre is to keep the discussion to the subject as the author treated it, and not to stray into any speculations likely to arise because one's personal experience fills an awkward vacuum.

The first move is to see that the play is not written within any known realistic convention, for all that it starts almost in a vein of parody, at a level even more trivial than the level of the everyday. This, for example, is a Celia we are acquainted with, and are prepared to despise: 'Do tell us that story you told the other day, about Lady Klootz and the wedding cake.'[8] She is here certainly not the martyr-to-be. It remains a matter for doubt whether this initial scene, indeed, should be played with the realism of the modern drawing-room comedy, and not by stylized acting. The author is clearly making a travesty of Mr Noël Coward's cocktails-and-cigarettes drama. The inane repetitions of the opening dialogue are unmistakable burlesque:

> PETER. I like that story.
> CELIA. I love that story.
> ALEX. *I'm* never tired of hearing that story.
> JULIA. Well, you all seem to know it.
> CELIA. Do we all know it?
>   But we're never tired of hearing *you* tell it.
>   I don't believe everyone here knows it.
>   You don't know it, do you?
> UNIDENTIFIED GUEST. No, I've never heard it.

And so on. This dialogue should put us on guard. If Act I were played stylistically and formally, as I believe it was to a degree in a Frankfurt production, we should be the more prepared to accept, for example, the tonal change of Reilly's

Passing Judgment

conversation with Edward after the party, and with Celia in the consulting-room. The consulting-room would become the setting symbolic of a twentieth-century confessional. Formal playing would prepare us to accept the seemingly enigmatic Guardians as within the convention of the play. When they leave the drawing-room for the consulting-room, we should no longer be worried because they cease to be 'in character', applying that peculiarly realistic standard of judgment; we should be pleasantly surprised to discover that they fit. We are reminded of Mr Eliot's statement about poetic drama in 1945: 'It may use any device to show [the characters'] real feelings and volitions, instead of just what, in actual life, they would normally profess to be conscious of.'[9] If we are to admit the typical patients Celia and the Chamberlaynes into the consulting-room, then it seems important we should equally admit the symbolic agents Julia and Alex. They will then appear graphically as they are intended to appear: the unacknowledged ministers among whom we mix in ordinary life without realizing their power upon our future lives. If the play is free to move on the uncommitted theatrical plane its verse form suggests, then, too, we might be happier to accept the reversion to a near-realistic normality in Act III, and to accept the serious overlay of meaning after the events of Act II. Then, too, the shock of the news of Celia's death would achieve something of its full effect: the meaning of her martyrdom must infect and overwhelm us, and it cannot do this if we have reservations about the realism of the action. The play would take on the form of a penetrating experiment with the spectator's emotions, and leave him with a then-and-now, before-and-after understanding, following the structure of the play. It seems essential, if the long catalogue of misapprehensions is to be dispelled, that both the producer and the playgoer approach it as a play in a non-realistic convention. Unhappily, in an anxiety not to disturb his audience with an

The Elements of Drama

obtrusive verse, the author's hints at this kind of playing are so weak as to be almost a handicap, and have permitted great divergence in presentation.

Even allowing for the pliant design of the play, it is difficult not to feel that Mr Eliot has attempted to encompass more than its form allowed. The faults one would wish to comment on are therefore dramatic and technical ones, as these affect final values. The most prominent discomfort is felt in the necessary dichotomy between what Celia and the Chamberlaynes stand for. This divides the whole play, and all the efforts of the last act do not unite the segments. It may be that there has not been a complete fulfilment of his wish to break down his experience by his laws of the 'third voice of poetry', by which the poetic dramatist

> may put into [a] character, besides its other attributes, some trait of his own, some strength or weakness, some tendency to violence or indecision, some eccentricity even, that he has found in himself....Some bit of himself that the author gives to a character may be the germ from which the life of that character starts. On the other hand, a character which succeeds in interesting its author may elicit from the author latent potentialities of his own being.[10]

It is difficult for the spectator to sympathize with the small and thoroughly unexciting comedy of those who must

> Maintain themselves by the common routine,
> Learn to avoid excessive expectation,
> Become tolerant of themselves and others,
> Giving and taking, in the usual actions
> What there is to give and take...,

after his interest has been stimulated by a heroine who chooses the second way described so piquantly:

> The second is unknown, and so requires faith—
> The kind of faith that issues from despair.
> The destination cannot be described;
> You will know very little until you get there;
> You will journey blind...

Passing Judgment

The spectator must respond to the former as Celia herself does: 'it leaves me cold'. Yet the whole of the third act rests upon the Chamberlaynes in order that we might be persuaded that 'Neither way is better. / Both ways are necessary.'

To the point of Celia's choice, the picture of a civilized group of people frivolously hurting each other and themselves, but only half aware of their own chaotic triviality, adequately depicts our crowded contemporary irresponsibility. It is from this limited group that particular problems of a few misfits are to emerge until they become serious to us. The problems emerge, unfortunately not as complementary, but as two diametrically opposed, situations. Thus in the development of either, the force of one must check the other, and if there is no special measure of integration between them, it is inevitable that the more powerful story of tragic individuality will detract from the interest the author wishes to stimulate in the social normality of the other. Reilly says,

> Both ways are necessary. It is also necessary
> To make a choice between them.

This is something that is stated, but in terms of the theatre is not proved, because, with Celia so prominent, no choice is imaginatively left to us.

Thus the play sets itself the impossible task of persuading us both at the rational level of social comedy and at the emotional level of tragedy. Both must integrate to form the inclusive religious drama that Mr Eliot is working towards. The comprehensive value of the play will turn upon this integration. Not only Celia, but also the audience, is to be offered the alternatives, and we must be compelled to experience both in spite of their mutual competition for our interest. The two ways were planned to lend depth to the portrayal of the human condition, whereby we were to receive the suggestion that it was for ourselves to discover within ourselves aspects of Celia or Lavinia or Edward (or even Peter Quilpe?). At

The Elements of Drama

least we were to recognize, understand and tolerate them in others. These aims depended for their meaning and effect upon the way we were to accept such differences within the same image. Momentous as this revelation might have been in conception, it would have been of no consequence unless the organization of the last two acts was as indivisibly constituted as that of Act I. The author's endeavour to promote a growth and pressure of feeling and understanding to the fall of the last curtain amounted to and depended upon that.

The experience in the theatre is otherwise. We are always in danger of losing direction for our thoughts. There are no hints that the Celia of Act I will be the martyr of Act III; there are not enough stages in the shocking leap to her crucifixion, which is itself offered only at second-hand. The decisions of the consulting-room are presented externally, and embodied more by statement than by any action that might make them acceptable. We are not aware of struggle or pain: all the guinea-pigs have their choices made for them and face their futures too resolutely. The Guardians in their symbolic role are properly excluded from the self-revelations of Celia and the Chamberlaynes; they are the active ones, and they are explicitly uninvolved:

> You and I don't know the process by which the human is
> Transhumanised: what do we know
> Of the kind of suffering they must undergo
> On the way of illumination?

But by denying himself a means of dramatizing the sharing of suffering, the author throws away a chief asset of drama: ironic exchange.

The real test comes in Act III, where the lack of balance becomes fully apparent for the first time. Without doubt Mr Eliot was right to keep Celia out of this act for as long as possible: her presence or the remembrance of her reduces the Chamberlaynes to a status less than normal. It is unfortunate

Passing Judgment

for the ends of the play that Act II leaves us so strongly aware of Celia. Mr John Peter has pointed out the nature of the anticlimax the play suffers when the new Edward and Lavinia are presented to us:

> At the end of the play Edward is clearly on the way to regeneration, his relations with Lavinia clearly more unselfish, yet how is this presented? Partly, to be sure, it is a matter of contrast with their previous relationship. But the dramatist does not leave it there. He goes on to give Edward a string of compliments and 'thoughtful' remarks that are as monotonous as they are unconvincing—'I hope you've not been worrying'. 'It's you who should be tired.' 'I like the dress you're wearing.'[11]

The failure of integration of the two patterns of the play becomes striking when the news of Celia's death on an ant-hill is disclosed. At this crux, the play might be said to collapse. It was necessary to remove Celia from the scene in order that attention might be refocused on the Chamberlaynes. It was also necessary to provide a vividly physical shock to stress that Celia's martyrdom is not a fantasy of doubtful reality. Mr Eliot electrifies us into sudden awareness of the actuality of her situation. He also wishes to bring her, as it were, vicariously back to life, that we do not forget her contribution, but feel her presence. She is thereby to become the 'shrine' for the rest, through which they may come to 'understand'.

This is how the news is received:

> ALEX. It would seem that she must have been crucified
> Very near an ant-hill.
> LAVINIA.   But Celia!...Of all people....
> EDWARD. And just for a handful of plague-stricken natives
> Who would have died anyway.
> ALEX.   Yes, the patients died anyway;
> Being tainted with the plague, they were not eaten.
> LAVINIA. Oh, Edward, I'm so sorry—what a feeble thing to say!
> But you know what I mean.
> EDWARD.   And you know what I'm thinking.
> PETER. I don't understand at all.

The Elements of Drama

Edward and Lavinia are represented in theory as having returned to our level, though not quite to the level of the first scene. But in practice they have not. Their reaction is naturalistic: they can neither understand the new Celia nor what her death means. As a sacrifice, it seems to them one of appalling waste. Alex immediately and provocatively points out that 'the patients died anyway', but we have to wait before Lavinia begins to recognize the significance of the death, when she says that 'the way in which she died was not important'. Lavinia and Edward together stumble along with ineffectual remarks that stress their comparative littleness: it would seem they understand each other and that is enough. But naturally, though shocked like the Chamberlaynes, we do not respond as they respond. They cease to be our mouthpiece. Unlike them, we know from Reilly what Celia undertook. We recall his warning: 'It is a terrifying journey.' We were granted an insight into her state of mind when she chose this destiny, and to some extent we were prepared for a revelation, though not one of this kind. Our reaction, therefore, is one of greater understanding than theirs, and again, therefore, we are unsympathetic with them. We remain several moves ahead of them as they fumble towards the understanding of her 'happy death'. If we do respond in part to their admirable humility, we must detach ourselves from Celia and view her distantly as they do. She then becomes so much a creature apart, that her significance for us is restricted by the measure of that distance. In Act III *The Cocktail Party* becomes two plays to which we give divided allegiance, and in doing so damage and destroy the meaning and value of both.

Our sense of the texture and ordering of this important last act is the only valid test of the value of the play. But it is nevertheless likely that we reserve a strong residual effect from Celia's story. If the Chamberlaynes mean little to us, Celia

Passing Judgment

means more. The failure of *The Cocktail Party* as an assessment of the problems of the modern mind is a failure of a different order from the success of, say, *Outward Bound*. What has held large audiences during the performances of *The Cocktail Party* is probably the activity of conceiving Celia's religious experience. Although Mr Eliot does not dramatically succeed in making both ways equal or necessary, there is nevertheless in the conception of the play's idea a tension between the two in Act III that does affect us. There was perhaps sufficient imaginative power in the duologue between Reilly and Celia in the consulting-room to carry us through to the end. Mr Eliot's profoundly felt distinction between 'loneliness' and 'solitude', dimly perceived through the banalities of the first scenes, and loosely defined in Act II,

> Each way means loneliness—and communion.
> Both ways avoid the final desolation
> Of solitude in the phantasmal world
> Of imagination, shuffling memories and desires,

must grow sharp in Act III, by which we make the urgent comparison with the unhappiness of Act I. Perhaps the meaning of solitude reaches us as much through the poignancy of our own case, as through any understanding of Celia's: the situation of *The Waste Land* and of *The Hollow Men* is real enough to provide its own momentum. The consciousness of our predicament and the author's power of uncovering and touching the raw and sorer places must be felt, as in the poems.

The play offers us 'communion' through loneliness and tolerance, and although it fails when it has to indicate precise dramatic results for Celia and the Chamberlaynes, tending to present all of them as martyrs to their vocations, the circumscribed solutions necessitated by the realism of the last act are gently mitigated. They are softened by the sensation of life going on, either at the Gunnings' or at the Chamberlaynes' next party:

The Elements of Drama

> Sir Henry has been saying,
> I think, that every moment is a fresh beginning;
> And Julia, that life is only keeping on.

But they are especially softened by the peculiar tone of implication-without-statement that pervades the dialogue after the crisis: 'But you know what I mean...'; 'I think I begin to see your point of view...'; 'Now I think I understand...'. The moral experience does not become a dogmatic one. Reilly, virtually untouched by the action, assumes a grandeur we cannot resent, and when he addresses the Chamberlaynes in their world 'of lunacy, / Violence, stupidity, greed...', he is speaking of our world and addressing us too:

> If we all were judged according to the consequences
> Of all our words and deeds, beyond the intention
> And beyond our limited understanding
> Of ourselves and others, we should all be condemned.

The Cocktail Party has a partial success in spite of its self-imposed technical awkwardness, in that it volunteers, if uncertainly, a new experience. At the last stage of judgment we should recall Dr Richards on the feelings of the reader facing a poem:

> The personality stands balanced between the particular experience which is the realized poem and the whole fabric of its past experiences and developed habits of mind. What is being settled is whether this new experience can or cannot be taken into the fabric with advantage. Would the fabric afterwards be better or worse? Often it must be the case that the new modification of experience would improve the fabric if it could be taken in, but too much reconstruction would be needed. The strain, the resistance, is too great, and the poem is rejected.[12]

13

PLAYGOING AS AN ART

Playgoing *is* an art. It demands an active enthusiasm to join in an act of creation, the skill to interpret stage action, and the discipline of an artist to fashion the play in the mind. The skill and discipline required to enjoy a good play to the full are very much *part* of the sheer pleasure of the theatre.

But the act of creating drama is basic. Other provinces of theatre-study are dependent absolutely upon a primary appreciation of the play. Our interest in the acting ability of others, in décor and lighting, in stage design and costume, is subsidiary. How is an actor to be judged without knowing what he is undertaking and what demands are being put upon him? How is the effect of a colour-tone on a scene to be considered without an understanding of the intention of that scene? How is the degree of emphasis in light and shadow to be recognized without a feeling for the play's manner, and without an acquaintance with its processes? A concern for style, atmosphere and symbolism in the acting and setting of a play must follow, or at least go along with, but never precede, appreciation.

Researches into the theatre audience and the theatre building are perhaps close to the heart of drama as activities for those who wish to pursue their appreciation of the play: these considerations have helped to determine the subjects, acting conventions and style of drama at different periods. The playgoer attending a play of the past may wish to visualize both the audience and the stage for which it was first written. Some may even try to reconstruct the experience as if they were the particular audience in a particular theatre at a particular point

The Elements of Drama

in history. Such imaginative activity must prove illuminating. What are we to do in hard practice with an Elizabethan soliloquy on the modern proscenium stage? Or a Greek chorus? Such students may tell us the answer. Nevertheless, the ultimate test of a play is, happily, that it is still alive for a modern audience. These researches and interests are subsidiary also, dependent as they are upon a feeling for what a theatre experience is. If they are not so dependent, they must become sterile as a specifically dramatic activity: they become a branch of another study, history, catching perhaps the excitement of a discipline other than that of drama.

Interest in the interpretation of plays by other media must be a valid one. The film stresses the visual side in drama, with the wide range from vagueness to precision possible in camera work. For this reason, we may not wish to see the cinema contesting the theatrical assumptions of Shakespearian drama any longer. But film has as its special asset the remarkable potentiality, even now after several decades largely unexplored, of cutting from one shot to another, creating dramatic meaning by the juxtaposition of visual suggestions in immeasurable variety. Its special manner has led to a general belief that film drama is something different in kind from the stage play, even, in its medium, superior. To cite one typical half-denigration of the stage by the Russian director Pudovkin:

> The theatrical producer works with real actuality, which, though he may always remould, yet forces him to remain bound by the laws of real space and real time. The film director, on the other hand, has as his material the finished, recorded celluloid. This material from which his final work is composed consists not of living men or real landscapes, not of real, actual stage-sets, but only of their images, recorded on separate strips that can be shortened, altered, and assembled according to his will.[1]

We have made it clear that the dramatist has never been so bound, that he has since the beginning of the theatre been creating images he could shorten, alter and assemble 'according

Playgoing as an Art

to his will'. The methods of film structure are those of all drama. I like therefore to think that the playgoer interested in drama is also a filmgoer.

We are not so ready to believe the radio play to be different from the stage play, yet the blind medium of radio in its unique power upon the ear of stimulating the imagination makes for a kind of drama which can embrace subjects film and theatre may never approach. Its subtle and mercurial manipulation of sounds and words, allied to its quality of immediacy and intimacy with the listener, give it possibilities of development that await only the right dramatist. We think now of the poetic plays of Mr Louis MacNeice, of Dylan Thomas's *Under Milk Wood* and of Mr Samuel Beckett's *All That Fall* as tentative but real steps towards the discovery of radio drama's proper form. Can the playgoer fail to find this medium of help?

Television is the youngest and the least blessed of all the dramatic media, since its qualities are the narrowest. It suffers as yet from having few of the advantages of the theatre, the film or the radio. The physical immediacy and complexity of the live stage picture, the lightning speed of the edited frames of the film, the penetration of the pure aural effects of the radio are all denied it. One would like to guess that its quality of intimacy and thus its special power to present a character's thoughts in episodes of brief fantasy, will one day enlarge its range and produce its own dramatic form. But it awaits the arrival of a Stanislavsky or an Eisenstein to handle it.

So we return to our belief that playgoing is the basic activity, though many have reasoned that the only complete way of appreciating a play is to act in it. It is difficult to agree with this. The actor, even with the best of motives, is likely to have a limited view, since he must be governed eventually by his need to immerse himself in his part. Granville-Barker wrote,

The Elements of Drama

Study includes the obligation to criticize, performance the obligation not to. A company rehearsing must very soon drop its critical attitude towards a play.[2]

The playgoer must remain external to the play as a whole if he is to create it in his mind as a whole. Even the producer himself, interpreter and unifier, may not always necessarily be the 'sounding-board' for his actors, the 'ideal spectator', if he does not see the play freshly from the spectator's side of the footlights.

By contrast, the spectator has it within his power to be an ideal 'producer' in his imagination, and still represent the audience which is to suffer the theatrical experience. We again reach our paradoxical conclusion that the play is not on the stage but in the mind. When Granville-Barker saw that the student wanted a method of study 'involving all the preparations for a performance which we know from the beginning we shall never have to give',[3] he was in fact looking for a discipline also proper to the keen spectator.

Going to a play is not, as it is often taken to be, a passive pursuit: it is a live and fruitful activity. Playgoing is an act which, like the proper reading of a novel or the complete act of listening to music, expects us to make the contribution of what ultimate qualities of fine feeling and intellectual honesty we possess. Whether the play is Greek tragedy or kitchen comedy, or whether it is well or indifferently performed, our active contribution is required. What will follow, even from a bad play badly presented, is important: for judgment is choice. Undergoing a play, from its start to its finish and in its subsequent effect, is an act involving, in Dr Richards's frightening phrase, 'momentous decisions of the will'.[4] But what he claims for poetry is as applicable to drama, and I take leave to interchange these words:

If we do not live in consonance with good drama, we must live in consonance with bad drama. And, in fact, the idle hours of most lives are

Playgoing as an Art

filled with reveries that are simply bad private drama. On the whole evidence, I do not see how we can avoid the conclusion that a general insensitivity to drama does witness a low level of general imaginative life.[5]

To this responsible extent, then, going to the play is not to be thought of as an escape, certainly not a matter of living life at second-hand. Happily, we have a consuming curiosity about man, about his life, his problems, his loves and sorrows and aspirations, the whole range and sweep of the human spirit in its relationships and conflicts. We go to the theatre as one of the means by which we come to terms with life. It is exciting first-hand work, and an urgent part of living.

A SHORT READING LIST

DRAMATIC CRITICISM

This list is necessarily a short one. There are no books on systematic dramatic criticism that one would care to recommend, but there are a very few which contain pieces of close criticism of the play performed.

Unrivalled among these remain the five volumes of Harley Granville-Barker's *Prefaces to Shakespeare* (First Series: *Love's Labour's Lost, Julius Caesar, King Lear*. Second Series: *Romeo and Juliet, The Merchant of Venice, Antony and Cleopatra, Cymbeline*. Third Series: *Hamlet*. Fourth Series: *Othello*. Fifth Series: *Coriolanus*. Sidgwick and Jackson, 1927-47). These should be read, like all criticism of this kind, in conjunction with the texts of the plays. The author, writing as scholar and producer in one, contrives to give his account of the plays much of the vitality of the theatre. The introduction to the First Series gives a useful, if brief, account of Elizabethan stage conventions.

Mr Raymond Williams's *Drama in Performance* (Muller, 1954), mentioned in the text, indicates a profitable method, with examples of analysis, for studying Greek and Shakespearian drama (chapters I and III). The book has a tendency towards being thesis-ridden, and does less than justice to Chekhov.

It is sad that on modern drama there are almost no examples of dramatic criticism. Dr J. R. Northam's *Ibsen's Dramatic Method* (Faber, 1953) offers a helpful demonstration of the visual and verbal unity of the mature plays, and of Ibsen's working method of defining his characters and situations for performance. It contains some illuminating pieces of close dramatic criticism. One must also respect Miss Eva Le Gallienne's actors' guide to Ibsen's *Hedda Gabler* and *The Master Builder* in two prefatory studies to her translation of these plays (Faber, 1953 and 1955). They provide useful beginnings for study, but suffer somewhat from the dangers of character detection.

PRODUCTION COMMENTARIES

After this, where a producer has written down his approach to a particular play, we have the next best thing. Shakespeare again has had the most attention. The two books containing Stanislavsky's production scores for *Othello* and *The Seagull* (*Stanislavsky Produces Othello*, trans. H. Nowack, Bles, 1948, and *The Seagull Produced by Stanislavsky*, edited with an

Short Reading List

introduction by Professor S. D. Balukhaty, trans. D. Magarshack, Dobson, 1952) give an insight more into the ways of Stanislavsky than of Shakespeare or Chekhov.

Controversial but stimulating are Dr G. Wilson Knight's views on the production of Shakespeare's tragedies based upon his practical experience. These will be found in his *Principles of Shakespearian Production* (Penguin, 1949). Dr Wilson Knight is an original literary critic as well as an actor and producer of Shakespeare, and it is sometimes appropriate to read his studies in Shakespeare's symbolism in conjunction with his ideas on production.

While we must recognize doubts about his picture of Shakespeare's stage, Mr Ronald Watkins's book about his discoveries while producing Shakespeare in an Elizabethan-type theatre at Harrow School, *On Producing Shakespeare* (Michael Joseph, 1950), might well supplement in a practical way Granville-Barker's work. *Moonlight at the Globe* (Michael Joseph, 1946) is an account of his production of *A Midsummer Night's Dream*.

THEORY OF ACTING AND PRODUCTION

Stanislavsky's fundamental, though rather emotive, books, *An Actor Prepares*, trans. E. R. Hapgood (Bles, 1936) and *Building a Character*, trans. E. R. Hapgood (Theatre Art Books, New York, 1949), and especially the second of these, suggest incidentally how a text must be handled by the actor. *Stanislavsky on the Art of the Stage*, with introduction and translation by D. Magarshack (Faber, 1950) might also be read. Mr Michael Redgrave comments on the 'System' in his *The Actor's Ways and Means* (Heinemann, 1953), a book too general to be of real help to the playgoer. There is a further discussion of the methods of production of Stanislavsky and Bertolt Brecht in *Le Théâtre dans le monde*, IV, i, pp. 5–36 (The International Theatre Institute, 1954). Mr Eric Bentley discusses Brecht's 'Epic' approach fully in *The Modern Theatre* (Hale, 1948) and *In Search of Theatre* (Dobson, 1955).

Among the numerous books on producing plays, Mr John Fernald's *The Play Produced* (Deane) is particularly helpful and precise, and stresses the right approach to the text of a play. It also contains some detailed examples from *Othello* and *Uncle Vanya*.

REFERENCES

The numbers are those in the text.

INTRODUCTION (pp. 1–7)

1. T. S. Eliot in a letter to Ezra Pound, quoted in J. Isaacs, *An Assessment of Twentieth Century Literature* (1951), p. 159.
2. H. Granville-Barker in a letter to Jacques Copeau, *Theatre Arts Anthology*, quoted in M. Redgrave, *The Actor's Ways and Means* (1953), p. 85.
3. W. Archer, *Play-Making*, Preface to 1913 ed., pp. xi–xii.
4. R. Williams, *Drama in Performance* (1954), p. 12.
5. P. Brook, Preface to J. Anouilh, *Ring Round the Moon*, trans. C. Fry (1950), p. 7.
6. H. Granville-Barker, *Shakespeare's Dramatic Art*, in *A Companion to Shakespeare Studies*, ed. H. Granville-Barker and G. B. Harrison (1934), p. 84.
7. *Ibid.* p. 86.

1. DRAMATIC DIALOGUE IS MORE THAN CONVERSATION (pp. 11–26)

1. Shakespeare, *Othello*, v. ii. 7.
2. E. R. Bentley, *The Modern Theatre* (1948), p. 82.
3. Strindberg, Preface to *Miss Julie*, trans. E. Björkman, in *Eight Famous Plays*, p. 111.
4. C. Stanislavsky, *Building a Character*, trans. E. R. Hapgood (1950), p. 113.
5. *Ibid.* p. 124.
6. Ibsen, *Rosmersholm*, trans. R. F. Sharp, Act I.
7. Wilde, *The Importance of Being Earnest*, Act II.
8. Such a lapse occurs a few lines further on when Gwendolen says, 'The home seems to me to be the proper sphere for the man. And certainly once a man begins to neglect his domestic duties he becomes painfully effeminate, does he not?' For all that such confident paradoxes are part of the fun, they seem to me to encumber the progress of the scene and embarrass the actress.
9. W. Archer, *The Old Drama and the New* (1923), p. 125.
10. Shakespeare, *Romeo and Juliet*, III. v. 60.

References

2. DRAMATIC VERSE IS MORE THAN DIALOGUE IN VERSE (pp. 27–47)

1 T. S. Eliot, '*Rhetoric*' *and Poetic Drama* (1919), in *Selected Essays* (1934), p. 38.
2 T. S. Eliot, *A Dialogue of Dramatic Poetry* (1928), in *Selected Essays* (1934), p. 52.
3 T. S. Eliot, *Poetry and Drama* (1951), p. 32.
4 H. Granville-Barker, *On Poetry in Drama* (1937), pp. 16–17.
5 Shakespeare, *Hamlet*, I. ii. 133.
6 O'Neill, *Mourning Becomes Electra*, Part III, Act IV.
7 Shakespeare, *Hamlet*, I. ii. 139.
8 T. S. Eliot, *Murder in the Cathedral*, Part I.
9 Shakespeare, *Hamlet*, III. iv. 24.
10 T. S. Eliot, *Murder in the Cathedral*, Part I.
11 Shakespeare, *Othello*, IV. ii. 84.
12 *Ibid.* IV. ii. 34.
13 *Ibid.* V. ii. 304.
14 *Ibid.* II. i. 189.
15 *Ibid.* V. ii. 33.
16 *Ibid.* V. ii. 349.
17 C. Fry, *A Sleep of Prisoners*, p. 17.
18 M. MacOwan, *Radio Times*, 11 April 1952.
19 C. Fry, *A Sleep of Prisoners*, p. 5.
20 *Ibid.* p. 4.
21 L. Abercrombie, 'The Function of Poetry in the Drama' in *The Poetry Review*, March 1912.
22 T. S. Eliot, *A Dialogue of Dramatic Poetry* (1928) in *Selected Essays* (1934), p. 52.
23 H. Reed, 'Towards *The Cocktail Party*' in *The Listener*, 10 May 1951.
24 See R. Williams, *Drama in Performance* (1954), p. 109. The whole chapter 'Text and Performance' should be read.

3. MAKING MEANINGS IN THE THEATRE (pp. 48–63)

1 Marlowe, *Doctor Faustus*, scene V, line 53.
2 Molière, *The Miser*, Act II, in *Molière, Five Plays*, trans. J. Wood.
3 Keats, *Ode to a Nightingale*.
4 J. Fernald, *op. cit.* p. 10.
5 Synge, *The Playboy of the Western World*, Act I.
6 E. Wilson, *Axel's Castle* (1931), p. 43.

The Elements of Drama

4. SHIFTING IMPRESSIONS (pp. 64–85)

1. G. Melchiori has offered persuasive reasons for the unity of the play in *The Tightrope Walkers* (1956), pp. 265–6.
2. See P. Wilde, *The Craftsmanship of the One-Act Play* (1937), p. 302.
3. Shakespeare, *Romeo and Juliet*, v. iii. 102.
4. Maeterlinck, *Interior*, trans. W. Archer.
5. See S. M. Eisenstein, *The Film Sense*, trans. J. Leyda (1948), ch. II, 'Synchronization of Senses'. I am considerably indebted to this book of fine aesthetic perceptions. And recently Professor Ronald Peacock has elaborated a useful theory of what he calls the 'intertexture of imagery' in *The Art of Drama* (1957).
6. V. I. Pudovkin, *Film Technique and Film Acting*, trans. I. Montagu (1954), p. xiv.
7. Shakespeare, *Julius Caesar*, IV. iii. 58.
8. Shakespeare, *Romeo and Juliet*, III. i. 61.
9. H. Granville-Barker, *Prefaces to Shakespeare*, II (1930), p. 13.
10. Chekhov, *The Cherry Orchard*, trans. E. Fen, Act IV. I have kept the traditional spelling of the names of the characters.
11. Chekhov, letter to Suvorin, 4 May 1889, quoted in D. Magarshack, *Chekhov the Dramatist* (1952), p. 118.

5. THE BEHAVIOUR OF THE WORDS ON THE STAGE (pp. 86–117)

1. C. Stanislavsky, *Building a Character*, p. 164.
2. Shaw, *Pygmalion*, Act II.
3. J. Fernald, *The Play Produced*, pp. 16–17.
4. Shaw, *Pygmalion*, Act IV.
5. Shakespeare, *King Lear*, II. iv. 168, *Hamlet*, II. ii. 641, II. ii. 615.
6. T. S. Eliot, 'Christopher Marlowe' (1918) in *Selected Essays* (1934), p. 119.
7. See R. Speaight, *William Poel and the Elizabethan Revival* (1954), p. 62 ff.
8. Shakespeare, *Coriolanus*, II. iii. 57.
9. Shakespeare, *King Lear*, I. iv. 241, IV. vii. 69, V. iii. 311.
10. Shakespeare, *Hamlet*, III. iii. 73.
11. *Ibid.* I. v. 10.
12. T. S. Eliot, *The Confidential Clerk*, Act II, pp. 55–6.
13. C. Stanislavsky, *Building a Character*, p. 118.
14. S. Selden, 'Stage Speech' in *Theatre Arts*, July 1945. See also R. Peacock, *The Art of Drama*, p. 167.

References

15 M. Lamm, *Modern Drama*, trans. K. Elliott (1952), p. 252.
16 Shaw, *Arms and the Man*, Act I.
17 H. Pearson, 'The origin of *Androcles and the Lion*' in *The Listener*, 13 November 1952.
18 Shaw, *The Apple Cart*, An Interlude.
19 R. Williams, *Drama in Performance*, p. 106.
20 *Ibid*. p. 94.
21 Congreve, *The Way of the World*, Act IV, sc. i.
22 See especially A. C. Bradley, *Shakespearian Tragedy* (1904), p. 247. The reader should consult H. Granville-Barker, *Prefaces to Shakespeare*, I (1927) for the reply to Bradley.
23 Shakespeare, *King Lear*, III. iv.
24 *Ibid*. v. iii. 9.
25 J. F. Danby, *Shakespeare's Doctrine of Nature* (1949), p. 17.
26 See J. F. Danby, *op. cit*. pp. 180-5.

6. BUILDING THE SEQUENCE OF IMPRESSIONS (pp. 121-140)

1 Sophocles, *King Oedipus*, trans. E. F. Watling, p. 37.
2 Synge, *Deirdre of the Sorrows*, Act II.
3 Shakespeare, *Romeo and Juliet*, II. i. 7.
4 Shakespeare, *Macbeth*, I. iv. 45, I. v. 41, I. vi. 1.
5 Sheridan, *The School for Scandal*, Act IV, sc. iii.
6 Goldsmith, *She Stoops to Conquer*, Act III.
7 T. S. Eliot, *Murder in the Cathedral*, Part II.
8 Shakespeare, *Macbeth*, II. ii. 36.
9 T. S. Eliot, *Four Quartets*, 'The Dry Salvages'.

7. TEMPO AND MEANING (pp. 141-162)

1 Shakespeare, *Macbeth*, II. iii. 81.
2 Wilde, *The Importance of Being Earnest*, Act II.
3 Ibsen, *The Wild Duck*, trans. U. Ellis-Fermor, Act V.
4 Coleridge, *Biographia Literaria*, ed. J. Shawcross (1907), vol. II, p. 56.
5 Shakespeare, *As You Like It*, V. ii. 90.
6 Sheridan, *The School for Scandal*, Act III, sc. i.
7 Strindberg, *The Father*, trans. N. Erichsen, Act II, sc. v.

8. MANIPULATING THE CHARACTERS (pp. 163-187)

1 G. W. Knight, *The Wheel of Fire* (1930), p. 16.
2 L. C. Knights, *Explorations* (1946), p. 4.
3 R. Williams, *Drama from Ibsen to Eliot* (1952), p. 18.

The Elements of Drama

4 Strindberg, Preface to *Miss Julie*, trans. E. Björkman, in *Eight Famous Plays*, pp. 105-6.
5 Shaw, *Arms and the Man*, Act II.
6 D. H. Lawrence, in a letter to E. Garnett, 5 June 1914, in *The Letters*, ed. A. Huxley (1932), p. 199.
7 Chekhov, *The Bear*, trans. E. Fen.
8 Strindberg, *Miss Julie*, trans. E. Björkman, in *Eight Famous Plays*, p. 124.
9 See E. M. W. Tillyard, *Shakespeare's Last Plays* (1938), ch. III.
10 Shakespeare, *A Midsummer Night's Dream*, I. i. 9.
11 *Ibid.* v. i. 4.
12 See L. J. Potts, *Comedy* (1948), pp. 22-6.
13 Pirandello, *Six Characters in Search of an Author*, trans. F. May.
14 *Ibid.* trans. E. Storer, stage direction, in *Three Plays*.

9. BREAKING THE CONTINUITY (pp. 188-204)

1 H. Pearson, *Bernard Shaw* (1942), p. 289.
2 S. O'Casey, *The Plough and the Stars*, Act II.
3 D. Johnston in *Radio Times*, 13 September 1946.
4 T. Wilder, *Our Town*, p. iv.
5 J. Anouilh, *Ardèle*, trans. L. Hill, Act III.

10. THE MEANING OF THE PLAY AS A WHOLE (pp. 205-227)

1 C. Stanislavsky, *An Actor Prepares*, trans. E. R. Hapgood (1936), p. 271.
2 Chekhov, *The Three Sisters*, trans. E. Fen, Act IV.
3 See D. Magarshack, *Chekhov the Dramatist* (1952), p. 231.
4 *Ibid.* pp. 262-3.
5 Wagner, *Correspondence of Wagner and Liszt*, vol. I, Letter 125, 16 Aug. 1853, quoted in S. M. Eisenstein, *The Film Sense*, p. 156.
6 Henry James to H. Renbell, quoted in Swan, *Henry James* (1950), p. 87.
7 C. Stanislavsky, *Building a Character*, trans. E. R. Hapgood (1950), p. 175.
8 D. Johnston, *The Moon in the Yellow River*, Act I.
9 I. A. Richards, *Practical Criticism* (1929), pp. 355-6 (my italics).
10 See H. Granville-Barker, *Prefaces to Shakespeare*, II (1930), p. 130-43.
11 Shakespeare, *Antony and Cleopatra*, III. xi. 154. The succeeding four quotations are: III. xi. 191, III. xi. 199, IV. i. 1, IV. x. 19.
12 J. Anouilh, *Eurydice*, trans. L. Small, Act I.
13 J. Anouilh, *Antigone*, trans. L. Galantière.

References

14 J. Cocteau, *La Machine infernale*, quoted in J. Isaacs, *An Assessment of Twentieth Century Literature* (1951), pp. 140–1.
15 J. Anouilh, *Eurydice*, Act II.
16 *Ibid.* Act III.
17 I. Brown, *The London Observer*, 5 Nov. 1950.
18 E. O. Marsh, *Jean Anouilh, Poet of Pierrot and Pantaloon* (1953), p. 189.

11. AUDIENCE PARTICIPATION (pp. 231–255)

1 See J. Macleod, *The New Soviet Theatre* (1943), etc.
2 Brecht, *A Short Description of a New Technique of the Art of Acting which Produces an Effect of Estrangement. Le Théâtre dans le monde*, IV, 1 (1954).
3 Shakespeare, *Romeo and Juliet*, I. v. 45.
4 Johnson, *Preface to Shakespeare* (1765).
5 Coleridge, *The Progress of Drama* (1818) in *Literary Remains*, quoted in A. Nicoll, *The Theory of Drama* (1931), p. 35.
6 W. S. Maugham, *The Summing Up* (1938), p. 134.
7 J.-P. Sartre, *Crime Passionnel*, trans. K. Black, sc. v.
8 I. Brown, *Parties of the Play* (1928), p. 30.
9 G. Simmel, quoted in E. R. Bentley, *The Modern Theatre* (1948), p. 39.
10 O'Neill, quoted in A. Nicoll, *World Drama from Aeschylus to Anouilh* (1949), p. 885.
11 O'Neill, *The Hairy Ape*, sc. i.
12 *Ibid.* sc. viii.
13 V. Woolf, *The Common Reader* (1925), pp. 72–3.
14 U. Ellis-Fermor, *The Frontiers of Drama* (1945), p. 77.
15 Ibsen, *Rosmersholm*, trans. R. F. Sharp, Act I.
16 See O. Holloway, 'The Teller and the Told' in *The Listener*, 18 February 1954.
17 See also S. M. Eisenstein, *The Film Sense*, p. 35, and in many places through the text.

12. PASSING JUDGMENT (pp. 256–284)

1 Synge, *Deirdre of the Sorrows*, Act III.
2 Lamb, *On the Artificial Comedy of the Last Century* (1823).
3 Bridie, *Tobias and the Angel*, 2nd ed., Act I, sc. i.
4 C. Fry, *The Lady's Not For Burning*, 2nd ed., Act III, p. 91.
5 *Ibid.* Act II, pp. 42 and 61–2.

The Elements of Drama

6 Bridie, *Tobias and the Angel*, Act III, sc. i.
7 I. A. Richards, *Principles of Literary Criticism* (1924), p. 211.
8 T. S. Eliot, *The Cocktail Party*, Act I, sc. i.
9 T. S. Eliot, Introduction to S. L. Bethell, *Shakespeare and the Popular Dramatic Tradition* (1945), p. 13.
10 T. S. Eliot, *The Three Voices of Poetry* (the Eleventh Annual Lecture of the National Book League) (1953), p. 11.
11 J. Peter, 'Sin and Soda' in *Scrutiny* XVII, No. 1 (Spring, 1950), p. 63.
12 I. A. Richards, *Practical Criticism* (1929), p. 303.

13. PLAYGOING AS AN ART (pp. 285–289)

1 V. I. Pudovkin, *Film Technique and Film Acting*, p. 61.
2 H. Granville-Barker, *The Study of Drama* (1934), p. 27.
3 *Ibid.* p. 19.
4 I. A. Richards, *Practical Criticism*, p. 305.
5 *Ibid.* p. 320.

INDEX OF PLAYWRIGHTS AND PLAYS

Where a passage from the play is specifically discussed, the page reference is printed in bold type

Aeschylus (525–456 B.C.), 64, 243
  Agamemnon, 257, 271
  The Eumenides, 165
Anonymous (15th cent.)
  Everyman, 11
Anouilh, Jean (b. 1910), 4, 189, 190, 199, 255, 260, 263
  Antigone, 167, 221–2
  Ardèle (*Ardèle ou la Marguérite*), **198** ff., 238
  Point of Departure (*Eurydice*), **217** ff.
  Ring Round the Moon (*L'Invitation au château*), 255, 256–7
  Thieves' Carnival (*Le Bal des voleurs*), 257
  Traveller without Luggage (*Le Voyageur sans bagage*), 226
Aristophanes (*c.* 448–*c.* 380 B.C.), 232
Auden, W. H. (b. 1907), and Isherwood, C. (b. 1904)
  The Ascent of F6, 237

Barrie (1860–1937)
  Dear Brutus, 222
  Mary Rose, 222, 237
Beckett, Samuel (b. 1906), 255
  All that Fall, 287
  Waiting for Godot (*En attendant Godot*), 48, 255
Betti (1892–1953)
  The Queen and the Rebels (*La regina e gli insorti*), 165–6
  Summertime (*Il paese delle vacanze*), 257
Boland, Bridget (b. 1913)
  Cockpit, 232
Brecht (1898–1956), 231–2, 291
  Mother Courage (*Mutter Courage und ihre Kinder*), 188
Bridie (1888–1951)
  Daphne Laureola, 205
  Tobias and the Angel, 262, 263, **267** ff.

Chapman (*c.* 1560–1634), 243
Chekhov (1860–1904), 45, 46, 72–3, 121–2, 199, 255, 290
  The Bear, 175
  The Cherry Orchard, 11, **73** ff., 121–2, 169, 210, 263
  The Seagull, 103–5, 290
  The Three Sisters, 5, 52, **206** ff., 263
  Uncle Vanya, 291
Cocteau, Jean (b. 1891)
  The Infernal Machine (*La Machine infernale*), 221–2
Congreve (1670–1729), 101
  The Way of the World, 106–7, 169, 170, 238
Coward, Noël (b. 1899), 276

Druten, J. van (1901–58)
  I am a Camera, 205
Duncan, Ronald (b. 1914)
  This Way to the Tomb, 273

Eliot, T. S. (b. 1888), 64, 96, 135, 139
  The Cocktail Party, 42, 45, 126, 135, 196, **274** ff.
  The Confidential Clerk, 96 ff., 135, 205
  The Family Reunion, 196
  Murder in the Cathedral, 29–30, 31, 126, **135** ff., 189, 195, 232–3
Euripides (485–406 B.C.)
  The Trojan Women, 271–2

Farquhar (1678–1707)
  The Beaux' Stratagem, 260
Fry, Christopher (b. 1907), 269
  The Dark is Light Enough, 42
  The Firstborn, 238
  The Lady's not for Burning, 45, **263** ff.
  A Phoenix Too Frequent, 267
  A Sleep of Prisoners, **39** ff., 55, 56–7, 232–3

Index of Playwrights and Plays

Galsworthy (1867-1933)
   Strife, 274
Giraudoux (1882-1944)
   Amphitryon 38, 165
   Tiger at the Gates (*La Guerre de Troie n'aura pas lieu*), 167, 168
Goethe (1749-1832), 64, 243
Goldoni (1707-93)
   The Mistress of the Inn (*La locandiera*), 206
Goldsmith (1728-74)
   She Stoops to Conquer, 134-5
Greene, Graham (b. 1904)
   The Living Room, 238

Ibsen (1828-1906), 12, 45, 64, 226, 238, 263, 290
   A Doll's House, 165, 176, 237
   Ghosts, 169
   Hedda Gabler, 163, 290
   The Master Builder, 249, 290
   Peer Gynt, 257
   Rosmersholm, 14 ff., 24, 53, **249** ff.
   The Wild Duck, **149** ff., 159

Johnston, Denis (b. 1901), 193
   The Moon on the Yellow River, **212** ff.
Jonson (1572-1637), 101
   The Alchemist, 272
   Bartholomew Fayre, 244
   Volpone, 52

MacNeice, Louis (b. 1907), 287
Maeterlinck (1862-1949)
   Interior (*L'Intérieur*), 66-7
Marlowe (1564-93), 243
   Doctor Faustus, 48-9, 65
   Tamburlaine the Great, 45
Miller, Arthur (b. 1915)
   Death of a Salesman, 237
Molière (1622-73), 64, 263
   The Imaginary Invalid (*Le Malade imaginaire*), 206
   The Miser (*L'Avare*), 50-1, 54

O'Casey, Sean (b. 1884), 189, 190, 255
   Juno and the Paycock, 190-1
   The Plough and the Stars, 190, **191** ff.
   Red Roses for Me, 244
O'Neill (1888-1953)
   The Emperor Jones, 47, 248
   The Hairy Ape, **245** ff.
   Mourning Becomes Electra, 29

Strange Interlude, 158

Pinero (1855-1934), 102
   The Magistrate, 256
   The Second Mrs Tanqueray, 237
Pirandello (1867-1936), 129, 163, 190, 232, 243, 255, 263
   Each in his Own Way (*Ciascuno a suo modo*), 188
   Six Characters in Search of an Author (*Sei personaggi in cerca d'autore*), **180** ff., 188, 201
Priestley, J. B. (b. 1894), 217
   An Inspector Calls, 46, 197-8
   They Came to a City, 238

Rattigan, Terence (b. 1912)
   The Browning Version, 205, 270
   The Deep Blue Sea, 271
   Separate Tables, 270-1
Rice, Elmer (b. 1892)
   The Adding Machine, 245

Sartre, J.-P. (b. 1905), 64
   Crime Passionnel (*Les Mains sales*), **239** ff.
Sayers, Dorothy (1893-1957)
   The Zeal of Thy House, 233
Shakespeare (1564-1616), 1, 27, 39, 41, 64, 93, 95, 101, 104, 117, 129, 164, 195, 245, 263, 286, 290-1
   Antony and Cleopatra, 126, **214** ff., 290
   As You Like It, 153-4, 178, 180
   Coriolanus, 94, 290
   Cymbeline, 290
   Hamlet, 28-9, 30, 93, 95-6, 130, 164, 174-5, 206, 240, 271-2, 290
   Henry IV, Part I, 169, 178, 255
   Julius Caesar, 69-70, 290
   King Lear, 92, 95, **107** ff., 121-2, 132, 149, 163, 164, 176, 244, 290
   Love's Labour's Lost, 244, 290
   Macbeth, 51, 130-2, 138, 141-2, 149, 163, 164, 165, 178, 273-4
   Measure for Measure, 254
   The Merchant of Venice, 166, 290
   A Midsummer Night's Dream, 153, 170, **178** ff., 291
   Much Ado About Nothing, 166
   Othello, 11, **32** ff., 54-5, 132, 244, 290, 291
   Romeo and Juliet, 25-6, 66-7, **70-2** 129-30, 149, 166, **233-4**, 290
   The Tempest, 227

Index of Playwrights and Plays

Shakespeare (*cont.*)
   Troilus and Cressida, 255, 273
   Twelfth Night, 178, 180
Shaw (1856–1950), 13, 64, 87, 99–100, 107, 169, 263
   Androcles and the Lion, 188
   The Apple Cart, **101** ff.
   Arms and the Man, 100–1, 169, **170** ff.
   Caesar and Cleopatra, 107
   Candida, 107
   Getting Married, 236
   Heartbreak House, 214
   Major Barbara, 238
   Man and Superman, 107, 169
   Pygmalion, 87–8, **89** ff., 107
   Saint Joan, 126, **146** ff., 167, 178, 205, 255
Sheridan (1751–1816), 101
   The Critic, 273
   The School for Scandal, 133–4, **154** ff.
Sophocles (497–405 B.C.)
   Electra, 169
   King Oepidus, 51, **123** ff., 126, 257, 271
Strindberg (1849–1912), 12–13, 129, 163, 255, 263
   The Father, **158** ff.
   Miss Julie, 167–8, **176** ff.
Synge (1871–1909)
   Deirdre of the Sorrows, **126** ff., **257** ff.
   In the Shadow of the Glen, 237

   The Playboy of the Western World, **57** ff., 64
   Riders to the Sea, 257

Thomas, Dylan (1914–53)
   Under Milk Wood, 65, 244, 287
Toller (1893–1939), 217
   Masses and Man (*Masse-Mensch*), 46

Vanbrugh (1666–1726)
   The Relapse, or Virtue in Danger, 170, 260 ff.
Vane, Sutton (1888–1913)
   Outward Bound, 274, 283

Whiting, John (b. 1918)
   Marching Song, 206
Wilde (1856–1900), 21
   The Importance of Being Earnest, **20** ff., 53–4, **143** ff., 260, 292
Wilder, Thornton (b. 1897)
   Our Town, 189, 196–7
Williams, Tennessee (b. 1914)
   A Streetcar Named Desire, 271–2

Yeats (1865–1939), 163
   The Land of Heart's Desire, 237

Zola (1840–1902)
   Thérèse Raquin, 237

INDEX OF SUBJECTS

acting, actor, 14, 28, 56–7, 66, 73, 76 ff., 86–7, 91, 94, 96, 101, 103–4, 123, 124, 134, 142, 147, 148, 152, 156, 158, 164, 165, 166, 169–71, 174, 176, 178, 181 ff., 197, 206, 212, 231 ff., 253, 265, 267, 271, 276, 285, 287–8, 290–1
action, 94, 111, 121, 125, 130, 136, 142, 150, 160, 162, 174, 178, 185, 193, 205, 210, 222, 236, 254, 262, 285
actuality, reality, 11, 149, 154, 165, 169–70, 175, 260, 286
alienation, estrangement, 189, 231–2, 291
amateurs, 206
anachronism, 167
anaphora, 139
anticlimax, bathos, 33, 42, 80, 90, 102, 142, 172, 174, 175, 191, 223, 241, 244, 248, 268, 281
apron, 132
arena, *see* theatre-in-the-round
aside, 132 ff., 144, 158, 233
atmosphere, 2, 75, 140, 219, 232, 248, 285
audience, 125, 126, 131, 133, 134, 135, 162, 164 ff., 170, 171, 181 ff., 189, 190, 206, 216, 227, 231 ff., 256 ff., 285, 288
auditorium, 181, 231 ff.

bathos, *see* anticlimax
beliefs, 135, 214, 275
blank verse, 93
burlesque, 107, 171, 179–80, 195, 237, 273, 276
business, 50

catharsis, 2, 75
caricature, 171, 180
character, 3, 6, 13, 20, 50, 65–6, 73, 76, 79, 122, 123, 133, 152, 163 ff., 196, 197, 202, 207, 213, 226, 232, 235, 237, 238, 243, 244, 245, 250, 262, 272, 277–8
chorus, 30, 31, 136, 140, 183, 192, 195–6, 207, 210–11, 213, 219, 221, 232–3, 248, 249, 254, 286
church, 136, 195, 232–3
cinema, *see* film
cliché, 171, 173, 192, 218, 222, 271
climax, crisis, 72, 83, 88, 90, 107, 110, 137, 139, 141–2, 144, 147–8, 149 ff., 175, 186–7, 195, 213, 237, 244, 248, 266, 271
comedy, 75, 82, 84, 90, 101, 133, 146, 169, 179, 188, 190–1, 192 ff., 208, 232, 235, 244, 248, 254, 255, 256, 261, 262, 263, 267, 272, 276, 279; artificial, 90, 101, 155, 170, 178 ff., 260; kitchen, domestic, 271–2, 288; of manners, 199, 260; Restoration, 101, 132 ff., 170, 260–2; Shakespearian, 170
comic relief, 244
commedia dell'arte, 4, 50, 169
conceit, 189, 191, 195, 199, 203
confidant(e), 53, 253
consistency, 167, 174, 263
continuity, 189 ff., 245
contrast, 56, 58, 147, 153, 154, 160, 192, 215, 222,
convention, 6, 24, 25 ff., 90, 126, 188 ff., 226, 236, 238, 248 ff., 277, 285
conviction, 17, 20, 166 ff., 186–7, 213, 245, 275
costume, 50, 285
crisis, *see* climax
cue, 35, 147–8, 161

dance, 153–4
declamation, 93
décor, 19, 232, 285
destiny, *see* fate
detachment, 24
detective play, 16
development, 176 ff., 209
dialogue, 2 ff., 11 ff., 48, 50, 57, 66, 72, 75, 79, 86, 101, 103–4, 153, 159, 189
diffuseness, 22
direct address, 195
discussion play, *see* problem play
'dramatic', 2, 64 ff.
dramatis personae, 168–9

eighteenth-century stage, 132 ff.
Elizabethan stage, 108 ff., 117, 129 ff., 131, 214, 233–4, 248, 286, 290–1
emotion, 86, 93, 94–5, 126 ff., 131–2, 151, 181, 183, 187, 188, 191, 192, 196, 197, 198, 199, 202, 210, 227, 231, 232, 235,

302

Index of Subjects

emotion (*cont.*)
  239, 244, 248, 255, 271-2, 277
end-stop, 94, 139
entrance, 91, 212
Epic Theatre, 232, 291
estrangement, *see* alienation
Existentialism, 239 ff.
exposition, 15 ff., 217, 237, 253
Expressionism, 46, 168, 244 ff.
extravaganza, 188, 238

fantasy, 134, 153, 163, 178-9, 186, 201, 213, 226-7, 238, 246, 257, 263, 267, 287
farce, 6, 62, 133, 169, 175, 199-202, 243, 254, 255, 256, 260, 269
fate, destiny, 207, 220, 221-2, 246
feminine ending, 139
film, cinema, 64, 68, 164, 198, 206, 215, 286-7
form, 65, 188, 226, 255

gesture, 5, 24, 25, 30, 31, 52, 72, 98 ff., 107, 117, 133, 139, 148, 171, 172, 173, 174, 212, 242
Greek drama, 51, 103, 105, 123, 169, 222, 226, 253, 254, 271, 286, 288, 290
grouping, 105-6, 110-11

hero, 72-3, 165, 191, 216, 235, 240, 258
history, 7, 286
honesty, 269 ff., 288

iambic, 93, 94
identification, 84, 235
illusion, 179, 189, 235
image, 14, 63, 68, 86, 105-6, 122, 123, 128, 130, 134, 152, 157, 168, 174, 176, 189, 195, 203, 208, 210, 212, 215, 216, 223, 242, 244, 248, 280, 286
imagery, 27, 36 ff., 52, 85, 129, 131, 138, 159, 178-9, 189, 249, 258
imagination: aural, 14, 87, 157; motor, 99; visual, 14, 286
imitation, *mimesis*, 257
immediacy, 287
impersonality, 221, 259
impressions, 6, 49 ff., 64 ff., 86, 89, 94, 100, 105, 107, 115, 121 ff., 141, 148, 154, 164, 168, 169, 174, 175, 176, 192, 207, 209, 212, 213, 215, 216, 217, 221, 234, 244, 255, 256, 259, 263
incongruity, 75, 90
indirect address, 233

inflexion, *see* intonation
intention, purpose, 121, 122, 171, 187, 214, 245, 247, 256, 257, 261, 266, 274
interest, 14, 15 ff., 64 ff., 121, 133, 168, 173, 174, 181, 235, 239, 248, 256
intimacy, 231 ff., 287
intonation, inflexion, 18, 31, 52, 72, 86 ff., 92, 93, 95, 98, 105, 148, 156, 166
irony, 12, 19, 23, 49 ff., 68 ff., 83-4, 88, 100, 102, 104, 114, 116, 124, 127, 130-1, 133, 144, 145, 149 ff., 157, 172, 174, 180, 191, 201, 203, 209, 217, 218, 221, 222, 241, 247, 265, 268, 280

laughter, 75, 133, 134, 145, 154, 180, 195, 198, 201, 203, 205, 236, 243, 255, 261, 265-6, 272, 273
legend, *see* myth
levels, 178 ff., 185, 265, 273-4
lighting, 48, 285
location, 153, 189

make-believe, 188, 196, 199
mask, 50, 163, 169, 176, 187
meaning, 48 ff., 93, 94, 98 ff., 112, 122, 125, 137, 141 ff., 149, 151, 152, 175, 181, 193, 197, 205 ff., 238, 243, 254, 265, 268, 282
melodrama, 37, 123, 126, 130, 131, 165, 183, 190, 198-9, 236, 237, 241 ff., 254, 255, 274
memory, 16 ff., 249 ff.
message, 130, 197, 262
metaphor, 52, 56
metre, 29, 42, 93 ff.
mime, 15, 107, 196, 199, 203
mimesis, *see* imitation
monologue, 158
monotony, 158
mood, 73, 75, 152, 153, 189, 190, 191, 215
morality play, 44, 165, 198, 217, 267, 271
moralizing, 262
morals, 134, 227, 243, 261
motive, 24, 167-8, 241 ff., 249, 254
movement, 15, 25, 40, 56, 58, 86, 89, 91, 105 ff., 128, 139, 147-8, 150, 152, 172, 186, 197, 212
music, 4, 13, 14, 24, 44, 65, 68, 86, 154, 210, 215, 219, 288
myth, legend, 169, 222, 226, 259

naturalism (*see also* realism), 13, 16, 45, 79, 93, 189

Index of Subjects

non-realistic, non-representational, 28, 46–7, 94, 132, 134, 140, 149, 167, 169, 225, 238, 245
non-representational, *see* non-realistic
novel, 45, 70, 174, 198, 214, 239, 249, 250, 254, 288

'objectives', 206
obscurity, 44

pace, 42, 67, 86, 137, 142 ff., 195
padding, 124, 205
pantomime, 140
parallelism, 218
parody, 276
participation, 231 ff.
pause, 72, 81, 86 ff., 148, 151, 215, 253
personality, 168
'perspective', 87, 174, 212
pessimism, 227
philosophy, 64, 239 ff.
pitch, 86, 157, 195
'plane of reality', 178 ff.
'plastic' acting, 186
play of ideas, 255
play-within-a-play, 130, 183 ff., 188
plot, 3, 6, 121, 123, 153, 158, 238
poetic drama, *see* poetry
poetry, poetic drama, 11–12, 27 ff., 45, 47, 94, 96, 132, 162, 164, 195, 215, 245, 263, 275, 277, 278, 284, 287, 288
problem play, discussion play, 169, 237, 243
producing, producer, 36, 107, 117, 123, 158, 162, 231, 252, 288, 290–1
properties, 48, 196
proscenium, 132, 286
prose, 28, 31, 45, 103, 113, 195
psychology, 152–3, 158, 167 ff., 237, 238, 249, 255, 270–1
'puppetry', 21, 50, 187, 226
purpose, *see* intention

radio, 65, 99, 170, 287
realism (*see also* naturalism), 2, 12, 13, 28, 89, 90, 103 ff., 129, 149, 152–3, 158, 159, 168, 186, 188, 190, 196, 197, 198, 202, 211, 217, 232, 235, 238, 249 ff., 255, 259, 261, 276, 277
reality, *see* actuality
relationships, 73 ff., 92, 98, 103, 122, 147, 157, 160, 174–5, 177 ff., 181 ff., 249 ff.
relief, 152

religious drama, 43, 125, 135 ff., 254, 275 ff.
Restoration stage, 182 ff.
rhetoric, 27, 101, 137, 139, 192, 195, 222, 249
rhyme, 93, 139
rhythm, 11, 17, 19, 24, 34, 42, 92 ff., 103, 116, 129, 131, 133, 137, 141 ff., 249, 259
ritual, 11, 140, 196, 232
Roman drama, 169

satire, 23, 64, 126, 146, 214, 217, 243, 260, 272
scenery, 233
sensation, sensationalism, 6, 130, 135, 142, 190, 198, 219, 222, 242, 243, 271 ff.
sentiment, sentimentality, 84, 154, 179, 191, 193, 222, 224, 237, 243, 271, 274
sequence, 68, 76 ff., 121 ff., 141, 144, 148, 178, 186, 193, 215, 217, 218, 247
setting, 232, 285, 286
silence, 5, 42, 187
situation, 50, 65, 123, 133, 134, 164, 169, 177, 188, 191, 197, 210, 227, 239, 245, 256, 266, 268
soliloquy, 66–7, 133, 212, 233, 246, 249, 254, 286
sound effects, 210, 282
spectacle, 2, 243
speech, 5, 24, 56, 86, 89, 93, 94, 104, 122, 140, 148, 150, 152, 153 ff., 166, 171, 173, 186, 192, 212, 233, 245, 249
stage directions, 99, 107, 142, 147
stress, 93, 94, 137
stychomythia, 139
style, 257
stylization, 21, 25, 101, 130, 137, 140, 144, 153, 220, 276 ff.
sub-plot, 178
'subtext', 13 ff., 20, 45
suspense, tension, 67, 95, 102, 133, 136, 145, 150 ff., 158, 162, 217, 219, 222, 239, 244, 253, 283
symbol, symbolism, 40, 44, 75, 82, 84, 111, 125, 135, 137, 140, 152, 163 ff., 168, 179, 194, 202, 214, 225–7, 236, 237, 245, 247, 249, 277, 280, 285, 291
synthesis, 68, 121–2, 125, 135

television, 287
tempo, 2, 6, 34, 41, 56, 58, 137, 139, 141 ff.

Index of Subjects

tension, *see* suspense
theatre-in-the-round, 233
theme, 20, 39, 121, 123, 125, 135, 167, 168, 178-9, 181, 198, 206, 211, 213, 217, 219, 222, 238, 241, 245, 257, 272, 273, 274
time, 65, 75-6, 83, 131, 132, 155, 157-8, 169, 190, 207, 211
tone, 17, 24, 56, 88, 91, 93, 102, 126, 143, 145, 146-7, 154, 156-7, 192, 194, 253, 255, 267, 276, 284
topicality, 237
tragedy, 84, 123 ff., 128, 130, 132, 148, 165, 168, 190-1, 201, 217, 221-2, 225, 235, 247, 254, 255, 257, 259, 269, 271, 272, 274, 279
tragi-comedy, 255

trochaic, 94
types, 168, 170

unity, 94, 169, 178, 181, 205 ff., 272
universality, 65, 165, 197, 237, 261

values, 6, 93, 122, 135, 149, 153, 164, 165, 167, 197, 214, 231 ff., 256 ff.
verse, 27 ff., 92 ff., 103, 113-14, 152 ff., 277, 278
villain, 170, 237, 242
voice, 24, 28 ff., 56, 86 ff., 92 ff., 99, 105, 117, 137-9, 143, 154, 156, 170, 172, 244, 253

'well-made play', 122, 245
wit, 13, 126, 189, 201, 213, 238, 265, 268

INDEX OF CRITICS AND COMMENTATORS

Abercrombie, L., 45
Archer, W., 2, 25, 169
Aristotle, 2, 164, 257

Bentley, E. R., 12, 291
Bradley, A. C., 295
Brook, P., 4
Brown, I., 225-6, 244

Coleridge, S. T., 152, 235

Danby, J. F., 112

Eisenstein, S. M., 68, 287, 297
Eliot, T. S., 1, 27, 45, 93, 277, 278
Ellis-Fermor, U., 249

Fernald, J., 56, 89, 291

Gallienne, E. Le, 290
Granville-Barker, H., 2, 4, 5, 28, 71, 287-8, 290-1, 296

Holloway, O., 297

James, H., 212
Johnson, S., 235
Johnston, D., 193

Knight, G. W., 164, 291
Knights, L. C., 164-5

Lamb, C., 107, 260-1
Lamm, M., 99
Lawrence, D. H., 174

MacLeod, J., 297
MacOwan, M., 40
Magarshack, D., 211
Maugham, S., 236
Melchiori, G., 294

Northam, J. R., 290

Peacock, R., 294
Pearson, H., 188
Peter, J., 281
Poel, W., 93
Potts, L. J., 296
Pudovkin, V. I., 68, 286

Redgrave, M., 291
Reed, H., 45
Richards, I. A., 214, 273-4, 284, 288-9

Selden, S., 98-9
Shaw, G. B., 263
Simmel, G., 244
Speaight, R., 294
Stanislavsky, K., 13-14, 79, 87, 98, 103-4, 206, 212, 287, 290-1
Strindberg, A., 167-8

Tillyard, E. M. W., 178

Wagner, R., 212
Watkins, R., 291
Wilde, P., 66, 294
Williams, R., 2, 46, 103-4, 166, 290
Wilson, E., 63
Woolf, V., 248

CPSIA information can be obtained at www.ICGtesting.com
Printed in the USA
BVOW08s2315300614

357847BV00014B/354/P